Global Humility

Attitudes for Mission

Andy McCullough

malcolm down
PUBLISHING

Elaine Kent
July 2018

Contents

Endorsements

Immediately arresting, Andy's book is at once provocative, stimulating, eye-opening, game-changing, theologically rich and scholarly, but earthed in hands-on experience. Even to one who may not be called to cross-cultural mission, the call to humility in our walk and witness demands a response.
Terry Virgo
Founder of the Newfrontiers network and author of several books, including *God's Lavish Grace* and *Does the Future Have a Church?*

Don't let the title – *Global Humility: Attitudes for Mission* – set you back. This book is masterful in its approach, is rich and clear by use of biblical and contemporary examples and not least, is crafted by a superb writer. Andy McCullough takes up a stringed instrument, plays an ear-catching melody, all the while by logic, metaphor and Bible story, and strums a surrounding cadence of striking importance. Humility, not your usual fare, is given its core place in the forming of Christian character. This I recommend with enthusiasm, and hopefully with some humility. After all, it is what he writes that calls me to listen to, and replicate, this eternal note.
Brian C. Stiller
Global Ambassador, The World Evangelical Alliance.

Please do read Andy McCullough's book *Global Humility* if you are interested in learning from the global Church, care for the marginalised in society or are passionate about world mission and want to understand life from the perspective of a genuine biblical world view. Andy is a good friend of mine and someone I have seen develop a genuine ability to relate to other cultures with humility, to learn their language and to gain insights from Scripture that many of us have missed. I am happy to commend Global Humility.
David Devenish
Leader, Newfrontiers Together, and author of *Demolishing Strongholds, What on Earth is the Church For?* and *Fathering Leaders, Motivating Mission.*

This may be a future classic of how faith goes global and what it will look like. Few things have I read by 'missiologists' that excite me – this is the exception – because he gets the world and approaches it as a humble student, not an authoritative religious colonial expert. This is an incredibly rich book – I'm saving the manuscript to think deeply over.

Dr Bob Roberts
Founding and Senior Pastor, Northwood Church, Keller, Texas and author of several books, including *Bold as Love* and *Lessons from the East.*

Few things are more important in global mission than a comprehensive vision of humility, and there are few people I would rather read on it than Andy McCullough. With a wealth of insight from Scripture, sociology, history, missiology and personal experience, he sheds light on all sorts of areas we need to be aware of and, more importantly, what to do about it. If it was in my power, I would make this required reading for anyone involved in cross-cultural mission.

Dr Andrew Wilson
Teaching Pastor, King's Church London, columnist for *Christianity Today* and author of several books.

The idea of humility is a helpful starting point for considering mission as the process of entering into another's world on the other's terms. The chapters in this book offer snapshots on a range of issues clustered around perspectives on humility. Selected portions of the Bible and cultural examples allow a smörgåsbord of different slants on missional issues. Although the author adopts a low-key, colloquial style, he draws on a wide range of sources and authors who are familiar with the complexity and challenges of mission in the modern world, and through them offers insights on the practicalities of mission.

Dr Warren Beattie
MA Programme Leader at All Nations Christian College, Ware, UK, and author of *Ministry Across Cultures: Sharing the Christian Faith in Asia.*

Every time I have heard Andy speak I have been provoked by his breadth of learning both from scholars and the people that he has sought to reach in many different missional contexts. In truth, as he has reached them he has opened his heart to allow them to reach him – and change him. This reality sets this book apart. You will glean not just ivory-tower theory but the very real experiences of a man, a family, that has lived and breathed what it means to love and serve people from other cultures in the name of Jesus. Andy's love for people and for God's world shines out through these pages and I know that you will gain much from taking the time to read, study and absorb all that he has to offer here.

Simon Holley
Senior Leader, King's Arms Church and Catalyst Network.

Introduction

Sitting in their living room sipping sweet coffee from tiny cups, I asked my hosts, a Lebanese Christian family, 'You have observed so many missionaries come and go over the last thirty years. What kind of people should we send here? And what kind of people should *not* come?'

'That's easy,' replied my host. 'It's all about attitude. They must be prepared to learn good Arabic – that takes several years of hard work. They must live among us, not separate from us. They must come to serve, not to judge; to learn, not to dictate; to be amongst, not above. They will come and go, but the Lebanese Church continues. They must contribute to our story, not inflict their own.'

Being born and growing up in Cyprus, having been involved in church planting in India, multicultural West London, and Istanbul, and having had countless conversations like the one above, I am persuaded that the aspect that needs training, more than any other, in cross-cultural workers, is *humility*. How dare you turn up with all the answers when you don't even know what questions people are asking? Pride and mission are polar opposites. Pride pollutes mission. The mission of Christ is humble mission.

For a church planter, godly character is essential, skill in evangelism is key, and the ability to work as part of a team, vital. All of these would be true for mission in your own cultural context, and are also needed cross-culturally. But there is a particular perspective, a certain capacity, without which entering a new culture to bring the gospel is impossible. The requisite capacity is an ability to handle grey (anyone crossing cultures quickly learns that not everything is black and white and that categories from before cannot be used), an appreciation of diversity, an honouring of others. I am calling this *Global Humility*.

There are many dimensions to Global Humility. *Moral Humility* condemns the sins of attitude; ethnocentrism, arrogance and judgementalism, that are more with us than we realise. *Public Humility* transforms geography and history; every nation tells its own story of the world, but can we learn to see the world through other eyes? *Semantic Humility* motivates Christians to study language, and insists upon inculturation of the gospel. *Intercultural Humility* demands more than mere *acceptance* of the fact that different cultures think, relate, are motivated and feel differently, and proposes *celebration* of God's wisdom and purpose in cultural diversity. *Incarnational Humility* interrogates the role of leadership in cross-cultural church planting. Finally, *Theological Humility* challenges the way we teach the Bible. If different cultural 'lenses' cause people to read the Bible differently, how are we as Evangelicals to understand this difference? Is our theology so brittle that it shatters when thrown up against another approach, or are we able to learn and adapt?

Cynicism about experts and a 'cutting out of the middle-man'[1] is a common postmodern trait that has permeated into the world mission. More and more churches and networks are sending people directly into cross-cultural mission without going through a third-party agency. This in itself is not bad (Newfrontiers, the network I am part of, are sending people this way too), but it does mean that we need to work harder at exposing people to the wisdom and expertise that is available, if only you know where to look. So I have quoted liberally from a wide range of writers and practitioners in Missiology, World Christianity and Intercultural studies so that my friends can become your friends. Sometimes I have even quoted two sources where one would have been enough! Indeed, each chapter in this book is a painfully tiny introduction to an enormous field of study, and I have tried to point the reader to scholarly resources which will guide them as they move forward.

Global Humility draws on my experience of cross-cultural church planting in India, multicultural West London, and Istanbul, and was written in Turkey, Cyprus, Greece, Lebanon and the UK.

This book should be useful, and I hope provocative, for cross-cultural Christian workers and candidates, for those involved in multicultural cities in their own nations, for sending pastors, and for anyone whose ministry or

Christian walk takes them across cultural divides. I hope it leaves you with more questions than answers. I hope it challenges and even offends you. I hope it provokes you to further study. And most of all, I hope and pray that it envisions and equips you to pursue with your whole life the goal of Christian mission: indigenous expression of ancient truth.

Endnotes
1. Johnson, Ros, 'Cutting out the Middleman: Mission and the local church in a globalised postmodern world' in Tiplady, R. (ed.), *One World or Many: The Impact of Globalisation on Mission* (Pasadena, CA: William Carey Library, 2003).

Moral Humility:
Thinking About Sin

If I had to write a decalogue for journeys, eight out of ten virtues
should be moral, and I should put first of all a temper as serene at the
end as at the beginning of the day. Then would come the capacity to
accept values and to judge by standards other than our own... [and] a
leisurely and uncensorious mind.

Freya Stark[2]

I sat in the headmaster's office, slid a cash-laden envelope across the desk,
and I did it with a clear conscience. The first year I had resisted with all
my heart. Pay a bribe to make sure my daughter got a school place? How
corrupt! Never! Of course, 'bribe' was my language, the headmaster had
called it a 'donation'. In English we only use the one word – bribe – and it
is loaded with guilt. In Turkish there are many finely nuanced words – gift,
donation, investment, friendship, cigarette money – and they are part of
how relationships and power work. They are part of the system.

Istanbul schools are under-funded, so these parental donations help to
equip the school with necessary resources. In many countries, the police
are poorly paid because (or 'and so' – cause and effect is complicated) it is
expected that they will supplement their income with gifts.

The book of Proverbs understands this complexity. There are six
references to bribery in Proverbs: three positive and three negative.[3]
Adeney, in his classic book on cross-cultural ethics, writes:

While the extortion of bribes is roundly condemned, the giving of
bribes (or gifts to officials) is not condemned ... Such equivocation

in the Old Testament seems to reflect a recognition of the power differential between a poor person who gives a gift in order to stage off injustice and the rich who uses his power to exploit the poor. *The powerful and the powerless are not judged by the same abstract absolute.*[4]

It's easy to have an opinion from a distance. We could all be a better football manager or president from the comfort of our sofas! But when you get closer to things they seem more complex, more nuanced, more confusing.

You may have a very decided perspective on polygamy, until you live among polygamous people who are starting to come to Christ, and you have to pastor them through the politics of family and tribal loyalties, of who cares for the estranged wives, even of how to interpret polygamous heroes in the Old Testament!

You may be very strongly pro-Israel, until you visit the Middle East and meet displaced Palestinian Christians. Or you may be anti-Israel, until you meet Israeli Christians who believe that they have a God-given right to the land. Your view will become more refined. Softer, perhaps.

Perhaps you have had very absolute views on sexuality, and then met a passionate Christ-follower who struggles with same-sex attraction, and suddenly you are forced to think more delicately.

Proximity helps us to appreciate complexity. It begets empathy. It compels us to take responsibility. Tearing down is easy, but proximity means we have to help rebuild. Proximity prohibits simplistic solutions. It causes us to be invested emotionally in the issues. Proximity, then, should be a priority. Mission that is not up-close-and-personal is inadequate.

In order to develop meaningful appreciation of another culture, our understanding of sin needs to change in two areas. Firstly, with regard to our own attitudinal sins of superiority, ethnocentrism, judgementalism, arrogance. 'Why do you see the speck that is in your brother's eye, but do not notice the log that is in your own eye?'[5] Don't you see? Even if you only had a speck in your eye, it would block your vision because it is *in your eye!* Not while sitting reading this book, but only by crossing a border or crossing our cities and meeting new people, can these attitudinal sins be dealt with. That is why part of Jesus' discipleship strategy was to take his disciples across the northern border into foreign territory to minister to a woman there.[6] Bailey comments on this story: 'Evil cannot be redeemed until it is exposed. In his dialogue with the woman Jesus exposes deep prejudices in the hearts of his disciples.'[7] Jesus' discipleship strategy is the same today – those who cross cultures on mission testify to being made aware of logs in their eye. The Bible has a lot to say about these kinds of sins, and there is a recurring call for repentance, for those with ears to hear.

Secondly, having worked hard to remove our own eye-logs, we will come to a place where we are confronting cultural strongholds amongst those we are reaching, although with most entry strategies this should not happen in the first few years. *Most guests never earn the right to criticise the host.* But when we are evangelising, church planting, discipling or caring cross-culturally, we will encounter sin and require a framework to help people to be freed from its entangling power. In Chapter Five, I offer some thoughts on a definition of sin which should help us to develop compassion and empathy.

Moral humility is the opposite of moral superiority. It flows from our apprehension of grace. May grace be at work in us as we wrestle these issues through!

Endnotes

2. Freya Stark, *A Winter in Arabia,* cited in Storti, Craig, *The Art of Crossing Cultures,* Second Edition (London: Nicholas Brealey, 2007), 127.

3. Proverbs 15:27; 17:8; 17:23; 18:16; 21:14; 22:16.

4. Adeney, Bernard T., *Strange Virtues: Ethics in a Multicultural World* (Leicester: Apollos, 1995), 152, emphasis mine.

5. Matthew 7:3.

6. Mark 7:24-30.

7. Bailey, Kenneth E., *Jesus Through Middle Eastern Eyes: Cultural Studies in the Gospels* (London: SPCK, 2008), 266.

Chapter 1
Tamar: Voice from the Margins

One of the great sins of those who cross cultures, particularly those who travel from the powerful to the powerless, is the sin of judging. The centre judges the margins. The strong judge the weak. The missionary judges the heathen. The Christian judges the non-Christian.

That the Scripture condemns such a perspective is clear in the many Old Testament encounters between Israel and Gentile nations. But nowhere is it more dramatic, more emotive, than in the Genesis 38 encounter between Judah and Tamar.

This is a story of cross-cultural encounter on many levels: oppressor with oppressed, religious centre with margins, male with female, insider with outsider, proud with lowly, Jew with non-Jew.

The context is that the Holy Family have gone from being a tiny minority to a large, wealthy clan, and the rot of complacency has already begun to set in. Where Abraham and Isaac walked with God, Jacob's sons have sold their brother Joseph as a slave, and Judah, one of the key instigators, is in a downward spiral of sin. In Genesis 38:1-5 he separates from the brothers, perhaps from shame after selling Joseph into slavery, befriends Hirah – a bad influence – marries a Canaanite, produces evil sons, and ends up living in Chezib, which means 'deception'. Thus, in the first five verses of the chapter the writer sketches the decline of centre, comfortable religion.

God will do what he always does. He will raise up a voice from the *margins* to save the *centre*, to put the Holy Family back on track. That voice belongs to Tamar.

In the renewal and expansion of the church, the breakthroughs always occur on the fringe of ecclesiastical power – never at the centre. In every generation, in some obscure place, God is beginning something new. That's where we need to be.[8]

When Tamar is introduced in Genesis 38:6 she is named – a mark of honour (Shua's daughter in verse 2 was not named). Our interest is piqued by this Gentile woman.

Verses 6-11 require us to understand the system of Levirate marriage, common in the Middle East and parts of Africa even today. Otherwise the reader will just judge Tamar out of hand for what, by Western standards, seems like blatant sexual manipulation. Bible-reading is a cross-cultural experience, and this story is a prime example of condemning without understanding, of judging Tamar by the standard of our privilege ('if I had been in that situation, I would never have done what she did'). The point, of course, is that you are not in her situation! The powerful often assume that options are unlimited, the poor know that they are not.

It was Tamar's God-ordained and cultural right to be given, on the death of Son 1, to Son 2. And on the death of Son 2, to Son 3. This was for prolonging of the name (honour) of Son 1 through offspring, and for the care of the widow. Additionally, although not explicit in the Mosaic Law, there is some evidence that in Canaan, if there were no remaining sons, she should be given to the father-in-law for the same reasons.

> *Genesis 38:8:* Then Judah said to Onan, 'Go in to your brother's wife and perform the duty of a brother-in-law to her, and raise up offspring for your brother.'
> *Genesis 38:9:* But Onan knew that the offspring would not be his. So whenever he went in to his brother's wife he would waste the semen on the ground, so as not to give offspring to his brother.
> *Genesis 38:10:* And what he did was wicked in the sight of the LORD, and he put him to death also.

Onan sins against Tamar, against the memory of his dead brother, against the tradition and against God by not allowing Tamar to conceive. Her shame is compounded (the gossip in the community would have been that she was barren, now she is with Onan and still not pregnant), whilst Onan's reputation is intact (he appears to everyone as though he is doing the honourable thing). If you are not going to fulfil her right to conceive, at least don't sleep with her! But Onan takes advantage of her without taking responsibility for her. He takes without giving. He is more concerned not to jeopardise his own offspring and lineage than to do what is right in the eyes of God.

What Onan did to Tamar is a picture of the oppression of the powerless by the powerful.

Judah, similarly, sins by sending Tamar away instead of giving her to Son 3. 'This woman is toxic! I gave her to Son 1. He died. I gave her to Son 2. He died. No way am I giving her to Son 3!' By sending her back to her father's house he is essentially ending her life. She will live in shame. She will never marry or conceive. Her life is finished. No hope. No future. No options.

What Tamar does next is actually heroic. She should have stayed consigned to her fate, just rolled over and given up. Like many in the world today who could be called 'poor' or 'powerless', she has until now been the object of all the verbs and the subject of none, she has been used and discarded like a tissue. The people of God are supposed to be the heroes in Bible stories, but Judah and his sons are the villains here.

Tamar weighs up her options. It is her right to be under the protection of this family and to conceive by this man. She hears that Judah has gone up to the sheep-shearing festival, looking for a good time. He is pursuing pleasure whilst Tamar is pursuing survival. Again, what an indictment of the comfortable today, viz-a-viz the suffering. 'She took off her widow's garments.'[9] In Genesis, garments speak of identity, even of fate.[10] Joseph was clothed by his father as a sign of particular honour, and stripped by his brothers to shame him and condemn him to slavery. Tamar chooses against fatalism and resignation, which would have been so easy to succumb to, she takes off her widow's garments, and she does what she can with the limited resources at her disposal. She becomes the subject of several verbs for the first time. Tamar takes responsibility for herself where Judah had taken no responsibility for her.

The story praises a powerless woman for her initiative and courage in the face of enormous odds. And she is explicitly honoured for the second time in the story in verse 18, 'and she conceived'. This is a direct action, even vindication, by God.

When, in verse 24, Judah is told that Tamar is pregnant, he condemns her in two Hebrew words, 'Bring her, burn her.' Decisive. Hasty. Haughty. Wrong.

Tamar, dragged out to stand before her judge, Judah, presents the proof that he is the father. Even thousands of years later, we can still hear her poise, her dignity, her courage, her integrity in speaking truth to power. 'By the man to whom these belong, I am pregnant.'[11]

The margins confront the centre. The weak rebuke the strong. The lowly shame the proud.[12]

And Judah has a decision to make. Throughout this entire narrative he has not taken responsibility, not thought about anyone but himself.

Then Judah identified them and said, 'She is more righteous than I, since I did not give her to my son Shelah.'[13]

He confesses his sin. He declares her righteous. The phrase he uses is the phrase used for justification, for declaring righteous, for vindication by God. This is Tamar's third explicit honouring in the passage. Judah repents, takes responsibility, and begins to change. By the time he is reunited with Joseph in Egypt he is a changed, humbled man. The Holy Family gets back on track. And it was Tamar that God used to do it. This woman makes a man of Judah. She saves God's means of salvation.

And she has twins. And Perez forces his way out first, even though he was going to be born second to his brother. And he is named Perez, which means 'Making a breach', like his mother, who made a breach in her death-like widowhood and forced her way out, taking off her widow's garments and taking command of her own destiny. And isn't this just like Perez' great descendant Jesus Christ, who would refuse to surrender to the tomb but forced his way out that glorious Sunday morning? Tamar made a breach in her fate. Perez made a breach in the womb. And Jesus made a breach in death!

The fourth time Tamar is honoured in Scripture is when she is named in the genealogy of Christ.[14]

When North meets South

This story carries wisdom for those on both sides of the global divide. Luther wrote that it was recorded to rebuke presumption and to challenge despair: 'No one should be presumptuous about his own righteousness or wisdom, and none should despair on account of his sins.'[15]

The tendency for Judahs is presumption, and all the sins that follow: pursuit of pleasure, hasty condemnation, not taking responsibility for the poor, rejecting those whom God is accepting.

The tendency for Tamars is despair, or fatalism. The Global South, the downtrodden, the marginalised must do what they can with the limited resources available to them, and God will vindicate. It's all too easy to wallow in self-pity and in victim status. Tamar issues a call to take responsibility. Consider the following lines from Pakistani poet Iqbal:

In Rome an old monk said to me:
'I have a piece of wisdom, and I give it to you:
Every nation causes its own downfall –
You were destroyed by fate, we by our strategy.'[16]

Iqbal's meaning is this: each nation's great strength is also it's undoing. Muslims' submission to God[17] can become a passive fatalism; the West's confident strategising can become arrogant presumption.

Richards and O'Brien write, 'The point of collision is a priceless opportunity for learning.'[18] Whenever we meet at a cultural divide, mutual learning should ensue.

Let's understand the massive differences between Judah's world and Tamar's world, differences which have never been starker than they are today. In Genesis 38, the contrast between Judah and Tamar is drawn as follows.

Judah	Tamar
Centre	Margins
Views options/resource as unlimited	Options are limited

Pursues pleasure	Pursues survival
Big sin: judging	Big sin: fatalism
Should bring forth Christ	Does bring forth Christ
Needs humility and compassion	Needs courage
Can despise heritage	Newly come into heritage
Is rebuked by Scripture	Is honoured by Scripture

Judah, in the end, hears what Tamar has to say and is able to humble himself in response. God is always raising up Tamars, but very rarely does the Church at the 'centre' know what to do with these voices from the margins.

> The western church does not yet know how to deal with all of the input from the majority world, since it finds itself in a relatively new postcolonial era.[19]

Indeed, many in the Church in the West have not even been exposed to this 'input from the majority world'. For most of us, the authors on our bookshelves and the speakers at our conferences are like us. When we do begin to encounter Tamar's voice, the words of James are extremely important – 'quick to hear, slow to speak, slow to anger'.[20] If we will approach cultural fault lines to learn, rather than, like Judah, to condemn, if we will embrace rather than shoving away, then perhaps we will hear God speaking in unexpected places.

What does this passage teach about crossing cultural boundaries? Do not judge others according to the standard of your privilege. Humble yourself to listen, God could be speaking through an unexpected person. Travel to learn, not just to teach. Look to see whom the Holy Spirit is honouring, even if they don't fit your box. Know that Christianity is always changing at the margins more profoundly than at the centre, and position yourself accordingly. Know that churches or movements with no input from the margins will die.

It is, in the end, the marriage of Judah and Tamar that brings forth Christ! When Judah was proud, he nearly burned Tamar and would have forfeited her contribution to the story. When Judah humbled himself, he was able to learn and be changed. Reform movements so often start at the margins and create a synthesis with the centre. But can the centre heed the margins? This demands humility.

Endnotes

8. Addison, S., *Movements That Change the World* (Smyrna, DE: Missional Press, 2009), Kindle loc. 265.

9. Genesis 38:14.

10. Alter, Robert, *The Art of Biblical Narrative* (New York: Basic Books, 1981), Kindle loc. 198.

11. Genesis 38:25.

12. 1 Corinthians 1:27-28.

13. Genesis 38:26.

14. Matthew 1:3.

15. Luther, Martin, *Luther's Works*, vol. 7, 'Lectures on Genesis', Pelikan, J. and Poellot, D.E. (eds.) (St Louis, MO: Concordia, 1960), 11.

16. Iqbal, Muhammad, Armaghan-i Hijaz 851:3 in Iqbal, Muhammad (trans. Mustansir Mir), *Tulip in the Desert* (London: C. Hurst & Co., 2000), 144.

17. Muslim means 'one who submits'.

18. Richards, E. Randolph and O'Brien, Brandon J., *Misreading Scripture With Western Eyes* (Downers Grove, IL: IVP, 2012), 49.

19. Shaw, R. Daniel and Van Engen, C.E., *Communicating God's Word in a Complex World: God's Truth or Hocus Pocus?* (Lanham, MD: Rowman and Littlefield, 2003), 16.

20. James 1:19.

Chapter 2
The Sins of Jonah

The little book of Jonah is *the* classic picture of cross-cultural mission in the Old Testament. Jonah exhibits a whole catalogue of shortcomings, many of which are in his *attitude* towards the Ninevites. Jonah's story is Israel's story, is the Church's story, is *our* story. Many missionaries over the years have found they have identified deeply with Jonah. There is something about ethnocentrism, for example, that never comes to the surface while you are in your home environment, but that is exposed down to its rotten root when you are flung up on a distant shore.

Is the book of Jonah about God saving Nineveh, or about God saving Jonah? Veteran missionary James Frazer, when asked eagerly by a student, 'What was your biggest surprise when you went to China?' replied, 'Myself'.[21] I wonder if Jonah would have answered similarly.

> The proper traveller ... thinks it a waste to move from his own home if nothing happens inside him as a result. I mean something fundamental, like a chemical change when two substances come into contact.[22]

Humility is reading Scripture and identifying with its weak characters. If Jonah had such gaping flaws, the chances are we do too. Jonah does not have much to teach us about strategy, but a whole load to teach us about our hearts.

Sin 1. Judging whilst God is saving

Jonah 1:2: Arise, go to Nineveh, that great city, and call out against it, for their evil has come up before me.

The word 'evil' in this verse is often translated or read as Nineveh's 'wickedness' (NIV, KJV), while it could just as easily mean 'trouble, hardship, calamity, misery'.[23] In fact, Stuart comments on this verse that '"wickedness" is a less likely translation, especially since throughout the book God's attitude towards Nineveh is not denunciary but merciful, in sharp contrast to Jonah's'.[24]

Sin, of course, is both. It is wickedness that comes from within us and it is calamity that comes upon us. As we will see in Chapter Five, Sin as Tyrant and Humanity as Victim are very common themes in Scripture, and theologically essential for developing compassion.

Nineveh is like the 'man born blind' in John 9, when the disciples ask, 'Rabbi, who sinned, this man or his parents, that he was born blind?' and Jesus answered, 'Neither' (NIV).[25]

Perhaps this Hebrew word is ambivalent for a reason, suggesting that God meant one thing by his commission but that Jonah understood another! Jonah walks into Nineveh with condemnation in his heart, and God pours out salvation!

'It is significant', writes Schreiner, 'that Jonah comes after Obadiah, correcting a false conclusion that might be drawn from Obadiah.'[26] Reading Obadiah, it could be possible to forget that the purpose of Israel's election was for the nations. God's people are not supposed to rejoice when other nations are under judgement, but to take responsibility for their blessing.

What do you see when you look at the massive unreached cities of the world? Why are they lost? Whose fault is it? What message do they need to hear?

Sin 2. Turning the river into a reservoir

The story of Jonah is Israel's story, is humankind's story, is our story.

Jonah is commissioned to go (1:2). He disobeys and runs into a storm. God has to rescue him, there is a death-resurrection-type experience, and then God in his grace re-commissions him (3:1,2) and this time Jonah obeys.

Adam and Eve were commissioned to go into all the world, bearing God's image (Genesis 1:28). They disobeyed and ran into a storm (Genesis 3). God had to rescue them through the death-resurrection experience of the second Adam, Jesus. And then humankind was recommissioned (John 20:21).

God's intention has never been for blessing to stay in one place, but for it to be spread to others. The promise to Abraham in Genesis 12 was two-fold: I will bless you, and you will be a blessing to all the families of the earth... I bless you, you bless others. Sadly, there is a tendency for the blessed to forget the second fold of this promise. The favour of God was supposed to be a river: God to you, you to others... but often we dam up the river and make it into a reservoir.

I often hear church leaders, for example, talking about trying to close their 'back door'. Urban churches can have a big front door (many new people attending) but also a big back door (people moving on). What is sometimes meant by this is people backsliding without being noticed, which is a matter of genuine concern. However, at other times pastors are talking about the naturally high turnover of urban churchgoers. Trying to close this back door is analogous to trying to dam a river. Shouldn't this flow of people rather be seen as an opportunity to send blessing to other places via people who are moving on?

There is a significant church in a Turkish town where many refugees from Iran, Iraq and Syria wait to get their UNHCR approval to move on to European or North American destinations. They often stay in this town for up to three years. The church serves, feeds, helps and leads large numbers of refugees to Christ annually. They are part of the fellowship for a season, but then they move on. If the only goal was to build a big reservoir in that town, then the pastors would constantly be frustrated by the 'leakage'. But a missional perspective enables these leaders to see that sending is as important as gathering. If only all pastors were like this!

In 2014, when many from East Ukraine had to leave their homes and flee the region or even the country, my dear friend Andrey Bondarenko, who serves a number of churches in East Ukraine (and who also had to flee his home with his wife and two children), had to make a choice. He could be distraught that everything he had been *building* had been dismantled, or he could see this as an (albeit unexpected and painful) opportunity for *sowing*. 'We told our people they were not refugees. They were missionaries,' says Andrey. 'Church members have scattered all over the place, and wherever they go they are starting new congregations. We are even planting churches in India and Portugal as a result!'

Jonah is written as a rebuke to Israel who had forgotten that the blessing of Abraham was supposed to be a river, not a lake. Jonah is called by God to arise (1:2). He is called by the ship's captain to arise (1:6). God and the world are calling us, Church. Arise!

Catholic theologian Aylward Shorter affirms that

Israel's election was a constant call to universality that remained unfulfilled in the Old Testament. It was a continual challenge that the chosen people failed to take up fully. In fact, Israel was continually tempted to resist the obligations of universality and often the sins of the chosen people were caused by a too exclusive understanding of their election.[27]

Sin 3. Ethnocentrism

We think we are not ethnocentric until confronted with evidence to the contrary. Humankind was happy with a geo-centric universe until presented with indisputable evidence that the sun is actually the centre!

The English, for example, find Italians too emotional, Germans too serious but, by implication, themselves just right! Seeing yourselves as normal and others as extreme is an example of ethnocentrism – an in-built superiority of perspective.

The unfounded superiority in Jonah's heart is exposed over and over again. The sailors show the fear of God while Jonah is in denial (1:6). The King of Nineveh is portrayed as having better theological understanding than Jonah (3:9).[28] The Ninevites are repentant while Jonah is unrepentant (3:6). Israel isn't better than others!

This is written to challenge the Jewish idea that they were the only seat of revelation, that they had nothing to learn from other nations. How like us! We travel to teach, but not to learn. We assume that our way of doing things is the best, even the *only* way. We think that we have a monopoly on sound doctrine, and that by definition others must be unsound.

Christopher Wright's comment on Jonah really hits the nail on the head: 'The concluding open-ended question of the book is an enduring, haunting rebuke to our tendency to foist our own ethnocentric prejudices on to the Almighty.'[29]

David Devenish, in a seminar in 2012, said: 'We need people from other cultures who understand the gospel to set us free from similar prejudices. The gospel is not safe in any culture without a witness within that culture from beyond itself.'[30]

Peskett and Ramachandra comment on this also, making application to cross-cultural missions today:

> The unsettling thing for the reader of the book (and it ought to have been unsettling for Jonah too) is that the sailors and the Ninevites seem to have grasped something about God which the orthodox Jonah has not reached.
>
> Those who move from one culture to another, especially if they are moved by missionary loyalty to the One whom they believe to be the true and living God, often have to struggle with this largeness and surprisingness of God.[31]

Sin 4. Non-appreciation

This phrase is taken from Japanese theologian Kosuke Koyama, who in *Three Mile an Hour God* wrote:

> While Jesus Christ, the head of the church, has an appreciative mind, often his historical churches have displayed a non-appreciative or even anti-appreciative mind. *Only rarely is the church moved.* Often it has rejected, 'thrown cold water upon' the one who said 'all these I have observed from my youth.' The cultural values of Asia and the Pacific have not been appreciated. They were, in a package, decided to be against the values for which Jesus Christ stood, though in most cases such judgement has been given in terms of the values found in the Western life-style for which Jesus Christ does not necessarily stand. That which was unfamiliar to the church was condemned as anti-Christian. One of the few most critical problems posed to the life in the Christian faith is this lack of appreciation-perspective.[32]

Non-appreciation can be found anywhere. At one time we had a Christian lady from Georgia (the country, not the US state) staying with us. One of our Muslim friends popped round to visit my wife, who was unwell. When I say 'popped', I mean she travelled two hours across the city by bus, carrying with her large amounts of home-cooked food, visited for a short time, then travelled two hours home.

When our Muslim friend turned up at the house, our Georgian friend pulled me into the kitchen. 'Who is that woman?'

'She's a friend,' I replied.

'But she's… she's one of *them*!' She could not wrap her mind around anything good coming from a Muslim. It grated with her world view.

The issue here is one of common grace. Those who define things by in-or-out, like 'Christian and non-Christian', or 'us and them', miss a whole spectrum of grace that has been given to the non-Christian, which theologians call common grace.

According to John Murray, common grace is 'every favour of whatever kind or degree, falling short of salvation, which this undeserving and sin-cursed world enjoys at the hand of God'.[33]

In the book of Jonah we witness a large amount of common grace given to those whom the Jews would not have considered likely. I agree with Douglas Stuart:

> The book does not suggest universalism, that all peoples or nations are chosen, but does teach that non-believing peoples may still benefit in some ways from God's compassion. In this regard the book teaches the biblical doctrine of common grace (i.e. that some of God's blessings in this life are given to all people in general, not just believers).[34]

God clearly loves Nineveh. The parable of the vine in chapter 4, followed by the words 'and should not I pity Nineveh …' imply that God has been labouring over the growth of this pagan city, as he had over the vine.

> There is a wonderful implication here, a thought so novel it must have taken away the breath of any ordinary Jew of the period. Could the Prophet really mean that God, the God of Abraham, of Isaac, and of

Jacob, had 'laboured' for a heathen growth like Nineveh and 'made it grow'? This was indeed a strange extension of the uncovenanted mercies of God![35]

God is at work in the world, not just in the Church. Those who cross cultures, encounter new perspectives, enter into new expressions, should do so with appreciation, even awe, knowing that God has been at work long before we got there, expecting to discern God's grace, even beauty, in the lives of those whom we have gone to 'instruct'.

Sin 5. Projecting our idea of success onto God
Nineveh repents, God relents, and Jonah vents!

Jonah 4:1: But it displeased Jonah exceedingly, and he was angry.

Things not working out as you had planned is par for the course in cross-cultural missions. The instant you step off the plane, you are transformed from a high-functioning person to an infantile, laughed-at incompetent. You go from being able to achieve ten things in a day to aiming for two, and sometimes hitting one of them. Functioning in a second language is like driving with the brakes on (sometimes I can even smell the burning rubber coming from my brain). And when it comes to ministry, measures of success need to be totally redefined. Otherwise you end up like Jonah – angry.

God shows Jonah that this actually is an issue of identity. It's a fig leaf. When the plant is eaten by the worm, Jonah is angry. Ever since Adam and Eve, we humans have a habit of trying to cover our nakedness with something; for them a fig leaf, for Jonah a plant as a metaphor of his identity in something other than the righteousness of Christ. For us, competence, fruitfulness, successful ministry, or at least busyness in pursuit of success.

You find out what your fig leaves are if you get angry when they are eaten by worms. You get laid up sick and are frustrated because of not being able to work. Of the five people who you led to Christ, three of them fall away again. At one point I had four kids in four different schools around Istanbul and was spending three and a half hours a day in traffic on school runs.

31

That's when I realised that 'efficiency' was an idol; when you have no option of living efficiently you either spend every day angry or you surrender it to the worms.

Jonah needed to learn that obedience is success, and that results belong to God.

Sin 6. Missing God despite right theology

Jonah knows his Bible well, but does not know God well. He is able to quote from the prophets in 4:2, 'You are a gracious God and merciful, slow to anger and abounding in steadfast love, and relenting from disaster', but he had never considered that these Scriptures, written to Israel, could be applied also to disaster-relenting towards pagans.

First and foremost, Jonah's compassion is too limited and narrowly focused. He cares for what does not matter (or hardly matters) and does not care for what matters ... he only wants to be merciful where to do so is safe and carries no risk.[36]

The apostle James is ferociously committed to there not being a gap between what we know and what we do. Reading the Bible does not end with reading, but with doing; otherwise you haven't read properly.

Jesus said to the scribes, 'You search the Scriptures because you think that in them you have eternal life; and it is they that bear witness about me, yet you refuse to come to me that you may have life.'[37]

It is possible to know rightly without doing rightly. Doing enlarges and completes knowing. Knowing and not doing is sin. Orthodoxy without orthopraxy is dead. We are not judged according to what we know, but according to what we do with what we know. 'Everyone to whom much was given, of him much will be required.'[38]

Sin 7. Assumption of security

Jonah is sitting in the sun watching for judgement to fall on Nineveh. It is a fierce Iraqi sun, and it will kill him. To save him from certain death, God sends a plant to give him shade; a parable of gracious salvation. And Jonah rejoices in God's salvation. He sits in the shade waiting for God to judge

Nineveh. A rebuke to Israel; enjoying God's election whilst the 'non-elect' suffer wrath. May the Church never be like this!

The taking away of the plant is a prophecy, a terrible warning that God will not tolerate such complacency. It is a prophecy fulfilled some years later when the Assyrians came and took away Israel's shelter. And finally when Jesus said, 'The kingdom of God will be taken away from you and given to a people producing its fruits.'[39]

In the same way, it is a warning hanging over the Church. We know that Jesus removes lampstands. Movements and churches that miss the missional compassion of God miss God. Navel-gazing leads to stagnation which leads to destruction. Rejoice in the particularity of your election, but don't take it for granted. Don't ignore the great unreached cities of the world. Don't sit in the shade watching. Don't turn the river into a reservoir.

As the king of Nineveh asked in 3:9, 'Who knows?' There is much that we don't know. Let's learn from the sins of Jonah.

Endnotes

21. Crossman, Eileen, *Mountain Rain: A New Biography of James O. Fraser* (Littleton, CO: OMF International, 2011), Kindle loc. 1319.

22. Stark, Freya, Letters quoted in Storti, Craig, *The Art of Crossing Cultures*, Second Edition (London: Nicholas Brealey, 2007), 135.

23. Stuart, Douglas Jonah in Carson et al (eds.) *New Bible Commentary*, Fourth Edition (Nottingham: IVP, 1994), 820.

24. Ibid. 815.

25. John 9:2,3 NIV.

26. Schreiner, Thomas R., *The King in His Beauty: A Biblical Theology of the Old and New Testaments* (Grand Rapids, MI: Baker Academic, 2013), 408.

27. Shorter, Aylward, *Toward a Theology of Inculturation* (Eugene, OR: Wipf & Stock, 1999), 112.

28. Moberly, R.W.L., *Old Testament Theology: Reading the Hebrew Bible as Christian Scripture* (Grand Rapids, MI: Baker Academic, 2013), Kindle loc. 4587.

29. Wright, Christopher J.H., *The Mission of God: Unlocking the Bible's Grand Narrative* (Nottingham: IVP, 2006), 461.

30. Devenish, David, Main Session EFM 2012 in USA. Devenish is referencing Bailey, *Jesus Through Middle Eastern Eyes*, 166, who is in turn referencing Niles, D.T., *Upon the Earth: The Mission of God and the Missionary Enterprise of the Churches* (London: Lutterworth Press, 1962), 166.

31. Peskett, H. and Ramachandra, V., *The Message of Mission* (Leicester: IVP, 2003), 131.

32. Koyama, Kosuke, *Three Mile an Hour God* (London: SCM Press, 1979), 9.

33. Murray, John, *Collected Writings of John Murray* (Edinburgh: Banner of Truth, 1977), 2:96

34. Stuart, Douglas, *Jonah*, 814.

35. Caiger, Stephen L., *Lives of the Prophets: A Thousand Years of Hebrew Prophecy Reviewed in its Historical Context* (London: SPCK 1949), 292.

36. Moberly, *Old Testament Theology*, Kindle loc. 4852.

37. John 5:39-40.

38. Luke 12:48.

39. Matthew 21:43.

Chapter 3
The Men from James

The Men from James were probably good-hearted. It's not that they were evil. Most likely, they were of good standing in the Jerusalem church. And we obviously have no quarrel with James himself, the brother of Jesus! Indeed, James denied any knowledge of these men.[40] Neither did Paul pick a quarrel with James. He honoured him and loved him.

So why have the Men from James gone down in sacred history as grace-killers? How come Paul is so angry in Galatians? What is the sin of the Men from James?

The sin of the Men from James[41] was that they believed they could impose, or at least commend, Jerusalem Christianity to non-Jerusalem Christians. They had not understood that all expressions of Christianity are contextual, including their own. That the Pauline apostolic sphere of churches was parallel to, not contingent upon or subservient to the Yacoban sphere.[42] In short, that Christianity was becoming multi-centric.

So they commended Torah-keeping, and circumcision, and dietary constraints, and other Jewish 'cultural baggage', which were (arguably) appropriate for born-again Jerusalem Christians, but not for those in other churches.

'This is how we do it in Jerusalem,' they cried. And Peter, and Barnabas and the Antiochene and the Galatian Christians were listening to them! As Meeks and Wilken wrote: 'What Paul was resisting, in his confrontation with Peter, was the attempt of Jerusalem to extend its authority to Antioch.'[43]

Fast-forward 1,800 years to the height of the British Empire, and we see an identical dynamic at work. British missionaries to Africa, for example, bringing the gospel plus civilisation. 'This is how we do it in London! You need organs and bishops and three-piece suits.' I remember a conversation with a pastor from Tanzania when he said to me, 'You guys now mock us for wearing suits on a Sunday. You call us legalistic. But it was you who brought us the suits in the first place!'

Lamin Sanneh in his magisterial *Disciples of All Nations*, writes:

> The West's immense cultural achievement spawned the sentiment of cultural righteousness, and demanded maturity in converts as a condition of Christian acceptance. The call to repentance and faith was a call to renounce non-Western customs ...
>
> Mission as European cultural righteousness contradicted the gospel as God's irrevocable gift of salvation to all people.[44]

This is really important! See how easily it can happen? We believe our culture is the true expression of Christian culture. We want the best for our converts. So we bring the gospel plus something. And, as Paul contends in the first verses of Galatians, the gospel plus anything is a non-gospel. It enslaves rather than liberates. It produces slaves, not sons.

Today with ease of travel, technology and widespread access to English language, this phenomenon is as pronounced as it has ever been. People travelling from the West to plant or teach or partner with churches in other places will regularly say things like, 'This is how we do it back home.' Whether leadership techniques, worship styles, church organisation or theological training, the Men from James continue to assume that because this is how it was done in Jerusalem, that's how it should be done in Antioch.

This does not, of course, negate the giving and receiving of travelling ministries cross-culturally. The entire Pauline corpus is evidence to the contrary. Paul and Barnabas, while in Antioch, welcomed travelling prophets from Jerusalem (Acts 11:27). Both men are recognised and received from place to place as apostles, and part of their ministry was, of course, teaching. Paul even wrote to the Corinthians, 'This is my rule in all the churches' (1 Corinthians 7:17). Indigenisation is not the same as isolation.

The question that needs to be asked, then, is does the teaching or the example that is brought from outside direct the church towards a contextual maturity, or does it rather pull the church towards a non-indigenous way of doing things?

The difference is the difference between converts and proselytes, between freeholders and leaseholders, between first class and second class. Very rarely would any use this language, yet that is precisely the implication of the statement, 'This is how we do it in Jerusalem.' Too often in mission, Jerusalem is attempting to extend its control to Antioch all over again.

I would like to suggest five reasons why Men from James (let's be honest, I am talking about Christians from established churches in one place travelling to newer Christians in another place) bring so much cultural baggage with them when they travel. This is not a purely Western tendency, Nigerian or Korean churches can be equally at fault! Then I will suggest three reasons why newer believers in newer Christian contexts are prone to receive, even ask for, a 'Western Christianity'.

Export tendencies (Why the Men from James bring what they bring)

1. Blindness to the contextual nature of their own Christianity

Samuel Escobar, famously, has commented that 'all theology is contextual.'[45] How much of what you are used to as normal Christianity is actually culturally conditioned? How much of what you think is objective is actually subjective? The answer, as I hope to show in the chapters that follow, is: 'Much more than you think!'

> All theology was influenced, if not determined, by the context in which it had evolved. There never was a 'pure' message, supracultural and suprahistorical. It was impossible to penetrate to a residue of Christian faith that was not already, in a sense, interpretation.[46]

And so, believing that how they do it in Jerusalem is how it is to be done everywhere, Men from James export their brand of orthodoxy, declaring it to be The Orthodoxy.

2. Desire for results

Paul writes of the Galatian agitators:

Galatians 6:12: It is those who want to *make a good showing* in the flesh who would force you to be circumcised, and only in order that they may not be persecuted for the cross of Christ.

Galatians 6:13: For even those who are circumcised do not themselves keep the law, but they desire to have you circumcised that they may *boast in your flesh.*[47]

In other words, the Men from James are looking to 'make a good showing' or 'boast' in appearances. Sadly, the same can be true today. When missionaries measure success in Western terms, believers can be forced or persuaded into things other than the gospel. This can be micro-ethical milestones in discipleship (stopping smoking, having a 'quiet time', regular church attendance, even transitioning from polygamy to monogamy!), standards of leadership (attaining a certain level of evangelical orthodoxy or a certain degree of organisation), or church success measured as numerical growth. The battle for the cross-cultural worker, rather, is to resist their preconceived measurements and submit to Roland Allen's assessment, 'I do not trust spectacular things. Give me the seed growing in secret every time.'[48]

3. Paternalism

It is natural for those from established churches in nations with a long history of Christianity to think that they have a fathering role towards newer churches in newer Christian contexts. The post-colonial cry in many parts of the world, however, would be, 'We have grown up much more quickly than you think, and we have much to teach you too!'

It is difficult, however, for those who think they are centre to express anything other than (even benevolent) paternalism: 'Is the Western Christian academy's insistence on adhering to one particular method of biblical interpretation a form of hermeneutical neo-colonialism?'[49]

Philip Jenkins, in *The New Faces of Christianity*, writes that Christian libraries have books on 'Asian Theology', 'African Theology', etc., but that books written by Europeans or North Americans are just called 'Theology': 'We will know that the transition is underway when publishers start offering studies of 'North American theologies.'[50]

4. Not trusting the power of the gospel
Paul to the Asian elders when he told them he would never see them again, said:

> *Acts 20:32:* And now I commend you to God and *to the word of his grace*, which is able to build you up and to give you the inheritance among all those who are sanctified.[51]

The word of the gospel is able to keep and build the believers. All of the tree is in the seed. Everything in an enormous mature tree was originally in the seed; all the DNA necessary. A seed needs planting and watering and needs space clearing out for it to grow (James 1:21), but does not need adding to. So with the gospel of the grace of God in Christ!

To paraphrase Timothy Keller, the Men from James were saying, 'You have been saved by grace, which is the ABC of the Christian life. Now let's teach you the rest of the Alphabet.' Meanwhile, Paul is arguing that grace is the A to Z of the Christian life![52]

5. Not trusting the Holy Spirit
Roland Allen has written:

> When the activities usurp the place of the Holy Spirit, the Spirit is obscured and hidden, because He is in fact deposed from His rightful place. It is He who creates leaders, it is He who enlightens, it is He who uplifts, it is He who teaches men to 'live', whatever the conditions in which they live.[53]

Jesus' disciples hardly seemed ready for him to depart, but he entrusted them to the Holy Spirit: 'I will not leave you as orphans'.[54] In Acts, whenever the apostles checked out a new work of God, they would ensure that the Spirit had been received by the believers. And if not, they would lay their hands on them and make sure that they were filled with the Spirit. If Jesus did not leave his disciples with a rule book, but rather with the Spirit, the same must surely be true in church planting today.

Cross-cultural workers may have to leave again for many reasons, but the Holy Spirit will be with the Church forever! The local believers may not have you any more, but they do have God the Holy Spirit. His presence is more important than yours!

Import tendencies (Why newer believers receive the Men from James)

1. Desire to belong (cultic deprivation)

The Galatians had been pagans. Paul's problem, in part, is that in the ancient world, ritual and symbol was an indispensable part of religion. The Galatians' identity markers had been sacrifice, temple, ritual, and now all of these had been removed. So who are they now? What defines them? If Christianity is essentially a ritual-free zone (I relate to God through the work of Christ, not through ritual), then the Judaisers' offer of a system, of tangible symbols such as circumcision and Sabbath was immediately attractive to them.

This issue of identity is a key one in our cross-cultural church planting work today. We were 'A', defined by this holy place, these symbols, this religious-cultural matrix. We are now not 'A', so what are we? Grace-based Christianity does not tick the boxes of what a religion ought to be, we have no special buildings, no priesthood, no hierarchy, no geographical centre, and no ritual.

Interestingly, in contexts where Christianity does have some of these aspects, it is often more acceptable to national governments – it is definable, containable, such as the Three-Self Church in China, or the legally acceptable denominations in Jordan or Lebanon. In contexts where the gospel is unconstrained by these, e.g. church planting movements, highly contextualised forms, house church gatherings, it is understandably seen as more of a threat.

The Galatian believers were attracted to the idea of belonging to something with clearer boundary markers than Paul had given them.

Galatians 4:9: But now that you have come to know God, or rather to be known by God, how can you turn back again to the weak and worthless elementary principles of the world, whose slaves you want to be once more?

Galatians 4:10: You observe days and months and seasons and years!

Galatians 4:11: I am afraid I may have laboured over you in vain.

Likewise, national believers often will want a 'higher context' expression of Christianity. I have seen cross-cultural workers pushing further eastwards (into deeper forms of contextualisation) whilst their converts are pushing further westwards. In a desire to belong to the global Church, there can be a desire to express their faith in more Western forms. So whilst we are encouraging the writing of worship songs in the national language, local believers are listening to Hillsong on the Internet and asking, 'Can we use this song in church?'

2. Impressibility

The Men from James came from the 'centre', from Jerusalem. Their style was commanding and fluent, much more in tune with the accepted rhetorical norms of the day. Paul, by contrast, was living out cruciform apostolic example, holding up weakness as his badge of authenticity. Small wonder, again, that the Galatians were impressed and swayed by the agitators.

Paul's being true to weakness, servant leadership, crossing cultures with humility, his desire to raise sons, not slaves, left his converts open to influence and control by powerful, influential global ministries. The same is true today. 'I saw this on the Internet from America and we should do it here.'

Ignacio Ramonet, chief editor of *Le Monde Diplomatique*, writes in an article about secular American cultural hegemony:

Its mastery extends to the symbolic level, lending it what Max Weber calls charismatic domination. The US has taken control of vocabulary, concepts and meaning in many fields … its hypnotic charm enters our minds and instils ideas that were not ours. *America does not seek submission by force, but by incantation. It has no need to issue orders, for we have given our consent.*[55]

This is obviously not just true for America. 'Charismatic domination' is common in the Christian world today.

The glitz of megachurches, the 'success' of certain programmes or ministries can impress a pastor of a small struggling church. Of course we should learn from each other, but sorting gospel wheat from cultural chaff requires discernment.

3. Natural bias to legalism

The third bias, which is universal, is what Keller calls 'self-justification as the default mode of the human heart'.[56] This details a bias to legalism, because just relying on the gift of the righteousness of God through Christ goes against the natural mode of man, whatever his culture. Martin Luther wrote that 'if you do not build your confidence on the work of Christ you must build your confidence on your own work'.[57]

Friends, the Men from James are alive and well today. They want to tie new churches emerging amongst the unreached to an earthly 'Jerusalem', imposing a foreign Christianity. But Christianity has no earthly centre. Local churches must be free to express their faith in indigenous ways. That's what Galatians is all about.

One of the most wonderful moments in Galatians is 4:26. Paul has been arguing that the Galatians are not bound to the earthly Jerusalem. Then he says, 'But the Jerusalem above is free, and she is our mother.' If Christianity has a centre, if there is a mother-church that we should seek to imitate, it is the Jerusalem above! If there is a culture that we should seek to replicate in our churches, it is the culture of the Jerusalem above. Then our churches will be truly free! Let no Men from James rob emerging churches amongst the unreached of this freedom!

Endnotes

40. Acts 15:24.

41. I am assuming in this chapter that the 'Men from James' are coterminous with the groups commentators variously call the Circumcision Party, the Judaisers, the agonisers.

42. The group of churches served or influenced by the apostle James.

43. Meeks, Wayne and Wilken, Robert, *Jews and Christians in Antioch in the First Four Centuries of the Common Era* (Missoula, MT.: Scholars Press, 1982), 17.

44. Sanneh, Lamin, *Disciples of All Nations: Pillars of World Christianity* (Oxford: Studies in World Christianity, 2007), Kindle location 4749.

45. Greene, Gene L., 'Introduction' in Greenman, Jeffrey, P. and Green, Gene, L., *Global Theology in Evangelical Perspective: Exploring the Contextual Nature of Theology and Mission* (Downers Grove, IL: IVP Academic, 2012), Kindle loc. 63.

46. Bosch, D.J., *Transforming Mission: Paradigm Shifts in Theology of Mission*, Revised Edition (Maryknoll, NY: Orbis, 2011), 422.

47. Emphasis mine.

48. Allen, Roland, *The Ministry of the Spirit: Selected Writings*, David M. Paton (ed.) (Cambridge, UK: Lutterworth Press, 2011), Kindle loc. 425.

49. Greene, Gene L., *Global Theology in Evangelical Perspective*, Kindle loc. 585.

50. Jenkins, Philip, *The New Faces of Christianity: Believing the Bible in the Global South* (New York: Oxford University Press, 2006), Kindle loc. 112.

51. Emphasis mine.

52. Keller, Timothy, *Galatians for You* (Epsom: The Good Book Company, 2013), 9.

53. Allen, *The Ministry of the Spirit*, Kindle loc. 2036.

54. John 14:18.

55. Ramonet, Ignacio, 'The Control of Pleasure', *Le Monde Diplomatique*, May 2000, emphasis mine.

56. Keller, Timothy, *Center Church: Doing Balanced, Gospel-Centered Ministry in Your City* (Grand Rapids, MI: Zondervan, 2012), 116.

57. Keller, *Galatians for You*, 18.

Chapter 4
Softening Your Certainty

Inshallah is one of the words that immediately strikes the visitor to the Muslim world. 'If God wills.' 'We will come to dinner next week, *inshallah*. I will go to university, *inshallah*. The wedding is on 3 June, *inshallah*.' To the Westerner this can sound lazily fatalistic, but where Easterners seem non-committal or disorganised, consider – perhaps they are just humble.

The visitor to the West, conversely, is struck by overweening confidence. 'We will come to dinner next week.' How can you be so sure? Do you know the future? 'I will go to university.' 'The wedding is on 3 June.' But there are a million variables in play, myriad potential plan-breakers. For this reason, Westerners come across as arrogant as they travel eastwards. It's not just that they are sticking their heads up above the parapet of modesty, or attracting unwanted attention from the Evil Eye. They are being more confident than behoves a mortal. They are claiming knowledge of the future which only belongs to God.

Cross-cultural humility, however, will be more than just tagging a formulaic 'if God wills' onto the end of each sentence, although this habit of tongue could appease those with whom you are dialoguing. We need discipline of heart, not just discipline of grammar. Christianity is a religion of confidence, assurance, even of boldness – before people and before God. 'Let us then with confidence draw near to the throne of grace.'[58] But isn't Christianity also a religion of meekness, of humility? Can we communicate the latter without losing the joy of the former? In this chapter we explore some passages of Scripture which call us to soften our certainty. Some of our confidence is more cultural than biblical. In no sense does our confidence in the love of God through the grace of Christ waver, but does our Western experience create artificial, Scripture-surpassing confidence and security? This is the question we must seek to answer.

James 4 – softening tomorrow's certainty

James 4:13: Come now, you who say, 'Today or tomorrow we will go into such and such a town and spend a year there and trade and make a profit' –
James 4:14: yet you do not know what tomorrow will bring. What is your life? For you are a mist that appears for a little time and then vanishes.
James 4:15: Instead you ought to say, 'If the Lord wills, we will live and do this or that.'
James 4:16: As it is, you boast in your arrogance. All such boasting is evil.

Last year I had to pull out (due to unforeseen crises) of several events that had been in my diary for a year or more. I had been saying, 'Tomorrow, or next month, I will go to this place and do this...' just as James warns me to not to! Oh, how I wish had listened!

James says, 'You do not know what tomorrow will bring.' Nowhere was this more obvious than in our first Middle East Bible School. One of the key speakers, due to an unanticipated disagreement between his government and the country where the school was being run, was at the last minute unable to acquire a visa and could not come. In the Middle East, such last-minute changes are commonplace.

For many who live in poorer nations, life really is a mist, the future really is unclear, and 'if the Lord wills, we will live' expresses something that Syrian or Iraqi or Sudanese Christians might say every morning as they wake up. When I lived in Pune, India, I knew a brother who prayed Psalm 3:5 every day – 'Yesterday I slept and today I woke because you, O God, sustained me' – *and he meant it!* I have heard Andrew White, former Vicar of Baghdad, speak of how many members of his congregation he had to bury each year. Life is a mist, and unpredictability is a daily reality for many millions on our planet.

I don't think James is espousing fatalism or calling us to live in fear. One of the reasons James resonates so strongly with Global South Christians is that they identify – yes, my life really *is* a mist! I have a friend from a conservative Muslim background who visited churches and read the Bible for three years before finally putting his faith in Christ. The decisive moment for him was when he arrived at the book of James. 'Here,' he told me, 'I heard something that sounded like the voice of God, that sounded true, that identified with my daily reality.'

Anyone who has lived through a crisis knows that you cannot plan what you will do tomorrow, that you have to take one day at a time, that you have to say '*inshallah*' a lot. Crisis creates too many variables, there are just too many unknowns to be certain. Cross-cultural workers living in high-risk environments need to soften their certainty.

Sadly, crisislessness is a poor teacher. We assume routine is a right not a luxury, and we can get used to a degree of control over our lives that is globally and historically abnormal. In crisis, in risk, or in the Global South, James 4 takes on a whole new (actually the original?) meaning.

If you intend to live in a cross-cultural context, prepare yourself for less certainty, about just about everything!

Mark 8 – softening sight's certainty

In the teaching of Jesus, there is a deliberate and repetitive refrain, especially in his parables and aphorisms, designed to soften certainty, particularly of the comfortably religious. Those who think they will be inside find themselves outside. Those confident at the judgement are surprised.

> We always, with all others, are still *in via*. We have not arrived. We do not possess the truth. We are learners. And if one thing is made clear in the teaching of Jesus, it is that at the end we shall be surprised.[59]

In Mark 8, a blind man is brought to Jesus. Jesus spits on his eyes and lays hands on him, then asks him, 'Do you see anything?' The man has only partially received his sight. Then Jesus lays his hands on him a second time,

Mark 8:25: and he opened his eyes, his sight was restored, and he saw everything clearly.

Why the two-stage healing? Lack of faith is not mentioned. Jesus' lack of power cannot be the issue. What are we being taught?

Well, Mark tends to bunch lots of little accounts together in order to make big points, so we should zoom out and consider what the whole section is about. A major theme across this chapter is the theme of spiritual blindness and spiritual sightedness:

> *Mark 8:17,18:* Do you not yet perceive or understand? Are your hearts hardened? *Having eyes do you not see,* and having ears do you not hear? And do you not remember?
>
> *Mark 9:1:* And he said to them, 'Truly, I say to you, there are some standing here who will not taste death *until they see the kingdom of God* after it has come with power.'
>
> *Mark 9:2:* And after six days Jesus took with him Peter and James and John, and led them up a high mountain by themselves. *And he was transfigured before them* ...
>
> *Mark 9:8:* And suddenly, looking around, *they no longer saw anyone* with them but Jesus only.
>
> *Mark 9:9:* And as they were coming down the mountain, he charged them to tell no one *what they had seen,* until the Son of Man had risen from the dead.

In the verses immediately following the two-step eye-opening, we have Peter's big moment of revelation – 'You are the Christ.' Finally, he has seen it! Yet, famously, straight after this Peter has another moment of totally missing the point, and Jesus rebukes him, 'Get behind me, Satan! For you are not setting your mind on the things of God, but on the things of man' (8:33). He had seen that Jesus is the Messiah, but not understood that he is the *suffering* Messiah.

What Peter learned through this back-to-back encounter (first the action-teaching in the blind man receiving sight, then the words-teaching; receiving revelation and then being called Satan) is this: 'I was blind. Jesus touched me and now I see. But I only see in part. My sight is not yet perfect. I can still make mistakes. There are still gaps in my knowledge.

One day Jesus will touch my eyes a second time, and only on that day will I see perfectly.'

As Christians we rejoice that we were blind but now we see. What Peter needed to learn, though, is that the sight we have received is only partial. All revelation is in part. One day we will see fully, but until then a healthy dose of humility, of maybe, of *inshallah*, is demanded of us.

1 Corinthians 13 – softening knowledge's certainty

Having already written that '"knowledge" puffs up ... love builds up' and that 'If anyone imagines that he knows something, he does not yet know as he ought to know'[60] the apostle Paul develops this theme of partial knowledge in his letter to the status-hungry, competitive Corinthians.

> *1 Corinthians 13:9:* For we know in part and we prophesy in part,
> *1 Corinthians 13:10:* but when the perfect comes, the partial will pass away.
> *1 Corinthians 13:12:* For now we see in a mirror dimly, but then face to face. Now I know in part; then I shall know fully, even as I have been fully known.

An overrealised eschatology can produce arrogance. We were blind. Jesus touched our eyes and now we can see – in part. On the final day Jesus will touch our eyes again and we will have perfect sight, perfect knowledge. So actually, when singing the line from the hymn 'Amazing Grace' that we were blind but now we see, in reality, we should add the parenthetical 'in part'. We see in a mirror *en ainigmati* (enigmatically); i.e. indirectly, with mystery, with unknowns. Love, says Paul, dethrones presumption, reminds us that Christianity is a 'religion of waiting',[61] that our eyes have been partially opened by Christ, but that our sight and our knowledge are as yet not complete. The 'not yet' of our eschatology must remain firmly in place when speaking of knowledge.

John 3 – softening power's certainty

Nicodemus, who was wealthy, powerful and from the religious centre, approached Jesus saying 'we *know* that you are a teacher come from God,'[62] and Jesus answered him, 'unless one is born again he *cannot* see the kingdom of God'.[63] There is a difference between knowing and seeing, and assumed knowledge is an obstacle to sight.

Nicodemus responds with a 'how' question – 'How can a man be born when he is old?'[64] And Jesus answers with another enigmatic, metaphorical statement, 'The wind blows where it wishes, and you hear its sound, but *you do not know* where it comes from or where it goes.'[65] Jesus seems to be being intentionally dissimulative here, deliberately mysterious and cryptic. Nicodemus is asking 'how' questions, which are the foundation of science. Jesus is looking for faith, which is not a science. Nicodemus approached Jesus with 'we know', and Jesus has replied with 'you do not know'.

There is a reference here to Ecclesiastes 11:5: 'As you do not know the path of the wind, or how the body is formed in a mother's womb, so you cannot understand the work of God, the Maker of all things' (NIV).

Theology is too confident when it presumes to predict or predicate what God will do. Missiology is in danger when it studies the work of God in the various places, and then concludes 'if we do these things, we too can see a move of God'. You cannot reverse engineer a work of the Spirit. Science makes people confident, but faith is not science. Faith makes people humble. Science is about black and white. Faith trusts God in spite of grey. We must beware 'how' questions like Nicodemus was asking. Jesus refuses to be drawn, refuses to answer the 'how' question, because where knowledge becomes idolatry it must be confronted, not accommodated.

Luke Timothy Johnson, on the danger of the idolatry of knowledge, writes:

> Among the idols that authentic faith must resist are the idols of human thought concerning God. Living faith remains aware that the most subtle and sophisticated of all idolatries might actually be the one constructed by theologians who claim to know and understand God.[66]

Softening strategy's certainty

One implication of the softening of our certainty will be in our approach to mission strategy. Is it possible to prepare strategy that honours James 4

*Ladies
Lunch ?.*

and John 3, that allows for the Spirit to blow wherever he pleases, and does not claim to know what will happen tomorrow, strategy that is confident in the gospel and the ultimate vindication of the purposes of God, that avoids on the one hand the errors of fatalism and laziness, and on the other the arrogance that claims to predict, even to control, outcomes?

Particularly when pioneering, when crossing cultures, when contextualising the gospel, strategy must be flexible, open to the leading of the Holy Spirit, able to respond to setbacks and new learnings. Consider an Eastern example.

The Japanese don't use the term 'strategy' to describe a crisp business definition or a competitive master plan. They think more in terms of 'strategic accommodation', or 'adaptive persistence', underscoring their belief that corporate direction evolves from an incremental adjustment to unfolding events.[67]

These phrases: 'strategic accommodation', 'adaptive persistence' and 'incremental adjustment' are so helpful when we approach the process of living and ministering the gospel cross-culturally. With James, we learn to say 'if God wills', with Peter we discover that we are capable of both stunning revelation and demonic blindness (even on the same day!), with the Corinthians we are cautioned against the presumption of knowledge, and with Nicodemus we are reminded that to understand the ways of God is impossible. What we do not know is so much more than what we do know. Our greatest theologians have only read the first line of the first page of an infinite library which is the knowledge of God. May our speech, our self-perception and our approach to God and others be softer!

Endnotes

58. Hebrews 4:16.

59. Newbigin, Lesslie, *Signs Amid the Rubble: The Purposes of God in Human History* (Grand Rapids, MI: Eerdmans, 2003), 74.

60. 1 Corinthians 8:1,2.

61. Wilson, Andrew and Rachel, *The Life You Never Expected*, (Nottingham: IVP, 2015), Kindle loc. 233.

62. John 3:2, emphasis mine.

63. John 3:3, emphasis mine.

64. John 3:4.

65. John 3:8, emphasis mine.

66. Johnson, Luke Timothy, *The Revelatory Body: Theology as Inductive Art* (Grand Rapids, MI: Eerdmans, 2015), Kindle loc. 87.

67. Lampel, Joseph B., Mintzberg, H., Quinn, J., Ghoshal, S., *The Strategy Process: Concepts, Contexts, Cases, Fifth Edition* (Harlow, Essex: Pearson, 2013), 215.

Chapter 5
Humanity as Victim

How can we avoid, then, this massive proclivity to judge? Because we are good Western Evangelicals who see the world through a guilt-innocence lens, and we want to start our gospel presentation with 'all have sinned and fall short of the glory of God',[68] we tend to define Sin as Choice, and Humanity as Guilty.

This is true, of course. But it is an inadequate definition of sin, and an inadequate view of man.

Choice implies power, a tacit assumption of the West. We don't even think about not having a choice. Many, however, are not so fortunate. And much of biblical narrative acknowledges this. The Bible, whilst teaching Sin as Choice and Humanity as Guilty, also teaches what I will call Sin as Tyrant and Humanity as Victim. They are not mutually exclusive. It is the latter, however, that tends to occur in the context of compassion, of rescue, of salvation. Strangely, I think that because we assume that every story must start with Guilt, we read it into stories, even when it is not there.

In Chapter Two we saw the story of Jonah, where we can read 'wickedness' instead of 'calamity'. The story of Ruth is another such example. I have heard many preachers blame Elimelech for leaving the promised land, for going to Moab, and to then build a story of redemption based on a return to Canaan. 'Man's story,' they say, 'is that we abandoned the presence of God and that we need to come back.' This is true. True for humankind. True for the prodigal son. But the book of Ruth does not mention blame. The author does not comment positively or negatively on Elimelech's migration. He simply narrates it.[69]

For many in the world, famine, unemployment, civil war are reasons for forced migration. They don't have a choice. There is no blame. The dark shadow of evil in the world is to blame. Consider an African perspective:

> The book of Ruth is loved because it has something for everyone in Africa. Africans read this book in a context in which famine, refugee status, tribal or ethnic loyalties, levirate marriages and polygamy are not ancient biblical practices but the normal realities of today.[70]

People hear Naomi's story and identify, 'We have suffered too. The Bible is a book that acknowledges our victim status.' Ruth is a story of a benefactor, Boaz, who takes responsibility for these powerless women. And hence a glorious metaphor of salvation in Christ! When read through a 'fear-power lens', Ruth is vulnerable as a widow and a foreigner, and she is 'saved' under Boaz' wings. Read through a 'shame-honour lens', Ruth's shame is absorbed by a noble patron. The gospel of Christ is foreshadowed in this story, but without the dynamics of guilt and forgiveness. And that's OK – because the gospel is bigger than forgiveness of sins, it is also rescue from fear and shame at work in the world as a result of Sin.

Another place where we often miss 'Humanity as Victim' is in the story of Jesus and the Samaritan woman in John 4. Why condemn her? The reality of the ancient world, sadly, is that she could likely have been widowed several times (as older guys married younger girls and the life expectancy was not high), or she could have been divorced several times (divorce was extremely common in the ancient world, at the male prerogative). She most likely did not have children, or else they would have been collecting the water for her or with her, and perhaps her barrenness was the reason for her divorces. The man she is with now is not her husband; more likely to be his fault than hers! Nowhere in this story does Jesus call her immoral. Later on, the fact that the townsfolk so readily accept her testimony is evidence that she was not considered immoral by the community. Sin is at work in her story, yes. She has been sinned against. She is a victim! And Jesus shows her his mercy.[71]

Stephen Motyer[72] demonstrates that the Samaritan woman has been let down, not just by a male-dominated world, but by the whole religious and historic context. The Gospel of John is portraying Jesus as the new temple,[73] and he goes to those who could not come to the temple because of their social marginalisation; the Samaritan woman, the official's son (chapter 4), the crippled man (chapter 5), the man born blind (chapter 9). The question in John 9:2, 'Who sinned, this man or his parents, that he was born blind?' is then a conclusion to this entire narrative section – a question that could be asked of all the marginalised. Whose fault is their marginalisation? The overall purpose of all of these stories is to demonstrate that these people are victims of a failing temple-centric system[74] and Jesus came to create access to the Father by *becoming the temple* for the socially and religiously marginalised. Of course the Samaritan woman is a sinner – we all are! But the purpose of this story in its narrative context is grace for the marginalised, not grace for the guilty.[75]

I wonder if we do this with Bathsheba too? Through our 'equality' lens we assume that she is just as much to blame as David for their adulterous fling, whilst the Scripture explicitly blames David,[76] and never Bathsheba. She was probably forcibly taken, then her husband was murdered, then David took her as a wife. In a culture where women were chattels, mere property, no one is thinking that Bathsheba played any active role in proceedings.[77] Reading situations through our Sin as Choice lens we are in real danger of condemning those whom God does not condemn.

The good Samaritan

Jesus' parable of the good Samaritan is a retelling of the story of humankind from the perspective of God's compassion. When reading this parable Christologically with Origen, Augustine, Ambrose, Matthew Henry or Kenneth Bailey, we encounter an important view of Humanity as Victim.

> We were like this poor distressed traveller. The Law of Moses passes by on the other side, as having neither pity not power to help us; but then comes the blessed Jesus, that good Samaritan; he has compassion on us.[78]

The Jesus of the Gospels often portrays humankind as beaten up, robbed, imprisoned or left for dead. 'The thief comes only to steal and kill and destroy' (John 10:10). There is no blame in this story. Yes, in other stories that Jesus told, there *is* choice, there *is* blame, and there *is* a call to repentance. But in *this* story, there is a helpless victim, and there is costly compassion. Cross-cultural compassion.

In the background of the good Samaritan we hear echoes of Ezekiel 16.

> And as for your birth, on the day you were born your cord was not cut, nor were you washed with water to cleanse you, nor rubbed with salt, nor wrapped in swaddling cloths. No eye pitied you, to do any of these things to you out of compassion for you, but you were cast out on the open field, for you were abhorred, on the day that you were born. And when I passed by you and saw you wallowing in your blood, I said to you in your blood, 'Live!' I said to you in your blood, 'Live!' (Ezekiel 16:4-6)

God's response in verse 8 is very much like Boaz' response to Ruth:

> *Ezekiel 16:8:* When I passed by you again and saw you, behold, you were at the age for love, and I spread the corner of my garment over you and covered your nakedness; I made my vow to you and entered into a covenant with you, declares the Lord GOD, and you became mine.

And verse 9 sounds like the Samaritan:

> *Ezekiel 16:9:* Then I bathed you with water and washed off your blood from you and anointed you with oil.

All of these passages show us the compassion of God.

Compassion has always been a significant missionary motif. To this end, missiologist David Bosch claims that Ezekiel 16:4-6 is 'one of the most powerful mission statements in the whole Bible, since it depicts God as the One who has compassion'.[79]

Here, like in the parable of the good Samaritan, humankind is lying helpless, a victim, and needs a Saviour from outside to draw near, to pity, to rescue. Bosch's conclusion? 'A faith in which compassion occupies so central a position is indeed missionary.'[80]

Rescue

Jesus famously framed his mission in terms of Isaiah 61, in which man is seen as oppressed and the Messiah as the Liberator.

He has sent me to proclaim liberty to the captives (Luke 4:18). We should not imagine that 'forgiveness of sins' here is a purely individualistic thing. In the light of the 'Nazareth Manifesto' (4:16-21), it seems clearly to extend to the jubilee principle, the release from all debts, the cosmic sigh of relief at God's new exodus achievement, rescuing people from all forms of slavery.[81]

If Jesus is indeed announcing the advent of Jubilee[82] in Nazareth, then the release that is announced includes a release from bondage to tyranny. The Greek word used by Luke for forgiveness, *afesis*, also carries the meaning of 'release'. So in Luke 24:47, when Jesus announces that forgiveness of sins should be proclaimed in his name to all nations, this means both forgiveness for Humanity as Guilty and release for Humanity as Victim.

What about Paul? Western theology has traditionally looked to the apostle, rather than to the Gospels, for its atonement theologies. Yet Paul, too, would speak of Sin as Tyrant alongside Sin as Choice.

Romans 6 – 8 is, in the words of N.T. Wright, 'a massive retelling of the exodus-narrative'.[83] There is deliverance from the power of sin as Pharaoh (Ch. 6) passing through the Red Sea in baptism (Ch. 6), the giving of the law at Sinai (Ch. 7) and the promised inheritance (Ch. 8). For Paul, the work of Christ delivering humankind from the power and captivity of sin is fundamental to the telling of the story of the world.

This is sometimes described as the 'apocalyptic' view of salvation; that at the cross God smashed the power of Sin, and set humankind free. Just as Israel were 'slaves' in Egypt, but after the Exodus became sons, so now we are 'sons, not slaves' (see Galatians 4:7) because Pharaoh was beaten at the cross.

The idea that Sin ('Sin-as-a-power') has been 'condemned' is precisely an 'apocalyptic' theme. Paul has built up to this very carefully through chapter 7, so that by the time we reach 8.1-4 we know that 'Sin' is virtually the equivalent of 'Satan'. And 'Sin' is condemned. Significantly, once this sentence has been declared we hear no more of Sin.[84]

Ethical bricks without gospel straw

Humankind without Christ is under the power of a harsh taskmaster, being ordered to make bricks without straw, enslaved. When you enter another culture, and don't find bricks there, will you judge? They haven't been given any straw for generations – how are they supposed to make bricks? When you see people who have been lied to and robbed and beaten up, you will get angry. You should get angry. But to whom, at what, should your anger be directed?

In one context where we are working, dysfunctional, broken marriages have been the norm for generations. Domestic violence, abused children, and lack of trust have been endemic. When people come to Christ, is it fair to expect them automatically to be able to build godly families? When new believers from this kind of background still end up divorcing, why is that surprising? The Holy Spirit will bring transformation in this area, but it will take time. We will fight and teach and pastor for biblical marriage (not Western marriage!), but we don't discount the place from which people are starting, and we come with compassion and patience.

Two of my children are on the Autistic spectrum. There are some things they just can't do. So we parent them differently than we do our other kids, and we are aware that sometimes they get things wrong, not because of bad choices, but because they can't do any better. Yes, there are times they are Guilty. But other times they are Victims of their particular psychological make-up. We have grace for them.

We must not forget that Sin as Tyrant is as big a theme in the biblical witness as Sin as Choice. The latter is still true, and the Christian formulation of sin includes both, but one of the things that makes Christianity unique as a world religion is the picture of sin as a power oppressing humankind and hence necessitating a Saviour. Islam, for instance, would teach Sin as Choice but not Sin as Tyrant. We, however, have a Saviour who came not to judge but to save the world![85]

If we can see people in this way, then instead of blaming we will serve, and instead of judging we will empathise.

The 'Christus Victor' view of the atonement describes the work of Christ as victory over the oppressive power of the Evil One in order to set free those who are in Christ. The very first statement of the gospel in Genesis 3:15 uses this type of language – 'he shall bruise your head'. Gustaf Aulen claims that Christus Victor was the ruling idea of the atonement for the first 1,000 years of Christian history. According to Aulen, this view began to be replaced by the guilt-innocence scheme in Europe as culture changed with the Enlightenment, from metaphorical to rational, from communal to individualistic, from dualistic to monistic, from metaphysical to materialistic.[86]

Recovering this view of the story of humankind will help us as we cross cultures. It will help us to point people to the Deliverer who comes to clothe and restore and carry and heal, at great cost to himself. Perhaps then, as Jesus exhorts at the end of the good Samaritan parable, we will 'go, and do likewise'.[87]

Endnotes

68. Romans 3:23.

69. Ruth 1:1,2.

70. Kanyoro, Musimbi, 'Reading the Bible from an African Perspective', *ER* 51 (1) (1999), 18-24.

71. Capes, David B., Reeves, Rodney and Richards, E. Randolph, *Rediscovering Jesus: An Introduction to Biblical, Religious and Cultural Perspectives on Christ* (Downers Grove, IL: IVP, 2015), 75.

72. Motyer, Stephen, 'Jesus and the Marginalized in the Fourth Gospel', in Billington, Anthony, Lane, Tony and Turner, Max (eds.), *Mission and Meaning: Essays Presented to Peter Cotterell* (Carlisle: Paternoster, 1995), 70-89.

73. John 2:21.

74. See Chapter Eight, 'Nimrod Versus Abram'.

75. There is a deliberate contrast between Nicodemus in chapter 3 and the woman in chapter 4. He is Jewish, male, honourable and named. She is Samaritan, female, shameful and unnamed. Yet where he fails to understand, she succeeds. 'In John's Gospel, the unnamed disciples are the heroes.' Capes, Reeves, Richards, *Rediscovering Jesus*, 74.

76. 2 Samuel 11:27; 12:7.

77. Clements, E.A., *Mothers on the Margin? The Significance of the Women in Matthew's Genealogy* (Eugene, OR: Pickwick Publications, 2014), 121.

78. Church, Rev. Leslie F. (ed.), *Matthew Henry's Commentary in One Volume* (Grand Rapids, MI: Zondervan, 1960), 1449.

79. Bosch, David J., 'Reflections on Biblical Models of Mission', in Gallagher, Robert L. and Hertig, Paul (eds.), *Landmark Essays in Mission and World Christianity* (Maryknoll, NY: Orbis Books, 2009), 8.

80. Ibid. 9.

81. Wright, N.T., *When God Became King: Getting to the Heart of the Gospels*, Kindle Edition (London: SPCK, 2012), 233.

82. Leviticus 25.

83. Wright, N.T., *Paul and the Faithfulness of God* (London: SPCK, 2013), 659.

84. Wright, N.T., *Paul and His Recent Interpreters, Some Contemporary Debates*, Kindle Edition (London: SPCK, 2016), 210.

85. John 12:47.

86. Aulen, Gustav, *Christus Victor: An Historical Study of the Three Main Types of the Idea of the Atonement* (London: SPCK, reissued 2010), 144.

87. Luke 10:37.

Public Humility:
Thinking About the World

All good people agree
And all good people say,
All nice people, like us, are We
And everyone else is They:
But if you cross over the sea,
Instead of over the way,
You may end by (think of it!) looking on We
As only a sort of They![88]

In 1275, a young Marco Polo first set foot in Kublai Khan's Xanadu. Marco came from a world where Rome was centre, and everything else was periphery. All of public life took this shape; geography, politics, history and religion were all centred in Rome; everything else was inferior and provincial by degrees. Being from a wealthy Venetian family, Marco was close to the centre.

And then he journeyed to Kublai's court, a man who ruled from Russia to the Pacific, over half of humanity, the most powerful king who had ever lived. Superior in technology and infrastructure and civilisation. *And the West had known nothing about him.* Kublai had his own orbit, his own gravity, and it operated completely independently of the Pope's.

Imagine two independent planets, each with its own gravitational field. To move away from your own planet and into the thrall of another is to enter a totally different way of seeing the world. Whenever East has met West, the ensuing clash of world views has been absolute.

In the Middle Ages, Crusaders travelling East were terrified of the Arab science *al-jibra*, which they feared was a type of sorcery. Actually, it was 'algebra', the foundation of mathematics! We fear difference because it does not fit our cosmology, but perhaps ours is the one that needs changing.

Culture-crossing is about getting out of your story (where you/your people/your values play the main character), and getting into someone else's story where *they* are the main character, and you realise you are just a cameo, your culture a caricature. It is to move from the centre of your story to the periphery of someone else's. To become Robin to someone else's Batman (or, more usually, to become the Joker or Poison Ivy – an enemy!). In your own view of the world, your people are the heroes. In another view, you are the villains.

Watching the Turkish movie *The Conquest: 1453* (2012) about the 'liberation' of Istanbul by the Muslim Turks from the Christian Byzantines was uncomfortable for me. After a lifetime of watching movies where 'my people' are the good guys, it was a strange feeling to see the invading Muslims portrayed as noble and courageous, and the defending Christians as debauched and cowardly. On reflection, the uncomfortable thing was realising that all the movies I was used to do exactly the same thing, only the other way around!

This section aims to prepare future Marco Polos to step into Kublai's court. It may seem inappropriate to raise political issues in a Christian book about cross-cultural encounter; suffice to say the people you are seeking to reach will almost certainly view the world more holistically and politically than you. Can you place yourself in the thrall of another planet's gravity? Can you allow yourself to be subsumed as incidental in another people's plotline? Are you prepared to admit that your story of the world is not the only story?

Endnotes

88. Kipling, Rudyard, 'We and They', *The Collected Poems of Rudyard Kipling*, (Wordsworth Poetry Library) (Ware, Hertfordshire: Worsdworth Editions Ltd, 1994), 790.

Chapter 6
Whose Story?

It's a great mistake to assume that historical truths are like mathematical truths where there is one right answer and all others are wrong.
Bernard Lewis[89]

The 1995 movie *Braveheart* takes as its subject the life of William Wallace. For the Scots, Wallace was a hero, a freedom fighter. For the English, he was a terrorist. So, was he a hero or a criminal? Depends which side you are on!

History is not objective. Those who record events choose what to include and what to omit. What the British called the 'Indian Mutiny' of 1857 is remembered by others as 'India's First War of Independence'.[90]

Perspectives differ. Iran says to America, 'You are decadent.' America replies, 'We are free (and you are not).' These are non sequiturs, a dialogue in which each party misunderstands the other's language, world view and concern.

World view comes from a story, a baseline narrative that we have believed, 'our' history. Our story tells us where we have come from, who we are now, and where it is all going. One of the biggest shocks in cross-cultural encounter is the realisation that your view of history, and therefore ability to make sense of the world, is not the only one.

History of the world
Tamim Ansaray's book, *Destiny Disrupted*, is the story of the world told from an Islamic perspective, written by someone who has lived in and appreciates the West. Ansaray's point is that the way Muslims view the

history of the world is discontinuous with the Western view, that they are completely different narratives with different emphases.

World history is always the story of how 'we' got to the here and now, so the shape of the narrative inherently depends on who we mean by 'we' and what we mean by 'here and now.'[91]

The Western narrative assumes that its current values have been the goal of history, i.e. democracy, liberty, equality, and therefore tells the story from this perspective. The world has always been moving towards our kind of society, and everyone else needs to catch up!

It renders us vulnerable to the supposition that all people are moving in this same direction, though some are not quite so far along – either because they started late, or because they're moving more slowly – for which reason we call their nations 'developing countries.'[92]

China is rapidly becoming the world's largest economy (again). It is not hard to imagine a Chinese point of view being something like this: 'We were the world's largest economy for 5,000 years, the upstarts Europe and America have had a tiny few hundred years in the ascendency, and now things are reverting to how they have always been.' Remember, China's name for itself is 'The Middle Kingdom', meaning, essentially, 'The Centre of the World'.

If our history is us-centric, so is our geography. Our map of the world has Greenwich at 0 Longitude, i.e. at the centre. When I was a kid some Australian friends had a large world map with Australia at the centre (such an Australian thing to do!)[93] in front of which I spent hours, utterly bewildered.

That which we call the Middle East is only east if you are standing in Europe. Presumably, if you were in India, the same area should be called Middle West?

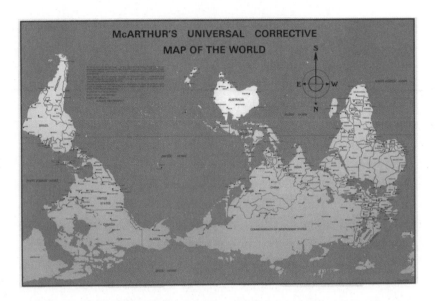

There is a classic episode of TV drama *The West Wing* in which Dr John Fallow, of the fictional Organization of Cartographers for Social Equality, lobbies White House staff about changing the maps used in schools. He describes the relative benefits of the Gall-Peters projection world map over against the widely-used Mercator projection. After having established that Africa is in reality fourteen times the size of Greenland (they look the same on the Mercator projection), Fallow moves on to relative location, explaining that Germany should actually be in the Northernmost quarter of the earth, not near the centre. The usually bright White House staff look completely bamboozled as they realise that nothing is where they thought it was![94]

The contention of those seeking to 're-draw the map' is that North is associated subconsciously with good, wealth and power, and South is associated with bad, poverty and underdevelopment. 'An inaccurate image of world geography … perpetuates colonial mind-sets.'[95]

Turkish friends have described to me a map they used at school, with the Central Asian Turkic heartlands in the centre, and arrows going north, south, east and west, depicting how Turkish migration and influence had spread throughout the world. They were taught that Turkic peoples had travelled as far as the Americas, that 'Niagara' was actually from the Turkish *Ne yaygara*, meaning 'What a racket!' and that 'Amazon' derived from the Turkish *Ama uzun*, meaning 'But it's long!'

Part of all cross-cultural conversation must be a desire to see the world from another's perspective. Everyone is 'us-centric', but not everyone realises it!

In the bazaars of Istanbul I learned the Turkish-centric history of the world and coffee. The Arabs discovered coffee and in eating the beans became more energised than other tribes, were able to conquer them, and the Arab Empire emerged. Then the Ottomans got hold of coffee, started to brew it as a drink, and the Ottoman armies conquered large territories – the Ottoman Empire. When the Ottomans departed from the gates of Vienna, on the threshold of Europe, they left behind bags of coffee, and that's how coffee got into Europe – and the rise of the European empires. And now, which country is the most powerful in the whole world? And where does Starbucks come from?

So the 'theft' of an idea has resulted in global shifts of power. Everyone has a history of the world in which their country plays a significant role, and in which their nation would have been the most powerful... if only certain historic villains had not intervened!

Bernard Lewis, the greatest Middle East historian of our time, who is himself Jewish, relates the following anecdote in his memoirs:

During my travels in Arab countries I heard again and again the line of argument: 'We have time, we have patience, history is on our side. We got rid of the Crusaders; we got rid of the Turks; we got rid of the British. We'll get rid of the Jews in due course.' Finally, I heard it once too often and sitting with a group of friends, I think it was in Jordan, I said: 'Excuse me, but you've got it wrong.' They said, 'What do you mean? That's what happened.' I said, 'Not quite. The Turks got rid of the Crusaders. The British got rid of the Turks. The Jews got rid of the British. I wonder who's coming here next?'[96]

History of Christianity

My view of Christian history used to be something like this: Christianity spread rapidly from Jerusalem into Europe, then in the Dark Ages not much happened, then with the Protestant Reformation 'justification by faith' was rediscovered and everything was OK again, then William Carey going to India was the beginning of modern missions, now the gospel is gradually filling the world, there are a few unreached peoples left, and then the end will come – hallelujah!

This is a classically us-centric (in this case Protestant-centric and Eurocentric and twenty-first-century centric) way of doing history. It is naïve. It is arrogant. And it is faulty.

I am not a historian, and it is not within the scope of this book to relate the history of world Christianity(!), but I would like to suggest a few helpful models that will help us to think about Christian history in a humbler way.

Christianity is multi-centric, and each centre has contextual differences

The movement of the gospel across the cultural boundary from Jerusalem to Antioch was a paradigmatic moment within the story of Christianity. It is when Christianity became a truly global movement.

Antioch transitioned within several generations from being a dark, pagan, unreached and ungodly city (Juvenal called it 'the sewer of the Empire' for its moral decrepitude)[97] to becoming the centre, or more precisely *a* centre, of the Christian faith. When Chrysostom was born there 300 years later, the majority of the population were registered Christian.[98] The Antioch church became an apostolic centre for the extension of Christianity eastwards along the Silk Road as far as China, as well as in all other directions. There are churches today who still trace their patriarchate back to second century Antioch (e.g. the Syrian Orthodox Church).

In the third and fourth centuries, Syriac was the third international language of the church. It was the vehicle of Christian missionary expansion on Persia, Armenia, Georgia, India and even in Ethiopia.[99]

From very early on, Christianity had more than one centre. This principle sets Christianity apart from every other world religion. The geographical heartlands of Hinduism, Buddhism and Islam are still where they have always been, and the faithful go there on pilgrimage. Not so with Christianity. 'Its conception of faith as grounded in the sovereign conscience of the individual was radically new.'[100] Jerusalem continued to be a centre (intellectual, theological, ecclesial), but other parallel centres emerged, with different emphases: first Antioch, then Ephesus, Rome, Alexandria, and so it has continued.

That is why the debates around the contextual nature of Antiochene Christianity (Galatians 2, Acts 15) are so important in the story of the Church. Antiochene Christianity needed to be uncoupled from Jerusalem's control if it was to indigenise and flourish. 'The church of Antioch from the outset had an ethos quite distinct from that of the Jerusalem church.'[101]

Thus the centres of Christianity today are not what they were 500 years ago. And what is today unreached will someday be centre. This is a dynamic unique to the Christian faith. It is the hope of missions.

Christianity is a movement of movements

The Church through history has been in a constant state of upheaval and change, decline and resurgence. Christianity is a movement of movements ... each new movement has a unique contribution to make to the kingdom – its 'founding charism.'[102]

As a centre begins to become established, complacent, overstructured and inflexible, God finds a new shepherd boy on the fringes, far from the centre of ecclesiastical power, anoints him with the Holy Spirit and begins a fresh movement with a freshly rediscovered emphasis. Whether St Patrick giving the Irish the gift of non-Roman Christianity, monasticism with its emphasis on devotion, the Franciscans' gift of God's heart for the poor, Pentecostalism and the baptism of the Holy Spirit, Watchman Nee churches and their deep spirituality, all of these have begun at the margins and breathed a revitalising power into the greater family.

In this way, the margins are the place where God is at work, they are the R&D department of the global Church. As Philip Yancey writes:

> As I travel, I have observed a pattern, a strange historical phenomenon of God 'moving' geographically from the Middle East, to Europe to North America to the developing world. My theory is this: God goes where He is wanted.[103]

The relationship between Christianity and culture is seasonal

Timothy Keller, observing the many different models of how the Church relates to culture, proposes (following Niebuhr) that Christianity in any given place grows through seasons in relation to the culture, and Christians should be aware of which season they are in as to how they see themselves.

1. Winter describes a church that is not only in a hostile relationship to a pre-Christian culture but is gaining little traction; is seeing little distinctive, vital Christian life and community; and is seeing no evangelistic fruit. In many cultures today, the Church is embattled and spiritually weak.

2. Spring is a situation in which the Church is embattled, even persecuted by a pre-Christian culture, but it is growing (e.g., as in China).

3. Summer is what Niebuhr described as an 'allied church,' where the Church is highly regarded by the public and where we find so many Christians in the centres of cultural production that Christians feel at home in the culture.

4. Autumn is where we find ourselves in the West today, becoming increasingly marginalised in a post-Christian culture and looking for new ways to both strengthen our distinctiveness and reach out winsomely.[104]

In this way, Christianity in Syria and Turkey experienced a spring in the early centuries of Christianity, a summer under Constantinanism (the

Byzantine Empire endured 1,000 years, monumental by any modern standard), an autumn as it began to decay under the Ottomans, a winter as a dwindling minority over the last few hundred years, and by the grace of God a new spring is beginning with Muslim Background Believers and fresh contextual forms of Church.

The house church movement in China, numbering by some accounts as many as 90 million, has come out of its winter and is well into spring. Many sub-Saharan African contexts would be at the height of summer. And post-Christian Europe would be in late autumn, even winter.

Why should this drive us to global humility? Because we realise that we are not the crown or centre of history, that the Church had glory and suffering before us, and will have after us. Because we realise that this family is much, much bigger than our movement or denomination or perspective. Because we realise that we are not the centre.

Where are we today?

Of the 2 billion Christians in the world today, the majority are in the Global South (510 million in Latin America, 390 million in Africa, 300 million in Asia). This southward movement will become even more emphatic over the coming years.[105] The Roman Catholic Church, the world's largest, has two-thirds of its members in the South (not counting people of the global South residing in the North). The biggest urban churches in Europe are African. Spanish has been the majority global Christian language since around the 1980s, followed by English, with Mandarin, Hindi and Swahili growing fast.[106] By 2050, for every ten Christians on the planet, only two will be non-Hispanic whites. The 'normal' Christian, if there is such a thing, will be a young, poor, South American woman. If you asked an alien to visit Earth and research Christianity they would most likely choose as typical a Chinese peasant farmer.

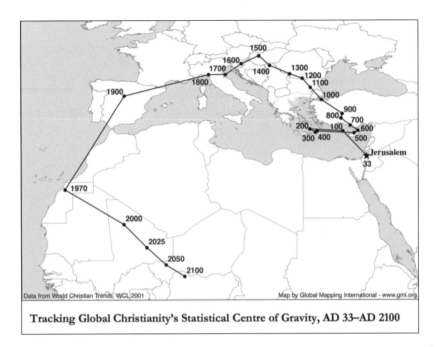

Tracking Global Christianity's Statistical Centre of Gravity, AD 33–AD 2100

The map of the 'Statistical Centre of Gravity of Global Christianity'[107] works with the assumed number of believing Christians globally each century, plotting an approximate statistically central point. We can clearly see the centre moving southwards and eastwards during the last century, to a point near Timbuktu today (ironically, the 'centre' is a place where there are hardly any Christians at all!).

If you are reading this book, in other words, you are likely a very non-typical, statistically outlying type of Christian!

Timothy Tennent writes: 'We must expand our *ecclesiastical cartography* … The Western Church has not yet fully absorbed how the dramatic shifts in global Christianity are influencing what constitutes normative Christianity.'[108]

Awareness of the bigger picture should make us aware that if we are not centre, neither are we normative, that there is much that we do not know, that our way of doing things is neither the only way nor the best way. It should make us humble.

Endnotes

89. Lewis, Bernard, *Notes on a Century: Reflections of a Middle East Historian*, Kindle Edition (London: Weidenfeld & Nicholson, 2013), 140.

90. First popularised by Vinayak Damodar Savarkar in his 1909 book, *The History of the War of Indian Independence* (Bombay: Sethani Kampani).

91. Ansaray, Tamim, *Destiny Disrupted: A History of the World through Islamic Eyes* (New York: PublicAffairs, 2009), xviii.

92. Ibid. xix.

93. For example, see McArthur's Universal Corrective Map of the World (1979). http://www.odtmaps.com/ (accessed 1.11.17).

94. *The West Wing* Season 2, Episode 16, 2001.

95. De Armendi, Nicole, 'The Map as Political Agent: Destabilizing the North-South Model and Redefining Identity in Twentieth-Century Latin American Art', *St Andrews Journal of Art History and Museum Studies*: 2009, 5-17.

96. Lewis, *Notes on a Century*, 227.

97. Juvenal, Satire 3.62.

98. Kelly, J.N.D., *Golden Mouth: The Story of John Chrysostom – Ascetic, Preacher, Bishop* (New York: Cornell University Press, 1995), 2.

99. John Meyendorff, preface to *Ephrem the Syrian: Hymns* (trans. Kathleen McVey) (New York: Paulist Press, 1989), 1.

100. Sanneh, Lamin, *Disciples of All Nations*, 4.

101. Bruce, F.F., *Paul: Apostle of the Heart Set Free* (Grand Rapids, MI: Eerdmans, 1977), 33.

102. Addison, S., *Movements That Change the World*, Kindle loc. 254.

103. Philip Yancey quoted in Addison, *Movements That Change the World*, Kindle loc. 440.

104. Keller, Timothy, *Center Church*, 237

105. Jenkins, Philip, *The New Faces of Christianity: Believing the Bible in the Global South* (New York: Oxford University Press, 2006), 9.

106. Johnson, Todd M., *World Christian Encyclopaedia, Second Edition* (New York: Oxford University Press, 2001), 12-15.

107. Johnson, Todd M. and Kim, Sandra S., 'Describing the Worldwide Christian Phenomenon', *International Bulletin of Missionary Research* 29 (2) (2005), 80-84.

108. Tennent, Timothy C., *Theology in the Context of World Christianity* (Grand Rapids, MI: Zondervan, 2007), Kindle loc. 176, emphasis mine.

Chapter 7
On Memory

In a recent conversation with a Central Asian man, he told me, 'We don't care for the environment because our ancestors were nomads.' I thought, 'You have been sedentary for 800 years!' But I was *underestimating the role of memory* in forming identity.

In any conversation about religion with a Muslim they will raise the painful issues of the Crusades and of the State of Israel. If we are not prepared for these, we are *underestimating the role of memory* in world view.

During the 2015 battle for Kobane on the Syrian/Turkish border, Western Powers were urging Turkey to arm Kurdish fighters. But it was only a generation ago that Kurdish separatist bombings were the terror of Turks. They were *underestimating the role of memory* in foreign policy.

When cross-cultural church planters struggle to see local leaders emerge and blame a 'lack of initiative in the local culture', they are *underestimating the role of memory* in global relationships. In some places people are so used to the colonial masters calling the tune that they will back off and wait to be led.

When introducing yourself to someone from a high-context culture, they don't just want to know who you are as an individual, but who your father and grandfather were, where your people came from originally, where your ancestral village is. Third generation urban migrants will still talk about their village, even if they have never been there. To know you, people need to know your family history. One of the major differences between identity in the East and West is the role of memory.

Fritz Kling is an American pastor who conducted a global 'Listening tour', travelling the world to learn from Christians in many countries, and to record his learnings in a book called *The Meeting of the Waters: 7 Global Currents That Will Propel the Future Church*. One of the global currents he observed is 'Memory'. Kling writes: 'Americans are generally characterised by short-term orientation, in that they believe that they owe little to history. Their past does not define their future.'[109] When an American says, 'That's history!' he means, 'It's all over.' In another context it can be a call to arms!

Memory makes individuals who they are today. But it also makes nations what they are today. In 2015 I visited Yerevan, Armenia, accompanying courageous Turkish pastors who were visiting Armenian churches as part of a reconciliation trip for the atrocities committed 100 years previously. Flowers were laid and prayers were said at the Genocide monument, on top of a hill right in the centre of the city. The centrality of this monument shows something of the centrality of the pain of those events in the identity of Armenians even today. In the Middle East, 100 years is a very short time. We saw many people who had been bound up by the pain of what their parents and grandparents had suffered experience the power of forgiveness and reconciliation during those few days.

'Postcolonialism is the world's strongest form of memory', claims Kling. I find this to be an incredibly powerful and helpful statement. Sugirtharajah defines the term 'postcolonialism' as 'a resistant discourse which tries to write back and work against colonial assumptions, representations, and ideologies'.[110]

When my grandfather was alive, roughly 85 per cent of the world's territories were ruled by European powers as colonies, protectorates, dominions and commonwealths.[111] This is very recent history. And it impacts perception. Perception of Christianity as an immoral, crusading, oppressive religion. Perception of you.

You may not like what follows, but like the Turkish pastors who travelled to Armenia to seek reconciliation, we must take responsibility for memory, not hold it at arms' length.

To devalue, or worse, to ignore the social, political and economic structures in which we work is seriously to limit the practical usefulness of our theological thinking.[112]

The postcolonial world slopes from West to East. It is not a level playing field. The ongoing values-dump from the West, combined with 'English linguistic imperialism'[113] and a past of oppression and stifling control shapes the world view and sense of identity of many millions on the planet. For instance, I have been in meetings where highly capable, gifted men from post-colonial countries will take a backseat and defer to others, just because they are European. This is excacerbated by the use of English in international contexts: native English speakers have another automatic advantage and the world slopes even further.

All this affects the way in which Westerners should approach mission today.

Today's pain is from yesterday's wounds

Sixteenth May 2016 was the 100th anniversary of the Sykes-Picot agreement, which began a nine-year process carving up the post-Ottoman Middle East and the drawing of many borders that are still on maps today. Wherever you see a ruler-straight line on a map in Africa or the Near East, the chances are it was drawn in a colonial office somewhere, almost arbitrarily, taking no account of ethnic groups or grazing lands or minority religions. Decolonisation has often been extremely painful.

The imposed borders of Syria and Iraq (Sykes, famously said, 'I should like to draw a line from the "e" in Acre to the "k" of Kirkuk') still produce pain today. The Syrian Civil War and refugee crisis. The Iraqi wars. 'Hundreds of thousands have been killed because of Sykes-Picot and all the problems it created. It changed the course of history – and nature.'[114]

It's amazing how often #sykespicot or similar will come up in a Twitter argument in the Middle East. After a terrorist bombing in Istanbul on 11 December 2016, I was reading British Ambassador to Turkey, Richard Moore's Twitter feed. He condemned the attacks, receiving angry responses from several indignant people who claimed that this was hypocrisy because the British 'definitely had a hand in the bombings'. Two respondents quoted sayings that are very common in the Middle East, and which reflect common (though by no means unanimous) sentiment. One was, 'History is comprised of repetition,'[115] and the other, 'If two fish fight in the Tigris, the British are behind it.'[116]

Of course, not everyone subscribes to conspiracy theories, and you cannot accommodate every extreme view, but the point is that in the Middle East such proverbs are very common, and their existence is a form of memory enshrined in language.

If many Arabs today will not trust a British person, the reason ostensibly is that: 'You asked us to fight for you in the First World War, and promised us self-determination afterwards. We fought the Ottomans for you, and then you did not give us our independence. You lied to us.' There is truth to this. However, there is also a 'lost in translation' issue. The crucial letter from British Governor of Egypt, Sir Henry McMahon, to Sharif Hussein of Mecca on 24 October 1915 making this promise on behalf of the British government contained a qualifying phrase, essentially, 'you can rule these lands, unless we need them as a buffer for British interests', which was deliberately woolly. It was only five years later, when Winston Churchill and Lawrence of Arabia examined the English and Arabic versions of the letter side by side, that they realised this nuance was entirely missing from the Arabic, that there had been a 'sleight of hand'. By that time the damage had been done.[117]

For an East African perspective on historic pain we go to Mzee Jomo Kenyatta:

When the missionaries came to Africa, they had the Bible and we had the land. They said, 'Let us pray.' We closed our eyes. When we opened them, we had the Bible and they had the land.[118]

As a foreigner living in, or ministering to, people from post-colonial countries, you cannot ignore the effect of memory. Read history, yes, but know that history written in the English language says different things to the history written in other languages. Know that people will hold you responsible. They will blame you. Work out how to take responsibility for what 'your people' have done.

Our airbrushed colonial history[119]
Imagine a British person wants to go and preach the gospel in Alexandria, Egypt. He will need to read some history. He will see that in 1882 British

warships had bombed and totally sacked the city, an attack in which five British and 2,000 Egyptians died. This was how Britain invaded and then occupied Egypt for seventy years!

Why did Britain enter Egypt? For financial gain. The Suez Canal. Prime Minister Gladstone had 37 per cent of his personal portfolio invested there and a further sixty-five MPs had investments in Egypt.[120] So we invaded, killed and oppressed for personal gain. We are the unjust oppressor!

Lord Cromer said, referencing Egypt, 'Civilisation must, unfortunately, have its victims.'[121] Just like that! The Portuguese novelist Eca de Queiroz wrote of that era, 'The world is becoming Anglicised. The English are everywhere, that is why they are detested, they never integrate or de-Anglicise themselves.'[122] And historian Philip Mansell, 'There may be arguments in favour of the British Empire. The bombardment of Alexandria and the occupation of Egypt are not among them.'[123]

Alexandria is not a one-off example, of course. We had just sacked Delhi (1857) and Peking (1860).

The point is this: whether or not you are aware of your history, the people you are reaching will be. Our preacher to Alexandria comes from the powerful. His grandparents killed their grandparents. And now he wants to declare Christ to them! He may be individually humble, but he comes from a historically arrogant nation. Will individual humility be sufficient to compensate for this?

The presence of fierce nationalism in many cultures

Over the last century one of the major challenges that cross-cultural gospel preachers have faced is nationalism; strong anti-foreign sentiment. Our Alexandria incumbent will face this too. Whether President Mugabe's land reforms in Zimbabwe, or Iranian anti-American rhetoric, or the expulsion of foreign aid workers from Morocco, the West in many ways is reaping what has been sown.

Countries become suspicious of outsiders because for several centuries prior, Western nations took advantage, overpowered, lied, stole, profited. Some benefits of colonialism could be argued, but the point is what people believe the story to be. Nationalism and mistrust, embodied in the big national saviour who 'stood up to the West', threw out the foreigners and forged the nation, then become centres, almost cults, of identity (Kenyatta, Ataturk, Gaddafi, Castro, Mugabe, Gandhi, Khomeini).

If we own our history, then this will make us more understanding, more gracious and patient when encountering suspicion, mistrust, difficult bureaucracy, visa difficulties. Nationalism will be one of the big cultural strongholds that we encounter in everyday life, let alone evangelism and discipleship, in many unreached nations. Understanding its roots can help us approach this edifice circumspectly, instead of just spraying right and left with the machine gun of demonisation. Indeed, the contemporary growth of nationalism in Western nations calls for further sober consideration – we must ensure that anti-foreign sentiment does not percolate into our churches either.

Jesus was constantly working to set his disciples free from an us-them world view. One of the goals of discipleship is to attain to 'one new man in Christ', but this is not achieved overnight and expectations should be adjusted accordingly. New disciples will not instantly forget their history, old animosities, deeply entrenched prejudices, and it is unreasonable to expect them to do so. We demolish strongholds and work towards maturity but we understand how deep-seated some of these are, and that at least part of the blame rests with *our* fathers.

I once watched a well-meaning English brother preach in Beirut from Ephesians 2:15 on 'one new man in Christ'. There are few cities as divided and sectarian as Beirut, where the painful memory of civil war is still fresh. Even the Church is deeply fragmented, let alone the wider fabric of the city. To call people to forget their differences and come together is good sentiment, but as I watched the congregation it felt like trying to stick a plaster on a deep, gangrenous wound. And the fact that it was an Englishman preaching made the notion seem even more unattainable – alien somehow. We must be circumspect about the discipleship journey, appreciate the power of history, and set our expectations accordingly.

Watch your world view

Because of the colonial legacy, the massive spread of English, and a West-East power flow, Westerners have a tendency to assume that their view is the 'right' or even 'global' view. 'West is best' might not be said, but is felt.

In our time, direct colonialism has largely ended; imperialism, as we shall see, lingers where it has always been, in a kind of general cultural sphere as well as in specific political, ideological, economic and social practices.[124]

There is a perceived ongoing superiority of attitude, a kind of hangover from colonial times. Novelist Chinua Achebe, when remarking that Western critics often fault African writing for lacking universality, writes sarcastically:

> But of course it would not occur to them to doubt the universality of their own literature. In the nature of things the work of a Western writer is automatically informed by universality. It is only others who must strain to achieve it.[125]

To assume that my view is *the* view is enormous arrogance. Yet for many Christians travelling to preach in other places this is too often a given. No wonder when this flows eastwards and southwards it often gets labelled neo-colonial!

Power-sensitivity

Whatever you think about postmodern, feminist and postcolonial discourses, one of their positive contributions is an increased sensitivity to power dynamics.[126] This *power-sensitivity* needs to be an essential part of the cross-cultural Christian's armoury. Power-blindness is unacceptable in the twenty-first century. Those who assume that the world is a level playing field, that everyone's opportunity is equal, that history does not still exercise power in the present are naïve, dangerously so.

The pride of the Westerner runs very deep. If he is not aware of it himself, his non-Western friends sense it in him, assume it of him, ascribe it to him. Mission in a post-colonial world must take this into account, must own its history. The Westerner must strive to understand how others see him. We can't change our history, but we can, and must, allow it to humble us, create empathy and grace in us, to reform our world view to make us better servants of the gospel.

Endnotes

109. Kling, Fritz, *The Meeting of the Waters: 7 Global Currents That Will Propel the Future Church* (Colorado Springs, CO: David C. Cook, 2010), 176.

110. Sugirtharajah, R.S., *Asian Biblical Hermeneutics and Postcolonialism: Contesting the Interpretations* (Maryknoll, NY: Orbis, 1998), ix-x.

111. Said, Edward W., *Culture and Imperialism* (London: Vintage, 1994), 6.

112. Parratt, John, *A Guide to Doing Theology* (London: SPCK, 2012 reprint), 66.

113. Crystal, David, *English as a Global Language*, Second Edition (Cambridge, UK: Cambridge University Press, 2003), 69.

114. Nawzad Hadi Mawlood, the governor of Iraq's Erbil Province, reported by Wright, Robin, 'How the Curse of Sykes-Picot still haunts the Middle East', *The New Yorker*, 30 April 2016.

115. *Tarih tekürrürden ibarettir.*

116. *Diclede iki balık kavga ediyorsa arkada İngiliz vardır!*

117. Barr, James, *A Line in the Sand: Britain, France and the Struggle that Shaped the Middle East* (London: Simon & Schuster, 2001), 118.

118. Kwiyami, Harvey, 'Umunthu and the Spirituality of Leadership: Leadership Lessons from Malawi', *Journal of Religious Leadership* 12, No. 2, Fall 2013.

119. This phrase is from Dalrymple, William, 'One Sure Way for Britain to Get Ahead: Stop Airbrushing Our Colonial History', *The Guardian*, Wednesday, 2 September 2015. Courtesy of Guardian News & Media. Ltd https://www. theguardian.com/commentisfree/2015/sep/02/britain-colonial-history-islam-white-mughals (accessed 5.10.17).

120. Mansell, Philip, Levant: *Splendour and Catastrophe on the Mediterranean* (London: John Murray, 2010), Kindle loc. 2437.

121. 'The Government of Subject Races', Political and Literary Essays, 1908-1913 (London: Macmillan, 1913), 44 cited in Asad, Talal, *Formations of the Secular: Christianity, Islam, Modernity* (Redwood City, CA: Stanford University Press, 2003), Kindle loc. 1744.

122. Mansell, Philip, *Levant*, Kindle loc. 2656.

123. Ibid. 2628.

124. Said, *Culture and Imperialism*, 8.

125. Achebe, Chinua, *Hopes and Impediments: Selected Essays* (New York: Doubleday, Anchor 1989), 76.

126. Kang, Namsoon, *From Colonial to Postcolonial Theological Education in* Werner, Dietrich et al (eds.), *Handbook of Theological Education in World Christianity: Theological Perspectives, Regional Surveys, Ecumenical Trends* (Oxford: Regnum Books International, 2010), 31.

Semantic Humility:
Thinking About Language

We were recruiting a team to move with us to Istanbul, learn Turkish, and plant a Turkish-speaking church. I remember sitting across the table from each potential team member, looking them in the eye, and asking them to commit five years. Why five? Well, there would be no point coming with us for two years, because for the first two all we would be doing was studying language!

There are so many reasons to shortcut language learning. It is exhausting. For most of us non-linguists we are using a part of our brain which we never usually use. It is slow, inefficient and disheartening. For those not well-funded, the temptation to get a job teaching English is very real, but it is so difficult to teach English and learn another language at the same time. And to make matters worse, so many people speak English to a higher level than our second-language attainment will ever reach. Surely we could plant an English-speaking church more quickly, more easily and more competently. Why keep going?

Walter Brueggemann, in his commentary on the Babel story, writes:

Language is decisive for the shape and quality of human community. More than anything else, language determines the way in which human persons care for each other. Language shapes the ways in which human communities conduct business and arrange power. Language is the way in which we bestow upon each other the gifts of life and death (James 3:10).[127]

When I was first preaching in Turkish, I was on forty hours of preparation *per sermon*. Language-learning is disparagingly slow. And yet, it is essential to the missionary enterprise, imperative for those seeking to get to know a culture, and indispensable to church planting. If we will plant national churches, we must learn local language.

In this section, *Semantic Humility*, I will argue for a *positive* view of language and linguistic difference. God's purpose has always been that people receive the gospel in their heart language, worship and pray in their mother tongue. Because language is the key to culture, and all translation is to some extent interpretation, linguistic diversity begets cultural diversity. And this, too, tells us something beautiful about the universality of the gospel of Jesus Christ. As the story of the cross is told in different languages in different places, different aspects of the story resonate, different truths come to the fore. 'There is something unique about the Bible that makes it infinitely translatable like no other literature.'[128]

Semantic humility expresses that different languages have different strengths and weaknesses, that we need each other's perspectives to round-out our knowledge of God, and that in the eternal kingdom, linguistic diversity will endure.

> *Revelation 7:9*: After this I looked, and behold, a great multitude that no one could number, from every nation, from all tribes and peoples and *languages*, standing before the throne and before the Lamb, clothed in white robes, with palm branches in their hands ... [129]

Endnotes

127. Brueggemann, Walter, *Genesis: Interpretation, A Bible Commentary for Teaching and Preaching* (Atlanta, GA: John Knox Press, 1982), 102.

128. Shaw and Van Engen, *Communicating God's Word in a Complex World*, 18.

129. Emphasis mine.

Chapter 8
Nimrod Versus Abram

The mixing of languages at Babel is often thought of as a curse. I don't think that's right. I think it was a blessing.

The Bible's story of language begins in Genesis 10. When they staggered out of the ark, God commanded Noah and his sons, 'Be fruitful and multiply and fill the earth' (Genesis 9:1,7). This was a reissuing of the command given to Adam and Eve in the beginning. What Adam had failed to do, God now recommissions humankind's newest representatives to do, albeit under the shadow of sin. So, will they obey this time?

Throughout chapter 10, as Noah's descendants spread out on the earth, there is a running refrain, 'each with his own language, by their clans, in their nations'.[130] The seventy nations listed here represent the whole world; seventy became the symbolic number meaning 'all the nations'.

Each tribe had its own language. Language is the key to culture, the 'intimate, articulate expression of culture',[131] and this scattering, this diversity of linguistic and cultural identities was *good*, it was God's purpose, a fulfilment of the 'multiply and fill the earth' command. It is important to note the possessive; for a nation to have their own language demonstrates their freedom, independence and dignity.

Old Testament scholar Walter Brueggemann, commenting on the Hebrew word for 'scattered' (*pus*) in this chapter, writes: 'The idea of "scatter/spread abroad" (*pus*), at least in this context, is not negative nor concerned with punishment. It can be argued that in this context (10:18), the intent of creation finally comes to fulfilment (1:28).'[132]

Then we meet Nimrod. In 10:9 he is called a hunter, a hunter of men; i.e. a warrior. He is a 'big man'; he has power: physically, politically. Nimrod, it seems, wants to save the world – in the way that Caesar or Hitler saw themselves as saviours. He establishes a 'kingdom' in Shinar – the first use of this word in the Bible, and it is used in opposition to God's kingdom. In an interpretation as old as Josephus,[133] Nimrod is the prototypical tyrant, using his power to establish a kingdom, the name of which will be Babel/Babylon, and which from Genesis through to Revelation will stand in opposition to the kingdom of God and of Christ. Babylon has its beginning here, and is only torn down at the end of Revelation.

And so when we come to 11:1, all the people had one language and the same vocabulary, we ask, 'What happened?' In chapter 10 each nation had their own language, but now there is one common language! Nimrod has done what so many tyrants after him through history chose to do: he has implemented one state language, quashing tribal expression and sentiment, outlawing the indigenous.

When the Spanish conquered South America and Spanish became the language of power, so much was lost, writes Argentinian Jose Miguez Bonino. 'To accept the new language meant to deny everything that gave meaning to their lives – stories, traditions, "the naming of things", the music of words, the sounds of love.'[134]

Imposition of language is a tool of empire which has been used since time immemorial; the Mandarin empire, the Soviet empire, the British,[135] the Turkish Republic, all have used language as a tool of control.

Nimrod's second tool of control was to 'build … a city' (11:4). Imperial cities can represent control through force (most likely the various subject nations were used as slave labour for the building project), or merely through a concentration of military, economic and political power – any subject needing anything would have to travel to the city. The imperative 'come' in verses 3 and 4 is highly significant. God has called people to scatter, but Nimrod is gathering them.

The third tool of control was religion. The 'tower with its top in the heavens' symbolises a bridge between the heavenly and earthly realms; it was a temple.[136] Like language and cities, religion has often been used to control people. One central temple and state-sponsored religion is wonderful for the powerful, but oppressive for the powerless.

One language, one city and one temple – the beginning of Babylon. Babel was about 'the perpetuation of a single culture – the human race, speaking one language, living in one place'.[137] It's foundations? Fear ('lest we be dispersed over the face of the whole earth'),[138] pride ('make a name for ourselves') and rebellion (doing the opposite of what God had commanded).

Against the argument that chapter 10 actually narrates events after chapter 11, and that these materials have been dischronologised to demonstrate the spread of sin, Arnold argues that the *toledot*-structuring device,[139] which opens this section at 10:1 and the next section at 11:10, makes these two chapters a self-contained literary unit.

> The Table of Nations in its current location fulfils the divine command to 'be fruitful and multiply, and fill the earth' (9:1, reflecting also 1:28), and is there predominantly a positive appraisal of human dispersion. The sons of Noah were fulfilling their purpose by bringing God's blessing to fruition. Had it been placed *after* 11:1-9, the Table of Nations in Gen 10 would of necessity been transformed into a sign of God's judgement.[140]

For those who remain unpersuaded that chapters 10 and 11 are presented chronologically, at least it must be accepted that the author(s) of Genesis meant them to be recorded and read in this order. Gerhard von Rad writes: 'the chapters must be read together, because they are intentionally placed next to each other, in spite of their antagonism.'[141] Even for those who wish to read chapter 11 in complete isolation from chapter 10, however, there is increasing scholarly interest in the horizontal (cultural) tensions present in the Babel story (centrifugal vs centripetal, homogenisation vs heterogenisation) rather than a simplistic vertical reading about man's Promethean attempt to storm the heavens.[142]

God's 'going down' in 11:7 is therefore an act of liberation, even an act of grace. He delivers the enslaved peoples, gives them back their languages, their freedom, their honour. He sets them free to scatter once more over the earth. *Mishpat*, the Hebrew word for justice, is always a double-sided coin in Scripture. It means both judgement on the proud, and grace to the poor.[143] In the Exodus, God shames Pharaoh and honours the slaves. The

Babel-intervention is the same: judgement on Nimrod and Babylon, but freedom and identity for the peoples. A multiplicity of languages, then – and this is the important point here – *is a blessing, not a curse.*[144]

Medieval scholar Abraham Ibn Ezra, who believed that the purpose of Genesis 11 was to explain the presence of cultural difference in a positive light, wrote, 'God scattered the people for their own benefit.'[145]

Where are you standing?

When studying Scripture, one of the key criteria to which many of us Westerners seem naturally oblivious is the dynamic of power. Those who have something, never having not had it, are often unaware of what they have. The history of interpretation of the Tower of Babel story is a case in point.

St John Chrysostom, preaching in Constantinople, in Greek, at the centre of the Christian Constantinian empire, viewed unity of language positively, and plurality negatively: 'So when the people in the present case, who had been dignified with similarity of language, used the privilege given them for evil purposes, [God] put a stop to the impulse of their wickedness through creating differences in language.'[146]

Chrysostom would naturally see it that way! Being in the centre, he saw all the advantages of 'one language, one city, one temple', because it was *his* mother tongue, the city in which *he* lived, and the church in which *he* preached!

Jose Miguez Bonino, writing in his Argentinian context, reads through the eyes of the oppressed. Naturally, Bonino will see homogenisation as evil and argue that God loves diversity of languages and cultures.

The position of the reader affects how they read. But the difference between the powerful and the powerless is this: the powerless know that their reading is context-conditioned; the powerful, often, are oblivious.

The way Babel has been interpreted is a prime example. Like Chrysostom, many Evangelical scholars have read Babel heterophobically. When, in 11:7, we read in our English translations 'let us *confuse/confound* their languages'[147] there is an unmerited value judgement in these translations, proposes Hiebert. This word simply means 'mix'. 'God makes a polyglot world.'[148] If a multilingual world was actually God's intention, then the implications for mission are significant.

Abram as the contrast to Nimrod

The next chapter is chapter 12; the call of Abram. God turns his attention away from the powerful Nimrod and his city, and begins a humble work at the margins. The Bible never mentions Nimrod and Abram meeting, although both the Talmud and the Qur'an attest to a tradition of a personal confrontation between the two.[149] In the Genesis context, however, when Nimrod and Abram are considered side by side, it becomes clear that a contrast between the two is explicit in the text. Nimrod represents man's salvation plan, Abram reflects God's.

> *Genesis 12:1:* Now the LORD said to Abram, 'Go from your country and your kindred and your father's house to the land that I will show you.
> *Genesis 12:2:* And I will make of you a great nation, and I will bless you and make your name great, so that you will be a blessing.
> *Genesis 12:3:* I will bless those who bless you, and him who dishonours you I will curse, and in you all the families of the earth shall be blessed.'

Nimrod sought to make a name for himself (11:4). God promised Abram that he would make a name for him (12:2). Babel was characterised by the imperative 'come'. God told Abram to 'go'. Babel's founders 'settled' (11:2) (the first use of this word in Scripture, and it is used negatively), Abram was called to an unsettled life. Nimrod built one central temple, Abram built altars wherever he went (12:7-8).

To leave his 'country and … kindred and … father's house' (12:1), for those viewing the world through an *honour-shame lens*, would be to leave all the sources of his honour, to become a landless wanderer, a gypsy. Honour is family- and land-embedded and Abram would have neither. His most precious commodity, his identity, would be abandoned.

Viewed through a *power-fear lens*, he was leaving his security and heading into the unknown, into a land populated by enemies, where he would be treated with suspicion as a potential threat and would have no natural allies.

Indeed, on arrival they immediately experience a famine (12:10). Abram and his family are vulnerable.

Nimrod, through building, sought to mitigate his own need for honour and for protection. Abram was called to abandon both.

Finally, in response to Nimrod's attempt to homogenise, Abram is called to mission through cultural pluralism. 'In you all the families of the earth shall be blessed' implies a preservation of the diversity of these families, rather than a unification of them. So 'going' dignifies diversity in a way that 'coming' does not. In Abram there is an obedient response to the Adamic and Noahic commands, 'Go and fill'.

> [Abraham] is the paradigm of a new people through whom all the families of humankind are to experience blessing, not by surrendering their ethnic identities but by being embraced within the saving purpose of the God who rejoices in the diversity of the creation.[150]

Abraham and Nimrod are set up as contrasting strategies.

Nimrod	Abram
'Come'	'Go'
One language	Plurality of language
Homogenisation	Heterogenisation
Gather to one temple	Build altars wherever you go
Build a city	Leave a city
Settled	Lived in tents
Power	Vulnerability
Make a name for ourselves	Entrusts his honour to God
Resists fear of being scattered	Embraces fear of unknown
Rebellion	Obedience
Judged	Blessed

Pentecost: 'I love your languages!'

As previously noted, the symbolic significance of the number seventy carries through Scripture. Moses sees the Spirit given to seventy elders, prophesying that all nations would be included.[151] When the Lord Jesus later sent out the seventy two by two,[152] it was again a demonstration of the action of the missionary Church taking the gospel to all nations.

On the Day of Pentecost, the religion of Jerusalem had become no different from the plan of Nimrod; there is *one city, one temple* and *one sacred language.* That's why the city was filled with pilgrims from the many nations described in Acts 2; you had to 'come' to the temple at Jerusalem, you had to pray in Hebrew. And just as at Babel, the Spirit of God comes down to honour a multiplicity of languages, to reheterogenise worship. 'No longer any need for a holy temple, city and language!' declares the Spirit through this prophetic sign. They marvel at hearing the wonders of God in their mother tongues because the implications are staggering. No longer one sacred language! A tacit rebuke to Jerusalem, and a sign of the gospel being preached to all the families of the earth in their languages.

At Pentecost, as at Babel, God actively came down to reinstate plurality of language. Humankind's tendency is still, like Nimrod, to seek to gather to one centre, to build, to homogenise, and the Spirit's tendency is still to scatter, to diversify. Karl Möller writes: 'The sin of Babel was its quest for unity – one interpretation, one reading, one people – which was an abandonment of creational diversity and plurality in favour of exclusion and violence.'[153]

And at the very end, in the great vision of Revelation, there is a representation of 'every language' around the throne.[154] Linguistic diversity, and the cultural diversity it begets, will endure into the new creation. There shall exist a new creation unity; Jesus' blood will take these many languages and cultures, redeem them, and make them into 'a kingdom and priesthood',[155] not by homogenising but by rendering them one in Christ. Nimrod had assumed the answer to humankind's problem was to build a 'kingdom' and he was right, but the kingdom of God is very different to the kingdom envisioned by Nimrod.

Implications for Christian Mission

1. Christianity was never supposed to have a centre
Where there is a centre there are degrees of proximity, and where there are

degrees of proximity there cannot be equality. An Israeli and a Palestinian can break bread together, but whose language will they use, and on which side of the border will they meet?

The first Christians, in the early days, continued to meet in the temple to pray (Acts 3, 5). It seems they had not fully understood the implications of Christ being the new temple. It took the destruction of the temple (in AD70) and persecution[156] finally to scatter them. Much later, Peter would write 'you yourselves like living stones are being built up as a spiritual house'.[157]

The problem with one central temple is *access*. Some people can't get there. In fact, the people who need it the most can't get there. In John's Gospel, Jesus is clearly portrayed as the new temple, and he 'goes' to people who could never 'come'. As mentioned earlier, the Samaritan woman in chapter 4, the crippled man in chapter 5 and the blind man in chapter 9; none of these could come into the temple, so in Christ the temple came to them!

That is why Christian mission must be dominated by an Abrahamic 'go' rather than a Nimrodian 'come'. In the multicultural cities and towns of Europe the same dynamic is true. There are many in your town who can never come to your church, the geographic, linguistic, cultural barriers are too many. You may think your church is accessible because it has a good website and a wheelchair ramp, but what about emotional and cultural accessibility? Instead, you must go to them!

2. God loves diversity

> The Babel story contains a peculiar dialectic. Human beings strive to maintain unity, God's action effects diversity. Human beings seek for a centre, God counters with dispersion. Human beings want to be safe with homogeneity, God welcomes pluralism.[158]

The implications of Babel are pretty straightforward. God loves the diversity of languages and intervened to stop the homogenising work of Nimrod. Not that God is just academically linguaphile, but he has always desired each nation to have its own dignity, history, traditions, music, dance, customs, sayings. Language births and sustains culture. Christianity, as an incarnate religion, acknowledges this by seeking to embody truth within cultural forms.

3. Mission should be centrifugal not centripetal because of the power differential

As long as there are powerful and powerless, mission is best expressed by the powerful 'going', not by expecting the powerless to 'come'. In Christianity, it is the strong who should change, and not the weak. The way heaven invades earth is centrifugal ('let your kingdom come on earth as it is in heaven') not centripetal (trying to save disembodied souls from earth to heaven). When it comes to language, English-speakers should learn the language of the people they are reaching, and not the other way round, because language is power, language is dignity, language is identity.

4. Going is a vulnerable endeavour and goes against natural human inclination

Nimrod versus Abram teaches us that humans keep wanting to settle and God keeps calling them to unsettle. Humans keep wanting to get their identity and honour from being part of something big, something visible, some tangible measures of success, yet God keeps calling us to leave those things behind and trust him for honour and a name. Our tendency is to stay away from fear, God calls us into unsafe situations. We are risk-averse (like Nimrod), yet God calls us into danger. Like Abram, we are sent 'like lambs among wolves'.[159]

Endnotes

130. Genesis 10:5; 20; 31, emphasis mine.

131. Sanneh, Lamin, *Translating the Message: Missionary Impact on Culture, American Society of Missiology* (Maryknoll, NY: Orbis, 1989), 3.

132. Brueggemann, *Genesis*, 98.

133. Josephus, *Antiquities* (1:113-114).

134. Bonino, Jose Miguez, 'Genesis 11:1-9: A Latin American Perspective', in Levison, John R. and Pope-Levison, Priscilla (eds.), *Return to Babel: Global Perspectives on the Bible* (Louisville, KY: Westminster John Knox Press, 1999), 13.

135. Brian Friel's elegiac play *Translations*, about the renaming of Ireland with English place names, has counterparts in the stories of many cultures.

136. The Ziggurat in Babylon was called Etemenenki, 'The House of the Foundation of Heaven and Earth' and was part of the Marduk temple complex.

137. Hiebert, Theodore, 'The Tower of Babel and the Origin of the World's Cultures',

Journal of Biblical Literature 126, No. 1 (Spring 2007), 40.

138. Josephus writes of the tower being waterproof. Against the still-fresh memory of the flood Josephus implies a note of fear in Nimrod's motivation.

139. 'These are the descendants of (personal name)' as section-headings throughout Genesis, specifically: 2:4; 5:1; 6:9; 10:1; 11:10; 11:27; 25:12; 25:19; 36:1; 36:9; 37:2.

140. Arnold, Bill T., *Genesis (The New Cambridge Bible Commentary)* (Cambridge, UK: Cambridge University Press, 2009), 118-119.

141. Von Rad, Gerhard, *Genesis* (trans. John H. Marks; OTL; rev. ed.) (Philadelphia, PA: Westminster, 1972), 152.

142. Hiebert, 'The Tower of Babel', 30.

143. Luke 1:51.

144. Bonino, *Return to Babel*, 15.

145. Ibn Ezra, Abraham, *Ibn Ezra's Commentary on the Pentateuch* (trans. H. Norman Strickman and Arthur M. Silver) (New York: Menorah, 1988), 143.

146. Louth, Andrew (ed.), *Ancient Christian Commentary on Scripture: Genesis 1 – 11* (Downers Grove, IL: IVP, 2001), 169.

147. Emphasis mine.

148. Hiebert, 'The Tower of Babel', 43.

149. It can be argued that Terah's family's escape from Nimrod is a prototypical Exodus story. The Semites escape from a Hamite tyrant, just as they later would in Egypt.

150. Anderson, Bernhard W., *From Creation to New Creation: Old Testament Perspectives* (Minneapolis, MN: Fortress Press, 1994), 178.

151. Numbers 11:29.

152. Luke 10:1.

153. Möller, Karl, 'Words of (In-)evitable Certitude?' in Bartholomew, Craig, Greene, Colin J. D. and Möller, Karl (eds.), *After Pentecost: Language and Biblical Interpretation* (Carlisle: Paternoster Press, 2001), 378 n.115.

154. Revelation 7:9.

155. Revelation 5:9-10.

156. Acts 11:19.

157. 1 Peter 2:5.

158. Anderson, *From Creation to New Creation*, 168.

159. Luke 10:3, NIV.

Chapter 9
Heart Language

At Pentecost, when the Spirit fell upon the disciples and they began to declare the wonders of God in other languages, the question was asked, 'What does this mean?'[160]

Up to a billion people in the world at the moment are learning English as a second language. Why not merely plant English-speaking churches, particularly in the major cities of the world? Why do we urge those who relocate to inefficiently spend time and money and energy learning the language, preaching in that language, planting in that language?

Apart from language-learning being quite obviously an expression of humility, of incarnation, of service, of honouring our hosts, of a basic expression of a whole host of Christian values, I hope, in this chapter, to add a few more thoughts about the power of bringing the gospel to people in their mother tongue. Digging into language is very hard work. Funding people to spend several years studying language seems a poor use of finances. We need to be deeply persuaded about its essentiality.

Mother tongue is how people get their world view

If people receive the gospel in English, not via their mother tongue, it will not displace the loyalties and defaults of their previous identity. It cannot pass into the deepest places in their being. It cannot move them. It cannot change them. If world view is a story, the gospel cannot replace this with a better story whilst it resides in a separate compartment of their life.

Maybe this is the reason why Christians in some places could notoriously respond to Christ and yet engage in internecine atrocities. Their Christianity received in the trade language was unable to undermine their tribalism received via the mother tongue. When faith language is different to tribal language there is a conflict of identity. Gareth Bowley, pastor of one of the most wonderful multicultural churches I know in South Africa, says that culture kicks in at various stress points (weddings, funerals, crises, conflict), and that at these points people are tempted to default to their mother-tongue loyalties.[161]

This means that someone's English could be excellent, but they still need the gospel in their heart language.

Language is power

When our church-planting team of non-locals transitioned to a leadership team that included local guys who had been recently saved with us, we changed the language of team meetings from English to Turkish. This instantly changed the power balance in the room; local team members became more vocal, more opinionated, more in control. Foreigners, even those with excellent Turkish, had to take a back seat.

In any cross-cultural relationship, language is an invisible power differential. If our whole desire is to see local responsibility, local leadership, local ownership in the Church, one of the most decisive ways to achieve this is local language.

The foreign church-planting agent will be forced to defer, to ask advice, to do mission 'with' instead of 'to', to become dependent upon, their local brothers and sisters. Locals will take front seat, foreigners will take back seat. And this points us in the right direction for the indigenisation journey.

The church born in each different language looks different

When 'doing church' in English it is easy to import songs, style, theology from the West. You will default to preaching as you preached in the West. To worshipping as you worshipped in the West. To discipling as you discipled in the West. 'Doing church' in local language forces creativity. Forces songwriting. Forces rethinking church style and structure. Forces an interrogation of your assumptions about church.

Author Elif Shafak writes in English and in Turkish. In an interview about language at the Edinburgh International Book Festival she said the following:

[Turkish] is so heavy. It comes with an identity, with a baggage, an historical baggage, a cultural baggage, so I realise when I'm writing in English, even though it's daunting, even though it's intimidating – you know you're so scared as a foreigner, as a latecomer because of this gap between the mind and the tongue. Your mind always runs faster and your tongue wants to catch up, you know? As foreigners we always want to say more, crack better jokes, and we're very much aware of that gap. But that gap, as intimidating as it is, can be very stimulating at the same time because it pushes you to pay more attention to nuances, those words that can't be translated from one language to the next. And then you start thinking, 'Why is that?' You start thinking about the culture surrounding the language.[162]

The gospel incarnating into a new language forces a creative process, a de-Westernising, indigenising process, which roots the Church more firmly into the local culture than is possible in English.

Language is not just a neutral vehicle for meaning

Words carry cultural and historical baggage, so that direct translation is sometimes technically possible (and sometimes not), but is rarely emotionally or culturally possible. Translation is interpretation.

And this is even more true in the world of religious terminology. For us, entering into an Islamic-based culture, many words like *sin, repentance, faith, God, heaven* come already filled with meaning, with a world view bias. These are the tools available to us for preaching the gospel, but every time we say one of these words, the picture that comes into the hearer's mind is not the picture that we want to put there. So we have to work hard at retelling the Big Story, at redefining terms.

Consider *sin* and *repentance*. In Islam, humanity is basically good, sin is small (acts, words, thoughts), and repentance is not dissimilar to regret. God's forgiveness is not hard to attain. I am clean, I get dirty, I am washed clean again. In the Christian narrative, however, humanity is fallen, sin is either something intrinsic to us (like cancer) or a power over us (like Pharaoh), and the mere washing of forgiveness is insufficient. Repentance means death. Our old nature needs to die (in baptism) and be born again, no longer under the power of sin but under the power of grace.

If you call a Muslim with the former understanding to repent and believe and be forgiven, they may readily assent to this, but for true conversion these words need refilling with Christian meaning which carries with it a Christian view of the world. The words *sin* and *repentance* in and of themselves are inadequate. They are not neutral.

Languages create meaning

Shafak says later in the interview, 'languages shape us. It is not the other way around'.[163] If we can humbly grasp this, that language is *creative*, then we will understand that in learning a new language we are shaped by the values which it confers upon us. The language imposes a culture upon us, some of which we will accept and be enriched by, some of which we will choose to reject.

And equally, when we enter an unreached people group, learn the language, and begin to proclaim Christ in that language, we are creating a Christian expression within that culture that has never existed before.

Different languages are able to do different things

'Imagine', says Bosnian writer Aleksandar Hermon (who writes novels in English and his column in Bosnian), 'vocabulary as a pile of house-building material. Different languages will give you different kinds of houses.'[164] Farsi is great for poetry, German for precise technical discussion, Japanese for subtlety and courtesy. All of these lose something in translation. Elif Shafak again, 'When I want to write about sadness I use Turkish. When I want sarcasm I use English.'[165]

Winston Churchill famously said of the French language:

Frenchmen talk and write just as well about painting as they have done about love, about war, about diplomacy, or cooking. Their terminology is precise and complete. They are therefore admirably equipped to be teachers in the theory of any of these arts.[166]

How exciting for worship! How endlessly creative for Christian expression! How challenging for theology!

Every language carries different insight about God

A friend of mine working in an Arabic-speaking context is mining some great insights regarding the Arab patronage system and implications for understanding the grace of God in its honour-shame New Testament context. He writes:

> Language and world view shape one another. Clearly a good way to understand the Arabic benefactor-client system is to explore the vocabulary Arabs use themselves to describe it. In Arabic, the word for benefactor/patron is *raa'i* pl. *rua'ah* and is exactly the same as the word for *shepherd* and *shepherds* in Arabic.[167]

Those who through Christ the relationship-broker come under the patronage (grace) of the Father come within range of his shepherding authority. What a glorious insight into the grace of God through Christ!

There is a Tajik Bible translation, but local believers can find the language archaic and stuffy in places. One Tajik brother, who is helping with a more accessible translation, told me that they are using an old Tajik word for God. The word is *Khudo*, which carries a literal meaning of 'He himself comes'. Choice of language has opened the door for introducing Emmanuel, the God who comes.

Languages have a lot of vocabulary for things which are important, and little or no vocabulary for things which are not

In English there are different words for the different states of a pig (pig, pork, sausage, bacon, ribs, chops, ham, gammon). In Indonesian or Urdu or Turkish, there is only the one word 'pig' to describe all these states – for obvious reasons!

In Indonesian there are different words for the different states of rice: fields of *padi*, bags of *beras* and plates of *nasi*. In English there is no difference. We have words for what we consider important.

This is not merely a matter of vocabulary but of values. The words we use are a good indication of what we consider important. As our values change, so does our language. When we really need a word, we invent one.[168]

Andrew Walls writes that one of the providences of the movement of the gospel from the Semitic thought-world to the Hellenistic thought-world was the ability of the Greek language to handle philosophical nuance around the time of the Great Creeds. Greek categories such as *ousia* and *hypostasis* facilitated specificity in Trinitarian debate in a way that Semitic languages were technically insufficient to do.

The theological process arose by asking Greek questions in the Greek language, questions that were neither raised nor settled by using Hebrew categories such as *messiah*. Subsequent cross-cultural movements of the Christian faith open the way to theological discovery by raising questions in other languages that have no answer in the terms of another culture.[169]

How to inhabit and redeem language

When we consider 'the [*logos*] became flesh and made his dwelling among us'[170] we see that God did not just send words, a book, as this would have come nowhere even close to expressing his heart towards humankind. We need to inhabit the language which we are learning. To allow it to limit us, and then redefine from the inside.

I have a friend who is learning the local classical art-form of tile painting. She would like to push the boundaries, to express things in this form that have not previously been expressed, to depict Christian truth. But first she has chosen to learn well the traditional expression, so that when she brings newness it will not be imposed from without but reshaped from within. That is how we must bring the gospel through language.

We can bring redefinition, and newness of expression. The presence of the gospel can sacralise otherwise areligious language, infusing it with meaning. Aleksander Hermon quips that when his first novel in English was being edited the proof reader said to him, 'We don't say it like that,' to which he replied, 'Now we do!'

Those coming from outside have the advantage of learning words without feeling their baggage, and acquired language users often have a broader vocabulary then native speakers, as they are more intentional about expression.

Strength to you as you learn! Understand that what you are doing is one of the most Christ-like, most missional, most important things you could be doing: you are part of making the gospel live in a new language.

Origen saw the crossing of the gospel into the Greek-speaking world (a theological process which took at least two centuries), as akin to the Israelites building the tabernacle in the wilderness. Where did they get the gold for the cherubim and the gold vessels? Or the cloth for the curtains? It is because they plundered Egypt![171]

> The theological task, in Origen's view, is to take the things that are misused in the heathen world and to fashion from them things for the worship and service of God.[172]

That is the task of mission. As Jesus took flesh in order to redeem and glorify flesh, we learn language in order to redeem and glorify language, in order creatively to bring forth praise and prayer and art and expressions of faith and conceptions of God that will uniquely exist in that language, in order to honour and sanctify local culture, in order to point the Church in the right direction for indigenisation, in order to see Jesus honoured in every tongue.

Endnotes

160. Acts 2:12.

161. In a private conversation.

162. Aleksandar Hemon and Elif Shafak at the Edinburgh International Book Festival. https://www.youtube.com/watch?v=7d0oSikTuR8 (accessed 5.10.17).

163. Ibid.

164. Ibid.

165. Ibid.

166. Churchill, Winston S., *Painting as a Pastime*, (New York: RosettaBooks, 2014), Kindle loc. 323.

167. O'Carroll, Richard, *Generosity, Benefaction and Grace: A Contextual Theology of Grace Comprehendible to All Arabs from Poor Peasants to Powerful Politicians* (unpublished paper).

168. Richards and O'Brien, *Misreading Scripture With Western Eyes*, Kindle loc. 742.

169. Walls, A., 'The Rise of Global Theologies' in Greenman, Jeffrey P. and Green, Gene L., *Global Theology in Evangelical Perspective: Exploring the Contextual Nature of Theology and Mission* (Downers Grove, IL: IVP Academic, 2012), Kindle loc. 156.

170. John 1:14, NIV.

171. The same gold and silver taken from Egypt that was used in building the tabernacle was also used in crafting the golden calf. Language can lead to idolatry just as surely as to worship. 'Theology tends toward idolatry because of the way words can seduce us into thinking that they adequately express and represent reality. Language is a great blessing, perhaps the most distinctive mark of our humanity, and it does many things well. But while language enables us to perceive and interpret our experience of the world, it does so at a cost. In the first place, language fixes what is in fact fluid and ever-changing – our experience of the world – into something that appears stable and secure.' Johnson, *The Revelatory Body*, Kindle loc. 93.

172. Walls, 'The Rise of Global Theologies', Kindle loc. 197.

Chapter 10
Translatability

The vernacular has lost its own dignity. This goes against the Pentecostal affirmation of every language.
Kosuke Koyama[173]

One of the most important things about Christianity is its translatability. I can talk to God in my own heart language. God can speak to me (through the Scriptures) in my own mother tongue. I don't have to learn a sacred language – the gospel invades my language and renders it sacred!

Having previously established that language creates meaning, is not just a neutral vehicle for carrying truth but exerts its own influence over and projects its own thought world onto that truth, we can marvel at a God who allows, even demands, that his words be translated. What if his intended meaning is lost? What if the word available in the new language does not fully capture the divine substance? Isn't translation a truly risky business?

And the answer, of course, is yes. Lamin Sanneh, arguing for the priority of the translation principle, writes: 'When one translates, it is like pulling the trigger of a loaded gun: the translator cannot recall the hurtling bullet. Translation thus activates a process that will supersede the original intention of the translator.'[174]

Sanneh is not just writing about the literal translation process, but by implication the change of shape that Christianity takes on as it enters a new culture. New idiom means new ways of seeing God, means new ways of being church, means new forms of Christianity. All translation is interpretation. Andrew Walls says, 'Theology is an act of adoration fraught with blasphemy.'[175] Any human language is limited in its expression of the divine, is too weak a vessel to bear the weight of glory. Language is a jar of clay for holding divine treasure.

Because of this risk, formal Religion has sought to control the language of Scripture and of worship. Whether Jewish classical Hebrew, Orthodox Greek, Roman Catholic Latin, Islamic seventh-century Arabic, or for several centuries the English Authorised Version, much religious tradition has sought to capture a snapshot of a particular language at a particular time and declare it sacred. Living Christian faith has repeatedly had to rebel against such control and fight for the translatability principle.

In Istanbul, on our introduction to Christianity course to which we invite seekers, the first session we teach is the story of how the Lord's Prayer came into being. The Alpha course is contextual to questions British people are asking, so Alpha week one is 'Christianity: Boring, Untrue, Irrelevant?'. The first question people in our Muslim city are asking is, 'Christianity: Western, Political, Imperialist?' and we have chosen to answer this from the Lord's Prayer.

When the disciples asked Jesus to teach them to pray they were expecting a formal prayer in classical Hebrew. When Jesus taught them to pray 'Our Father', the Greek vocative in Matthew and Luke can only be explained by understanding that Jesus had taught his disciples to use, as he is recorded as doing during his own personal prayers, the Aramaic word *abba*. Jeremias concludes after extensive research that this word is nowhere used in the Jewish literature on prayer. 'No Jew would have dared to address God in this manner.'[176] The Aramaic language was non-sacred, common, inappropriate.

The modern consensus among scholars is that the Lord's Prayer begins with the Aramaic word *abba* and therefore we can assume that Jesus taught his disciples to pray in the Aramaic of daily communication rather than the classical Hebrew of written texts. The Aramaic-speaking Jew in the first century was accustomed to recite his prayers in Hebrew, not Aramaic ... Both Judaism and Islam have a sacred language. Christianity does not. This fact is of enormous significance.[177]

Jesus' endorsement of everyday, non-religious, heart language as appropriate for prayer was revolutionary! He opened the door for the translatability of the gospel. He urged us to pray to our Father in our mother tongue.

For Muslims coming to faith this is revolutionary. I have often had the joy of sitting with a Muslim talking to God for the first time in their mother tongue. There is a nervousness, 'What if I get the words wrong?' (just like Walls' 'fraught with blasphemy') but also great freedom. We connect on an intrinsic emotional level of our being, singing or reading in our heart language, and this is the kind of connection our Father desires!

I know that although for Muslim background believers this truth is often massive and liberating, for many in the West there is no news here. You have been speaking to God in English since you were born again. The point I am seeking to make, and the call to humility, is that translation begets indigenisation, and that the Church submitting to *sola scriptura* in her own tongue will, under the sovereignty of the Holy Spirit, look very different in different contexts. And that this is right. As Philip Jenkins puts it: 'The use of vernacular Scriptures means that all Christendoms are equidistant from Jerusalem.'[178]

The recovery of translatability was, arguably, the engine of the Protestant Reformation. In 1408, Archbishop Thomas Arundell declared:

> It is a dangerous thing, as witnesseth blessed St. Jerome, to translate the text of the Holy Scripture out of one tongue into another, for in the translation the same sense is not always easily kept … We therefore decree and ordain, that no man, hereafter, by his own authority may translate any text of the Scripture into English or any other tongue … and that no man can read any such book … in part or in whole.[179]

Keep it in Latin to keep it safe! Keep it in Latin to keep it under Rome's purview. If people could read the Bible for themselves, just imagine what horrors could occur! As a response, men like William Tyndale made translation their life's goal.

> I defy the Pope and all his laws … If God spare my life ere many years, I will cause a boy that driveth the plow, shall know more of the Scripture than thou dost.[180]

The principle of translatability hardwires into the core of Christianity the truth that no one centre can control the Church. Indigenisation, expressed in the commonly held 'four selfs' principle (self-governing, self-propagating, self-funding and self-theologising) becomes the logical goal of church planting. This demands of us humility; organisational humility, as sending churches should not be seeking to influence local conditions, and church planting is more than just 'growing our movement', and individual humility. The cross-cultural seed-sower's attitude will be 'they must increase, I must decrease'.[181]

I don't remember the names of any of the midwives who delivered my children, although they played an important role. They were translating the babies from the womb to the world. Cross-cultural preachers are translators of the gospel from one context into another, midwives of the indigenous. Translators are not glamorous and they don't win Oscars, but it is essential that they do their job well.

An old Middle Eastern proverb states that 'Translators are Traitors'. Likewise, there is an Italian phrase with two words that sound almost the same, 'Traduttore, traditore' ('Translator, traitor'). Why? Because in politics or in business, entrusting your words to a translator means entrusting your honour to them. You are putting your very life in their hands. They are your voice, your face, your ambassador. To find a trustworthy translator is to safeguard yourself and your reputation.

When God made human beings in his image, he was equipping us to embody himself, to be his translators. We fallen, fragile creatures are his voice, his body, his ambassadors.

Is this risky? All my readers concerned with orthodoxy will cry, 'Yes! It's terribly risky!' But we must fight for translatability, it is a uniquely Christian treasure. In the parable of the talents, Jesus rebukes the stewards who buried the treasure in the ground, and commends those who made investments that gained a return. The Church is a steward of the gospel, not lord over it. Translatability means risk, not burying the gospel in your cultural norms, but also glorious returns in creative new contextual expressions of the family of God. Jesus endorses this. Church history affirms this. Let us then pursue this!

Endnotes

173. Koyama, Kosuke, 'Theological Education: Its Unities and Diversities', *Theological Education Supplement* 1:20 (1993), 101.

174. Sanneh, Lamin, 'The Significance of the Translation Principle' in Greenman, Jeffrey P. and Green, Gene L., *Global Theology in Evangelical Perspective: Exploring the Contextual Nature of Theology and Mission* (Downer's Grove: IVP Academic, 2012) , Kindle loc. 407.

175. Walls, 'The Rise of Global Theologies', Kindle loc. 111.

176. Jeremias, J., *Jesus and the Message of the New Testament* (Minneapolis, MN: Fortress Press, 2002), Kindle loc. 858.

177. Bailey, *Jesus Through Middle Eastern Eyes*, 95.

178. Jenkins, *The New Faces of Christianity*, 25.

179. Piper, John, *Always Singing One Note – A Vernacular Bible: Why William Tyndale Lived and Died.* 31 January 2006. http://www.desiringgod.org/messages/always-singing-one-note-a-vernacular-bible (accessed 5.10.17).

180. Ibid.

181. See John 3:30.

Intercultural Humility:
Thinking About Differences

Racism is the refusal to love others in their difference, and that is not Christianity. Universal love must recognise, and reckon with, cultural differences. A lived faith demands inculturation and the acknowledgement of other people's right to an inculturated faith.
Aylward Shorter[182]

It's pretty obvious, but people from different cultures *do things differently.* Iranians kiss on three cheeks, Turks kiss on two cheeks, and the English shake hands. I grew up being taught that finishing everything on my plate was good manners. In India, we would visit poor Marathi families in their lean-to shacks, sit on the floor, and they would serve us their finest food, which they could barely afford. I would finish my plate, then the host would heap more on. I would finish my plate again, and it would get loaded up again. It took me quite a lot of curry to realise what was going on – finishing my plate communicated that I was still hungry. The family would all watch me eating, because they would only eat when I finished, and at the rate the hungry white man was going there would be nothing left for them! I had to unlearn my English manners and leave food on the plate as a sign that I was satisfied!

Behavioural difference is obvious, and any attempt at contextualisation will take account of this. However, when we spend a little more time cross-culturally, we will look beneath the surface and notice that people behave differently because they *think differently, relate differently, are motivated differently* and *feel differently.* These have behavioural implications, but actually issue from deeper down in the culture's psyche, from values, beliefs, and ultimately world view.

(Kwast's 'onion model' of culture[183]).

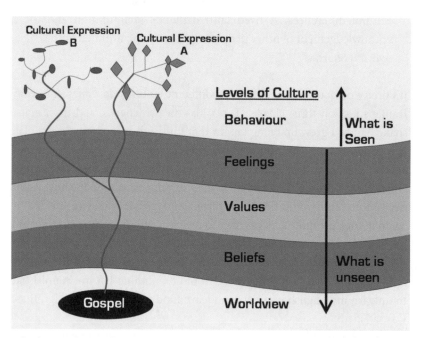

I have seen David Devenish helpfully using this diagram, which is an adaptation of Kwast's classic 'onion model' showing the layers of culture, changed in order to demonstrate 'behaviour' as the above-ground, visible aspect of culture, with the other layers representing the below-ground, unseen aspects of culture. Contextual mission will seek to see the gospel seed sown as deeply as possible, into the world view, or underlying narrative layer of culture. Otherwise, superficial conversion or change of feelings, even change of beliefs may result, but without world view change at the deepest level the gospel never takes root in a deeply felt place, so that it may transform whole individuals, whole communities and whole nations.

The study of anthropology has long helped missionaries to think about cultural difference in meaningful ways. Our question is, 'How should we understand cultural difference?' Our purpose, to bring the transformative power of the gospel of Jesus Christ to bear on that culture. And yet, when one sets out on this journey to understand difference, a wonderful thing happens. One begins to wrestle with the 'why' of difference. One begins to realise that difference isn't about superior and inferior, or more godly and less godly, or more developed and less developed, but exactly that – difference! *Intercultural Humility,* then, lifts us up and carries us from mere acceptance of the reality of difference, to celebration of, and even delight in, this difference. Contextualisation metamorphoses from an onerous duty (I need to study their world view so I can change it), into a delightful, creative enterprise, filled with surprise. Just as we are amazed by biodiversity, the myriad butterflies and vibrant colours of the rainforest, so let us marvel at ethno-diversity, no less part of the purpose of our creative God.

> Our first task in approaching another people, another culture, another religion, is to take off our shoes, for the place we are approaching is holy. Else we may find ourselves treading on men's dreams. More serious still, we may forget that God was here before our arrival.[184]

In this section, I will examine some of these differences. What I hope to contribute in these chapters is not just an introduction for those engaging cross-culturally to some ways in which cultures differ, but also the implications for evangelism, discipleship and the planting of Christ-following communities. Cultural difference, if not embraced, can create potentially fatal barriers for the transmission of the gospel. If, however, cultural difference is embraced, the potential for rich, creative, Spirit-led, biblically sound, indigenising Christianity is maximised.

Endnotes

182. Shorter, *Toward a Theology of Inculturation*, 78.

183. Kwast, L.E., 'Understanding Culture' in Winter, Ralph D. and Hawthorne, Stephen C. (eds.), *Perspectives on the World Christian Movement* (Pasadena, CA; William Carey Library, 1981), 397-399.

184. Warren, M.A.C. in Warren's Preface to the seven books in the Christian Presence Series (London: SCM Press, 1969-1966).

Chapter 11
Whose Reason?

Reason would have been chains to man;
If he had not had a heart within him.
Muhammad Iqbal[185]

One day an old farmer's only horse ran away. When his neighbours came to commiserate with him over losing his source of livelihood, he told them, 'Don't commiserate with me. Who knows what is good and what is bad?'

A few days later the horse returned, and following it was a wild horse. When his neighbours came to congratulate him on this surprising turn of events, the old farmer replied, 'Don't congratulate me. Who knows what is good and what is bad?'

The next day, when his son was out riding the wild horse, he was thrown and broke both his legs. As the neighbours came to offer their sympathy, guess what the old farmer said? 'Don't give me your sympathy. Who knows what is good and what is bad?'

Soon afterwards war broke out, and all the able-bodied young men from the village were conscripted. But the farmer's son was not taken, because of his broken legs. When the villagers came to congratulate him on his good fortune, the old famer repeated his refrain… 'Don't congratulate me. Who knows what is good and what is bad?'

This well-known Chinese story demonstrates some of the differences between Eastern and Western views of the world. In the East, what is significant is not the event, person or object on its own, but its relationships within its context.

When you get up close and personal with people from different cultures, working out how people think, and why they see the world the way they do, has enormous implications!

One day my wife let go of her shopping trolley and it scratched a fancy Mercedes. She left a note on the windscreen with her phone number so the owner could get in touch. The man found out our address, turned up at the door when I wasn't home, and reduced Jess to tears by shouting at her and demanding money. When I got home, I was incensed. I went to his house, gave him cash for the repair to his car, and told him what a shameful man he was for threatening my wife. His answer, I will never forget it, was, 'But I am a lawyer!'

'I don't care what job you do – the way you spoke to my wife was inappropriate.'

'But,' he puffed out his chest, 'I am a lawyer.'

A total clash of world views! For me as an English person, right and wrong are distinct categories, and what he had done was wrong. For him as a Middle Eastern male, he had a high-status job and good standing in the community. To isolate his actions from his context was impossible. Westerners atomistically examine each action on its own merit. Easterners view the complex whole. In the complex whole, he was a man, in his own neighbourhood, with high status. She was a woman, who is foreign, who was not a lawyer. Right and wrong didn't even come into it – he was a lawyer!

Cognition East and West

Cultural psychology is a large, and growing, field, exploring the variation in cognitive processes of people from different cultures. In this chapter, I hope to give a very broad introduction to the fact that *people from different cultures think differently*. There is not one rationality, one cognitive process, or one kind of intelligence. Neither are there superior and inferior ways of thinking.

> The notion of 'universal rationality' is today viewed by many as little more than a fiction ... There exist a variety of 'rationalities', each of which has to be respected in its own right; there is no privileged

vantage point, no universal concept of 'reason,' which can pass judgement upon them.[186]

We will examine some differences between East and West. This will inevitably involve some generalisations – in reality Americans think quite differently to Europeans, and Arabs differently to Chinese. Likewise, not everyone within the same national culture adheres to the generalisation. Yet research shows quite definitively that it is possible to speak of cultural cognitive difference. Here are some broad categories of difference.[187]

Black and White versus the Middle Way

The principle of contradiction is the foundation of Western logic. If A is true, and B is different, then B cannot also be true. The Greeks were very strong on this, perhaps because of their debate culture, where you had to be able to disprove your opponent's thesis and prove your own. Our ethics and our laws are based on the assumption of right and wrong, universal and inalienable.

For Easterners, contradiction is not a problem. The world is complex and wisdom is finding the best solution, the Golden Mean or Middle Way between two opposing views. 'The opposite of a great truth is also true' teaches Zen Buddhism. Seeing things as black and white is too simplistic, almost immature, according to Chinese philosophy. Classical Chinese culture, unlike the Greeks, had no history of debate, and was more concerned with *dialectical* thought than with logic.

> Dialectical thought is in some ways the opposite of logical thought. It seeks not to decontextualise but to see things in their appropriate contexts ... To think about an object or event in isolation and apply abstract rules to it is to invite extreme and mistaken conclusions. It is the Middle Way that is the goal of reasoning.[188]

One day, a petitioner came to Turkish folk philosopher Nasreddin Hodja to ask him to judge between himself and his adversary. 'You are right,' said the Hodja. The supplicant's adversary then came and presented his side of the story. 'You are also right,' decreed the Hodja. A third man piped up,

'Hodja, they can't both be right!' The Hodja stroked his beard and thought for a moment, before replying to the third man, 'Yes, my friend, you are also right!'

Before you pooh-pooh this, please consider that ancient Hebrews were probably closer to the Chinese than to the Greeks in the way they viewed the world.[189] The Bible expresses some contradictions that the authors were obviously able to hold in tension, because the Bible is an Eastern book. Consider these two consecutive proverbs:

Proverbs 26:4: Answer not a fool according to his folly, lest you be like him yourself.

Proverbs 26:5: Answer a fool according to his folly, lest he be wise in his own eyes.

Should you answer a fool according to his folly or not? Both. Depending on context.

Foreground versus background

In one piece of research, Japanese and American students were shown a picture of a fish in a tank. In the foreground the fish, in the background seaweed, stones, bubbles, etc. They were then shown subtle variations on this picture. In some variations, the background remained the same but the fish in the foreground was changed (facing right instead of left, spots instead of stripes). In others, the fish in the foreground stayed the same, but the background was varied (number of seaweed strands, position of stones, etc.). The American students noticed the changes to the foreground, but were oblivious to background changes. The Japanese students, conversely, noticed the background variation. Most tellingly, when asked what they had seen, the American students began their responses 'A large fish' and the Japanese students, 'A fish-tank...'[190]

This study, and others like it, demonstrate differences in perception. Westerners see the world atomistically, they 'zoom in' to the object; in this case the fish. Easterners see the world holistically. Their perception is 'field-dependent', meaning that the individual object is not significant; what is significant is its identity in context – the fish tank.

The Japanese word for 'I' is rarely used in conversation. Instead, there are many situational words for 'I' that are used depending on context and audience. Formal or informal, socially upwards or downwards, degree of intimacy all have varying words for 'I'. Why? Because who I am individually does not exist; rather it is who I am within the web of relationships.[191]

From a Near Eastern perspective, Greenlee seeks to explain Arab culture's holistic perspective as coming from its desert origins:

> In a desert the landscape is not cluttered with too many objects and therefore the eye is able to encompass vast expanses with great clarity … The mind develops an approach to knowledge that has a tendency to recognise the whole, not the part, of direct life experience.[192]

The point is that Westerners tend to decontextualise, to 'zoom in', whilst Easterners 'zoom out'. You can see this clearly in methods of Bible-reading; a strength of the Western tradition is to 'focus in' on exegesis of one verse, whilst a strength from the East is to 'broaden out' to grasp the narrative structure of the larger context.

Verbs versus nouns

Have you ever noticed that in the Old Testament there are very few 'photographic' descriptions of appearance, whether of people or of buildings?[193] But there is an obsession with the *process* of building. This is because in the East, verbs are more important than nouns. For the biblical writers, describing *what* the temple looked like was not as important as describing *how* it was made.

A researcher showed a picture of a cow to American and Chinese children. They were then shown two more pictures, a chicken and grass, and asked which one went with the cow. The majority of American children put the chicken and the cow together. I would have done so too. The reason being 'they are both animals'. This is a taxonomic categorisation. The Chinese children, however, put the grass together with the cow, 'because cows eat grass'. They saw a *relationship* between the two.

A   B

What goes with this? A or B

Example of item measuring preference for grouping by categories vs. relationships[195]

I think this is a great illustration of the differences between East and West. The way we Westerners group things together is static, it is about nouns of appearance. The Chinese children saw things in terms of verbs – 'cows *eat* grass'.

In Chinese, one would ask, 'Drink more?' In English, the same question would be, 'More tea?' For the Chinese, the noun (tea) is redundant. Of course it's tea! For the English, the verb (drink) is redundant. Of course you drink it!

This has significant implications for the way people think. It is a simplification, but Westerners tend to see the world in terms of objects, and Easterners in terms of dynamic relationships. When I, as a Westerner, learn another language, I find it easy to memorise nouns, because they describe something concrete and defined, and much more difficult to learn verbs. That's just the way my brain works! Nouns tend to have one-to-one equivalency with other languages, whilst verbs are much more difficult to translate. I struggled for ages with the many varied Turkish verbs for 'to use', 'to exploit', 'to take advantage of'. For example, '*sömürmek*' is the sucking up of the resources of the powerless by the powerful. The Turkish language apparently needs a high degree of nuance when discussing types of exploitation!

Rules versus relationships

For the Westerner, the world is relatively simple, and can be described by principles or laws: the law of gravity, the principle of human rights, and so on. For the Easterner, the world is constantly changing – you never step in the same river twice, because you have changed and the river has changed! So everything needs to be considered in its context.

For an Easterner, the idea of an immutable, objective law that can be imposed regardless of context verges on the immoral. As a citizen of pre-revolutionary China put it:

> A Chinese judge cannot think of law as an abstract entity, but as a flexible quantity as it should be personally applied to Colonel Huang or Major Li. Accordingly, any law which is not personal enough to respond to the personality of Colonel Huang or Major Li is inhuman and therefore no law at all. *Chinese justice is an art, not a science.*[196]

Before rejecting this out of hand, let's consider that New Testament Christianity was not a legalistic religion, that the apostle Paul wrote *occasional* (situational) letters, with emphases that although largely consistent, varied according to context, that there were certainly different rules for Jewish and Gentile Christians, and that God's justice does seem to take into account the situation and motives of people, not merely the action *prima facie*.

It is advisable, as this book argues in many different ways, to be slow to judge across cultures. There is a complexity to the world which resists a simplistic black and white analysis. Life really is more art than science, and all I am appealing for is a more cautious and nuanced approach to difference.

Assuming that your own way of thinking is superior is called ethnocentrism. Bernard Adeney, helpfully, in his classic *Strange Virtues: Ethics in a Multicultural World*, writes: 'A first step in overcoming ethnocentrism is the recognition that my own values are not necessarily the same as God's.'

The Lewis Model

One of the most helpful models for categorising cultural difference I have come across is that of Richard Lewis, the Lewis LMR model. Mr Lewis is an international business consultant. His wisdom is gritty, hard-won, (potentially) un-politically correct, but somehow winsome, honouring of difference, and has a ring of truth about it.

Lewis groups the cultures of the world broadly into three categories: Linear-Active (classic Western European), Multi-Active (classic Mediterranean or Latin) and Reactive (classic Far Eastern) personalities.

Linear-active people tend to be task-oriented, highly organised planners who complete action chains by doing one thing at a time, preferably in accordance with a linear agenda. Speech is for information and depends largely on facts and figures.

Multi-active people are loquacious, emotional, and impulsive and attach great importance to family, meetings, relationships, compassion, and human warmth. They like to do many things at the same time and are poor followers of agendas. Speech is for opinions.

Reactive people – good listeners – rarely initiate action or discussion, preferring first to hear and establish the other's position, then react to it and formulate their own opinion. Reactives listen before they leap. Speech is for creating harmony.[198]

Table: The LMR Model, The Three Major Cultural Categories

Linear-active	Multi-Active	Reactive
Talks and listens in equal degrees	Talks most of the time	Listens most of the time
Rarely interrupts	Often interrupts	Never interrupts
Confronts with facts	Confronts emotionally	Never confronts
Dislikes losing face	Has a good story	Must not lose face
Uses official channels	Seeks out key people	Uses network
Follows linear agenda	Diverges frequently from agenda	Follows circular agenda
Frank, direct	Indirect, manipulative	Indirect, courteous
Truth before diplomacy	Diplomatic, creative truth	Diplomacy before truth
Limited body language	Lots of body language	Hardly any body language
Cool	Excitable	Inscrutable
Promotes product	Promotes personal relationships	Promotes inter company harmony
Completes action chains	Completes human transactions	Harmonizes by action at appropriate times
Partly conceals feelings	Displays feelings	Conceals feelings
Speech is for information	Speech is for opinions	Speech is to promote harmony
Punctual, time dominated	Relaxed about time	Focuses on doing things in the correct order
Has individual goals	Has intimate circle goals	Has company goals
Task orientated	People orientated	Very people orientated
Does one thing at a time	Does several things at once	Reacts to partner's action
Respects facts and figures	Respects oratory, expressiveness, charisma	Respects age, wisdom, experience
Plans ahead step by step	Plans grand outline	Reacts to others' plans
Defines problems and solves in quick sequence	Goes for all-embracing solutions	Prefers gradualist solutions
Separates business and personal life	Intertwines business and social	Links business and social
Bad orders can be discussed	Bad orders should be circumvented	An order is an order
Admits own mistakes	Finds an excuse	Hides, covers up mistakes
Likes clarity and accuracy	Tolerates ambiguity	Likes ambiguity
Talks in turns	Often talks over the other	Takes turns slowly
Tolerates some silence	Cannot tolerate silence	Likes sharing silences

Any model like this will inevitably generalise, and should be seen as a tool to help equip, and not hard-and-fast scientific categorisation. Even the very act of presenting such ideas in tabular or graphical form is in danger of undermining or offending the diversity one is seeking to celebrate.

Implications of difference: Bible reading

Accepting that people think differently, and that one rationality is not superior to another, is all well and good, until we get to thinking together about things that we really care about. That's where the rubber hits the road.

Consider how we read the Bible. Everyone agrees that a certain degree of reason is used in biblical interpretation. But accepting cultural cognitive difference will lead to difference in hermeneutics, difference in interpretation, even difference in theology, differences emanating from cultural difference.

Linear-Actives seek to systematise and develop universal principles. Our models of hermeneutics are very Western; we read a passage, extract the 'theological principle', cross the 'principalising bridge' from the author's world into our world, and then make application.[199] Western theology over the last few centuries has produced Systematic Theologies, has treated exegesis as a science with fixed rules, and has only admitted an argument if it follows a logical development with proofs. The law of contradiction is essential: if something is true, then it must be universally true.

Easterners read the Bible very differently! Lewis writes: 'Multi-active truth is always contextual and is in the ear of the listener, as beauty is in the eye of the beholder.'[200] Multi-Active theologians use emotional arguments, anecdotal arguments ('this happened to me so it must be true') and experiential arguments (to be true it needs to *feel* true!). I have a good Middle Eastern friend who is an outstanding preacher. He can one week preach from Hebrews 6 and declare that free will is the most important thing about the gospel. The next Sunday, he will preach from Ephesians 2 and passionately proclaim that there is no free will, all is God's sovereign choice. Is he Calvinist or Arminian? Well, it depends which verse he is teaching! He doesn't need a system, he has the Bible. You may argue that he is inconsistent; he will reply that he is passionate. And who has the right to say whether passion or consistency is superior?

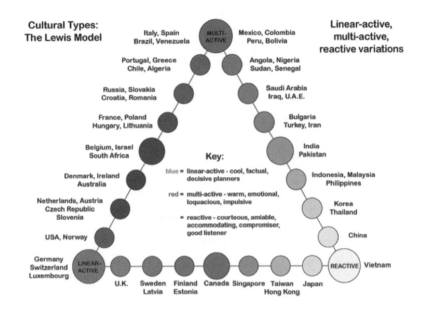

Cultural Types: The Lewis Model

Italy, Spain
Brazil, Venezuela

MULTI-ACTIVE

Mexico, Colombia
Peru, Bolivia

Linear-active, multi-active, reactive variations

Portugal, Greece
Chile, Algeria

Angola, Nigeria
Sudan, Senegal

Russia, Slovakia
Croatia, Romania

Saudi Arabia
Iraq, U.A.E.

France, Poland
Hungary, Lithuania

Bulgaria
Turkey, Iran

Belgium, Israel
South Africa

Key:

India
Pakistan

Denmark, Ireland
Australia

blue = linear-active - cool, factual, decisive planners

Indonesia, Malaysia
Philippines

Netherlands, Austria
Czech Republic
Slovenia

red = multi-active - warm, emotional, loquacious, impulsive

Korea
Thailand

USA, Norway

= reactive - courteous, amiable, accommodating, compromiser, good listener

China

Germany
Switzerland
Luxembourg

LINEAR-ACTIVE

REACTIVE

Vietnam

U.K.   Sweden   Finland   Canada   Singapore   Taiwan   Japan
       Latvia   Estonia   Hong Kong

© Roger Parry 2012. Reproduced by permission of Nicholas Brealey Publishing

Where Westerners tend to zoom in and focus on the detail, Easterners have the ability to zoom out and hold the whole big picture in their view. That means they will read the Bible differently.

Let's review what we are saying. A Western Evangelical hermeneutic may not be the only viable hermeneutic for people who would call themselves Evangelical. Systematic theology may not be universally translatable and applicable. Why? Because different rationalities work differently.

One of the great delights of living cross-culturally, not just for Bible-reading but for all areas of life, is the opportunity to benefit from a variety of perspectives. This is only possible, however, where we choose to celebrate that different cultures think differently, rather than defaulting to an ethnocentric, 'I am straight and you are skewed' perspective. This takes work, and time, and openness, but is wonderfully worthwhile.

Endnotes
185. Iqbal, *Armaghan-i Hijaz*, 848:1 in Iqbal (trans. Mustansir Mir) *Tulip in the Desert*, 134.

186. McGrath, Alister E., *Christian Theology: An Introduction* (Hoboken, NJ: Blackwell Publishing, 2001), 183.

187. Many, but not all, of the following examples are drawn from Nisbett, Richard E., *The Geography of Thought: How Asians and Westerners Think Differently – and Why*, Kindle Edition (New York: Simon & Schuster, 2003).

188. Nisbett, *The Geography of Thought*, Kindle loc. 490-492.

189. Boman, Thorleif, *Hebrew Thought Compared with Greek* (London: Norton, 1970), 17.

190. Nisbett, *The Geography of Thought*, Kindle loc. 1180.

191. Ibid. Kindle loc. 735-743.

192. Greenlee, David, 'Missiological Contributions from the Middle East' in Taylor, William D. (ed.), *Global Missiology for the 21st Century* (Grand Rapids, MI: Baker, 2000), 338.

193. Boman, *Hebrew Thought Compared with Greek*, 75.

194. Nisbett, *The Geography of Thought*, Kindle loc. 1711.

195. Ibid.

196. Lin, Y., *My Country and My People* (London: William Heinemann, 1936), 80. Emphasis mine.

197. Adeney, *Strange Virtues*, 23.

198. Lewis, Richard, *When Teams Collide: Managing the International Team Successfully* (London: Nicholas Brealey, 2012), 2.

199. Duvall, J. Scott and Hays, J. Daniel, *Grasping God's Word (Second Edition)* (Grand Rapids, MI: Zondervan, 2005), 23.

200. Lewis, *When Teams Collide*, 23.

Chapter 12
I Am Because We Are

Innovation is the root of all evil.
Arab proverb

My wife was working as a primary school teacher. She is strongly motivated, creative, a very good teacher. One day, to her dismay and confusion, the headmistress pulled her aside.

'I would like you to tone it down. Be less creative. Don't do such amazing craft projects with the children.'

She was stunned! She was being asked to be less excellent at her job. It made no sense! The headmistress explained, 'You see, you looking good makes the rest of the staff look bad.'

We are from an individualistic culture, where aiming high, individual expression, being the best you can, are very deep cultural values instilled from birth. We were living, however, in a collectivistic (group-orientated) culture, where the honour of the group is more important than the prowess of the individual. Her shining brightly made others look relatively duller. Her standing tall made others look relatively shorter. And this was wrong.

A Japanese proverb says, 'The nail that stands up gets banged down.' Others would call this the 'tall poppy syndrome'; in a field of poppies one taller poppy is seen as problematic for the others. Why? Because it makes the whole field look ugly. And because it uses up more sunlight and more nutrients than the others; an expression of the concept of *limited good*, at which we will look in a moment. Group-orientated cultures place a high value on conformity. This is all the more interesting, because individualistic cultures see conformity as a vice. Be yourself!

One of my most profound moments of feeling the truth of this was hearing Armenian pastor Karen Khachatryan telling the story of Peter through Matthew's Gospel. Peter, he said, is continually trying to be better than the other disciples, to stick out, to attract honour to himself. The most striking example is in Matthew's telling of the walking on the water story. I am used to this being told as a story of individual faith. 'While the others stayed in the boat terrified, Peter walked on water!' Pastor Karen, however, pointed out that Jesus never praises Peter for this act, he rebukes him. Essentially, Jesus is saying, 'Get back in the boat with the others where you belong. Stop trying to be better than everyone else.' In a collectivistic culture, what Peter was doing in trying to stand out from the crowd was unacceptable!

Bruce Malina argues that the cultural orientation in the New Testament world was primarily collectivistic; a first-century Mediterranean was 'essentially a group-embedded and group-oriented person'.[201] He helpfully lists some key differences between group-orientated preferences and individualistic preferences, which I have adapted opposite.[202]

Table: Communalistic vs Individualistic Preferences

Communalistic Preferences	Individualistic Preferences
People put high value on conformity	People put high value on independence
High-status people are of a different kind than low-status people	High-status and low-status persons are all 'people like me'
People born into extended families that protect them in exchange for loyalty, commitment, in-group solidarity	Everyone is supposed to take care of himself or herself and his/her immediate family
The individual is emotionally dependent on organisations and institutions, with identity based in the social system	The individual is independent of organisations and institutions, with identity based in the individual
Private life is invaded by in-group, kin group, and organisations to which one belongs: options are predetermined; individual conformity and group acceptance are foremost; group membership is ideal	Individuals have a right to a private life and to their own opinions; individual initiative and achievement are foremost, with leadership as ideal
Religion is part and parcel of the political system and the family system	Religion is separate from the political system and family system
Collectivist conversions	Individual conversions
Ideological, theory-oriented thinking is popular	Pragmatic, empirically oriented thinking is popular
Less questioning of authority in general	More questioning of authority in general

Nisbett would sum up the group-orientated mentality like this: 'The goal for the self in relation to society is not so much to establish superiority or uniqueness, but to achieve harmony within a network of supportive social relationships and to play one's part in achieving collective ends.'[204] This can't be dismissed as anachronistic anthropological gibberish in a globalised twenty-first century. In much of the world it is as current today as it has ever been.

De-individualising our faith, then, helps us understand the context in which the New Testament was written. It also helps us cross cultures into many world contexts, because the majority of cultures today would be less individualistic, more group-orientated, than European or North American cultures.

Limited good[205]

If the highest goal is the well-being of your group, then the concept of *limited good* comes in to play. Think about a village in the ancient world. Anything good is available in limited supply: land, livestock, wives for your sons. This means that if I get more (land, wives), less is available for others. In this way, my increase automatically means others' decrease. Thus village morals are fundamentally conservative; anyone excelling, acquiring or progressing is doing so at the expense of the rest of the community. So they should be considered evil.

In the book of Proverbs, for example, the rich are often considered evil. Why? Because the underlying assumption of *limited good* is that they have become rich at the expense of others.

Interestingly, the post-industrial West has in many ways begun to rediscover the concept of limited good. Starting with the 1972 publication of *The Limits to Growth* (which many say kicked off the modern environmental movement), we have begun once again to see the world as an interconnected system, that if some countries get rich it is at the expense of other countries which then become poorer, and that all that is good (productive land, crude oil, fresh water, the ozone layer) does indeed have limits. The global village works just the same way as an ancient Mediterranean village.

If good is unlimited, as assumed by capitalism, then individuals should excel, because my increase does not affect you. But if good is limited, then personal advancement harms others in the group, and the prime goal should then be the 'greater good', not individual good. So my wife should tone down her creativity for the sake of the other staff members, Peter should get back in the boat, and richer countries should slow their economic growth for the sake of the planet.

Conversion – group or individual?

As should become clear from this discussion, conversion in group-orientated societies is an extremely complicated issue. 'You believe in Jesus and you can go to heaven' is fraught with non sequiturs and cultural difficulties. 'For collectivistic people, choosing their religion in isolation from the group implies rejection of the group itself.'[206] Why would I want to go to a heaven where my family will not be? And what about the shame that I will bring upon my people?

In *The Samurai*, Japanese Catholic novelist Shusaku Endo has one of his characters, Father Valente, make a profound observation about the resistance of Japanese culture to the gospel. Valente sensed that many Japanese believed that the Christian teachings were good, but felt that they would be betraying their ancestors if they chose to go to a Paradise where their ancestors could not dwell.[207]

One of the Holy Spirit's answers to this problem is households coming to faith together. In the New Testament, and in our experience, group conversion does happen. We have had the privilege of baptising husband, wife, siblings, adult children all together on several occasions. But it does always require a pioneer, a family member who chooses to go against group pressure, investigate the gospel, then commend it to their family.

In this case, the role of the cross-cultural worker is to see this household as an embryonic church, and to coach the natural leaders of this community. All over the Middle East today, group conversions are leading to organically growing house churches, sometimes called Church Planting Movements. It is impossible to manufacture these kinds of movements, but where the Holy Spirit is bringing whole families to faith there is a natural context for discipleship and community which we would be foolish to overlook.

I recently heard a story out of Iran, about a prostitute who was ready to give her life to Jesus. The evangelist actually delayed 'leading her through' until many of her colleagues from the brothel were ready to come to faith – then they made their decision together. The evangelist's comment, tellingly, was, 'The devil would have been happy for us to just have the one lady believe, but we waited so that we could have her whole circle! Now she has an automatic support network.'

On another occasion, I was introduced to an Iranian sister, a small, unassuming woman. 'She has seen many from her family come to faith,' I was told. 'Upwards of 200 people!'

The first guy who came to faith with us in Istanbul was a well-known tattoo artist with a huge friendship circle. His shop was just around the corner from our church building. Within three months we had seen five from his circle come to faith, and there has been an ongoing trickle of believers to come through his witness. On one occasion we invited the Indian evangelist Ram Babu to come and hold some public evangelistic meetings in Istanbul. This tattoo artist invited a whole group of aunties and older ladies; all hard, secularised Muslims. They sat right in the front row, arms crossed and with stern expressions. At one point in the meeting there was an amazing sense of the presence of God, and many testified to gold dust and oil supernaturally appearing on their hands. This whole row of aunties had gold dust on them and were giddily exclaiming and showing each other. From that day onwards, his whole family circle were open to our team and to the church. God was removing his shame by showing the decision-makers in the family that there was substance to his belief.

In one of our churches, a young man had been a believer for about ten years before his first relative came to faith. His Muslim family had started by rejecting him pretty hard, then with time had come to accept and even appreciate the change in his life. One of our evangelists got alongside him and started to help him intentionally witness within his family group, and now there is a steady stream of relatives, family friends and work contacts coming to faith!

For this to happen, the evangelist needs to avoid the temptation to pull the individual out of their group. Mark 5 is a great example; the Gerasene man is delivered of his legion of demons and wants to get in the boat to leave with Jesus, but Jesus says no, and instructs him to bear witness in the Decapolis. Salvation is not to get us out of the world, but to get us into the world. Temple Gairdner of Cairo warned of 'extracting the leaven out of the loaf'.[208] Those preaching the gospel and planting churches in collectivistic societies need to ensure that, as far as possible, individuals who are converted are able to continue within their 'circle', rather than being pulled into the Church at the expense of their immediate kinship group.

Sometimes, of course, an individual who converts is rejected, persecuted, disowned by their family. The frequency of this in the New Testament, and in the world today, shows that God does sometimes call individuals to go against the group. There is a significant note in the teaching of Scripture about 'leaving'. Baptism is a decisive act, not just of individual faith in Jesus but of joining a new community.

In these instances, local church as family becomes hugely significant" a new source of honour, a new community, a new place to belong. We have learned that when Westerners talk about church as 'family' they mean something very different to what Easterners expect. If you are going to use that word, are you prepared to live up to the implications? Family pool financial resources to send a nephew to university, or to buy a married couple a house. Family find jobs for each other. Family is invasive, comments on everything, admits no no-go areas.[209]

Homogenous churches?

As is clear from the above discussion, there are no simple answers to evangelism, discipleship, or church planting within group-orientated cultures. Group conversion is beautiful, but it is the work of the Holy Spirit. It cannot be manufactured, although if the language used in evangelism is de-individualised (biblicalised?), this will be a step in the right direction. 'You will be saved, you and all your household' (Acts 11:14).

Group conversion can produce fast-growing, natural, homogenous churches. The Church Planting Movement (CPM) school is a grandchild of the Church Growth Movement founded by Donald McGavran.[210] One of McGavran's most controversial observations was that 'Homogenous Units Grow Faster'.[211] This was a sociological observation, not a theological conviction. 'McGavran's point is simply that people cannot demonstrate a kingdom ethic until they come into God's kingdom.'[212] The danger with the homogenous unit principle, and with CPMs more widely, is that where there exist cultural strongholds of racism or tribalism these are never confronted, that 'one new man in Christ' is never attained, and that the church, where there is 'neither Jew nor Greek ... neither slave nor free'[213] is never truly mature.

Missiologists are now observing that an exclusive focus on specific people groups (*ethne*) in evangelism and church planting can be problematic theologically and ecclesiologically. Professor Johannes Reimer writes:

> The church is not allowed to pick and choose the more receptive and leave the others out. Ecclesia can never be guided by a homogeneous unit principle (HUP) ... Such a principle may help to sharpen our missionary communication, but never determine our task.[214]

On the other hand, a forced multiculturalism, 'One new man in Christ must be expressed in the Sunday meeting,' can frustrate evangelism by creating unbiblical barriers to the gospel and prohibiting contextualisation. This issue is complex, painful and live today.

Individual conversion in collectivistic societies is always difficult. It requires great courage and conviction to rebel against cultural mores, history, identity, the honour of the group. As much as possible, individuals should be encouraged to remain and witness within their natural kinship group. The tendency to 'extract' should be avoided. Many come to Christ through the testimony of a family member or friend. But also, there are times when families reject, when dust should be shaken off feet, when the new community replaces biological family, and when a clear discontinuity occurs.

How do we know which approach to pursue when? We trust and follow the Holy Spirit. There is no one-size-fits-all in world mission.

John's Gospel is the most individualistic of all the New Testament books, with more than fifty aphoristic sayings about the individual and Jesus, such as 'The One who believes in the Son has eternal life,' where John seems to deliberately choose the word 'one' instead of using the plural form, 'those who believe...'[215] This gospel is characterised by explicitly private, individual conversations between Jesus and people (Nicodemus, the Samaritan woman, Pilate, Mary, Peter). John was an Easterner, writing in a group-orientated context, yet he chose to emphasise the possibility of individual, personal relationship with Jesus. Those who come to faith are coming to Jesus. Sometimes, in all the discussion about missiological approaches in collectivistic contexts, this is overlooked. In fact, reading the Bible through a non-individualistic lens makes such bold personal statements, such as those found in John, appear even more amazing!

> *The one* who loves me will be loved by my Father, and I will love him and reveal myself to him.
> John 14:21b (EHV, emphasis mine)

Endnotes

201. Malina, Bruce, *The New Testament World: Insights from Cultural Anthropology*, Third Edition, Revised and Expanded (Louisville, KY: Westminster John Knox Press, 2001), 62.

202. Ibid. 76-78.

204. Nisbett, *The Geography of Thought*, Kindle loc. 772.

205. Foster, George M., 'Peasant Society and the Image of Limited Good', *American Anthropologist*, April 1965, 67, No. 2: 296.

206. Georges, Jayson, *The 3D Gospel: Ministry in Guilt, Shame and Fear Cultures* (Jayson Georges, 2014), Kindle loc. 936.

207. Endo, Shusaku, *The Samurai* (trans. Van C. Gessel) (New York: New Directions Books, 1982), 164.

208. Gairdner, W.H.T., *Brotherhood – Islam's and Christ's* (London: Edinburgh House Press, 1923) cited in Allen, *The Ministry of the Spirit*, Kindle loc. 1873-1875.

209. Muller, Roland, *The Messenger, The Message, The Community: Three Critical Issues for the Cross-Cultural Church Planter,* Third Edition (Surrey, BC: CanBooks, 2013), 238.

210. Terry, John Mark and Payne, J.D., *Developing a Strategy for Missions: A Biblical, Historical and Cultural Introduction.* (Grand Rapids, MI: Baker Academic, 2013), 119.

211. McGavran, Donald A., *Understanding Church Growth* (Grand Rapids, MI: Eerdmans, 1970), 199.

212. Terry and Payne, *Developing a Strategy for Missions*, 123.

213. Galatians 3:28.

214. Reimer, Johannes, 'Church Planting Connected to Society' in Van de Poll, Evert and Appleton, Joanne (eds.), *Church Planting in Europe: Connecting to Society, Learning from Experience* (Eugene, OR: Wipf & Stock, 2015), Kindle loc. 1622.

215. Bauckham, Richard, *Gospel of Glory: Major Themes in Johannine Theology* (Grand Rapids, MI: Baker Academic, 2015), Kindle loc. 275.

Chapter 13
Honour Motivation

The rich young man *ran* up to Jesus, *knelt* in front of him and asked, with a flourish, 'Good Teacher, what must I do to inherit eternal life?'[216] In honour-shame societies, body language is more important than words, and *how* one speaks is often more significant than *what* is said. This young man is not sincere. Sincere searchers come at night like Nicodemus. This young man is dramatically kneeling in front of Jesus in the big crowd, so that everyone can see how religious he is.

Jesus can tell that this young man's treasure is honour; good standing in the eyes of everyone. He already has status; it is a land-based, not a cash-based economy. Being rich means that he has great lands. Being rich and young means that he has not acquired these lands himself, he is from a wealthy family. He is known in the village and has prestige due to his family. Yet, not being satisfied, he is trying to add to this prestige. He wants people to say, 'Not only is he wealthy, he is also devout. See how he is talking to Jesus!'

When Jesus tells him to sell all he has and give to the poor, Jesus is asking him to sell everything including his family lands. In the Middle East, no one would choose to sell their ancestral land. All the sources of honour, identity, name, genealogy are bound up in your lands. To sell them means that you are renouncing your heritage, your lineage. There is a Turkish proverb, 'A stone is weighty in its place.' Where you are from, where you are known, you have weight. Jesus is asking him to renounce all of this and become a rolling stone, a landless wanderer. In the words of Jerome Neyrey, 'Who would be so foolish as to choose shame for oneself and one's family? Yet that is what Jesus' remarks imply.'[217] His treasure is love of honour, Jesus calls him to renounce all his sources of honour, and he is unable to do this. He goes away sad.

We know this story is about honour because of its context. At the end of the passage in Mark 10, the teaching proverb 'But many who are first will be last, and the last first' is about honour. In Mark, the next story is about James and John competing for the highest status. In Matthew's telling of this story (Matthew 19), the next story is about the workers in the vineyard – a story about honour, competition and envy. We also know it is about honour because the Bible is a Middle Eastern book and in the Middle East, in the first century, as today, the dominant cultural value is honour-shame.

Guilt, fear, shame

Eugene Nida in 1954[218] observed that there are 'three different types of reactions to transgressions of religiously sanctioned codes: fear, shame and guilt'. In terms of moral motivation, people are persuaded to do good rather than bad for one of three reasons: they feel afraid, they feel ashamed, or they feel guilty.

Combinations of all three of these moral emotions are at work in all cultures, much as the three primary colours make up the many colours of the rainbow. However, each culture of the world is predominantly wired in one, or perhaps two ways.

Guilt-innocence societies (mostly Western) tend to be individualistic, and think in terms of rules: right and wrong, guilt and forgiveness.

Fear-power cultures (commonly tribal or African, or places where folk religion is widespread) choose to do good because of fear of harm, fear of consequences, fear of the spirit world.

Shame-honour societies (common in the East) tend to be collectivistic, and think in corporate terms about conscience: what is right for the group is right.

All three of these drivers, guilt, fear and shame, entered the world in Genesis 3 as a result of sin. Depending on your lens, the problem of humanity is that we are guilty, the problem of humanity is that we are vulnerable, or the problem of humanity is that we are full of shame. Depending on your lens, the gospel of Christ is good news for all: for the guilty, justification; for the shamed, an honourable Patron; for the fearful, a strong Deliverer.

Many of the unreached peoples of the world today have shame-honour or fear-power groupality.[219] But in many cases Western missionaries are only preaching a gospel of the forgiveness of sins. One of the basic skills for those ministering cross-culturally is to learn how to present the gospel to those from a different cultural orientation. What core question are they asking? How does the story of the world from the Bible's point of view, and the incarnation, death and resurrection of Jesus answer this question?

Honour and shame

In particular, in this chapter I would like to consider the world of honour and shame. In recent years there have been some great books written on this subject, both theologically (understanding that the Bible was written in an honour-shame context),[220] and missiologically (the implications for preaching the gospel in honour-shame cultures).[221] Increasingly, it is being understood that 'becoming literate in the Bible's language of honour and shame is a foundational skill for God's global mission'.

Remember that we want to understand cultural difference. And we want to understand what motivates people, to find out *why* they do what they do. We are approaching this difference with humility, seeking to understand, not judgementally, because 'cultural absolutism is simply a form of ignorance'.[223]

Shame is morally compelling pain. Discomfort at the opinion, or perceived opinion, of the majority. To understand the power of shame as a motivation, imagine living in a tiny village where everyone knows everything. Censure on your actions will be old ladies tut-tutting out of the window and the gossip in the coffee shop. You don't actually need an internal conscience, because everything is lived in the public eye and the village is your external conscience. If the village approves of your way of life, you will have honour (status, prestige, face, name). If they disapprove, you will be shamed (lose face). Everything that you do, then, is done for approval in the court of public opinion. 'Honour is all about the tribunal or court of public opinion and the reputation that court bestows.'[224]

One of my Turkish friends told me that her father raised her not just to do good but to be *seen* to do good. This reflects an honour-shame world view. Honour-shame societies have a sense of right and wrong, but it is defined by an external (corporate) conscience, not an internal (individual) one. 'What would the neighbours say?' is the most powerful motivation to good action in such societies.

Another friend of mine told me that his motivation not to do wrong was in the following ascending order of importance: 3. Law/rules (not very important), 2. Sin (fear of judgement by God), and 1. Shame (being ostracised by the community). He would happily break a law or commit sin as long as it did not bring him shame. Conversely, he would not do a shameful thing, even if it was neither a sin nor a crime. The strongest power operating in his life was the power of shame.

There is a Turkish joke illustrating this point. The driver of a two-metre-high car approached the entrance of an underground car park where there was a sign, 'Caution! Low Ceiling! Cars over one metre in height cannot enter.' He looked left and right, saw that no one was watching, and so he drove into the car park – wrecking his car!

Corporate conscience has advantages over individual conscience, which, according to Scripture, can be weak (1 Corinthians 8:10), defiled (1 Corinthians 8:7), evil (Hebrews 10:22), imperfect (Hebrews 9:9). Because conscience can be relative, just relying on guilt is insufficient ethical motivation. You end up with the fruit of individualism evident in the West, where each person decides what is right or wrong, and there are no moral absolutes. Communal conscience is more conservative, more resilient to change.

However, there are also problems with relying purely on shame as an ethical motivation. If *appearing* good is counted as *being* good, you end up with Phariseeism, hypocrisy, doing the right things in public but sinning behind closed doors, all of which Jesus confronted in the culture of his day. You also have a problem if God calls you to do something that the whole community considers shameful, such as when a Muslim chooses to come to Christ. There is a time to go to Jesus outside the camp, bearing the reproach he endured (Hebrews 13:13). There are times when individual conscience must trump corporate conscience.

The power of shame

Shame is a power, it can be used for good or evil. New Testament leaders knew how to harness the power of shame to motivate people to good behaviour. Jesus was happy to rebuke Peter in front of the other disciples, appealing to his sense of shame to bring change. Paul in 1 Corinthians 5:1-2 is shaming the community with the desire of provoking a change in behaviour. John, in Revelation, frequently employs a powerful rhetorical strategy to persuade those of a shame-honour orientation. John will paint two contrasting pictures, one honourable, one shameful. The Bride and the Whore. Jerusalem and Babylon. The Beast and the Lamb. These pictures in and of themselves are morally compelling. 'Which would you rather be a part of?' he is asking. John does not need to spell it out; these two contrasting scenarios are a 'morally compelling contrast';[225] because the power of shame and the power of honour are ethically compelling, they are forces which move one to change one's behaviour.

Even in the West, the rise of social media is bringing 'shaming' to the fore and demonstrating its effectiveness. There are increasing examples of shame outperforming guilt in its ability to change behaviour at a corporate level. When in receipt of poor customer service, tweeting about it is more likely to gain a hearing – 'shaming' via social media is increasingly showing its power. Environmental activists are realising that relying on individual guilt (recycling, reducing one's carbon footprint, buying fair trade and organic products) can only ever change a tiny slither of consumer behaviour. Increasingly, attention is being turned to attacking the reputation of giant corporations and indeed powerful individuals, seeking to bring the power of shame to bear.

> Consumers are swept up in using reusable bags and mugs and turning off the lights. This is like taking vitamin C after fracturing your skull in a car accident: it is not wrong; it is just so far from what is needed to actually fix things. For large-scale cooperative dilemmas, it is not sufficient that a small group of people feel guilty, and it is certainly not enough that this small group engage with that guilt as consumers. We need a tool that can work more quickly and at larger scales.[226]

So those engaging across cultures need, ideally, not just intellectually to assent to the massive role that honour and shame play in the lives of millions of people, but even to learn to feel their power.

My friend John (*not* the one who wrote Revelation!), who lives in the Middle East, tells the story of the first time he felt the power of Middle Eastern shame. His car broke down outside a school, in the main road, in the pouring rain. He had to leave it parked half-on, half-off the pavement, so that all the mothers collecting their children from school had to walk around the car, into the main road, getting drenched in the process. He was standing by the car, and every mother that walked past him tutted, 'Such a shameful man! Such a shameful thing to do! Shame on you!' In the end he felt so ostracised, so condemned, that he left the car there and went and sat in the coffee shop across the road, joining in the chorus, 'Who left that car there? What a shameful thing to do!' He felt shame's power and did something different as a result.

Only those who have felt the power of shame will be able to resonate with a gospel that delivers from shame. Here we come to the public aspect of Jesus' death. If the atonement were only a guilt-righteousness transaction, Christ could have died in private, satisfying God's wrath and bearing our punishment. The truth, however, is that he was not just bearing our guilt, he was also bearing our shame. The shame of the cross (Philippians 2:8), the shocking nature of crucifixion, the loss of face and loss of name reserved for the basest of criminals, the curse of those hung on a tree (Galatians 3:13), are all the language of shame-honour. Isaiah 53, prophesying the cross, as well as using strong guilt-language, also employs strong shame-terms: 'Despised ... rejected ... as one from whom men hide their faces ... we esteemed him not' (Isaiah 53:3).

The Honourable One became shameful that the shameful ones might be made honourable. Philippians 2:5-10 is another passage filled with honour-shame language describing Christ's self-humiliation and later vindication. Jesus chose shame for himself, the very thing that the rich young ruler could not do! Jesus, the true Rich Young Ruler, left behind all the sources of his honour. In a world where everyone is trying to go upwards in status, Jesus went downwards. While intrinsically shameful sons of man are trying to project honour, the intrinsically honourable Son of God chose public disgrace.

Kephar, the Hebrew root for atonement, literally means 'covering'. When, in Genesis 3, Adam and Eve realised their nakedness, they tried to cover themselves with fig leaves. All through the scripture, nakedness is shame and covering is atonement. The Lord God provided garments of skins for them (Genesis 3:21); the first sacrifice was an animal slain by God to provide a covering (atonement) for Adam and Eve. John's telling of the passion narrative has the soldiers taking Jesus' clothing for themselves (John 19:23); the Clothed One made naked so that the naked ones might be clothed. What an honour, now, to be covered with the garments of Christ!

In our increasingly globalised world, wrestling with the language of honour and shame, even for those not moving cross-culturally, is becoming more and more important. To preach the gospel in our multi-ethnic cities, preaching forgiveness for the guilty is insufficiently good news to satisfy those whose burning question is, 'How can I be free from shame?' At the same time, a growing scholarly emphasis on the honour-shame dynamics of the New Testament world are shedding helpful light on otherwise misunderstood passages of Scripture, and this will only increase in the years to come. Honour-shame will continue to be a hugely important area.

Endnotes

216. Mark 10:17, emphasis mine.

217. Neyrey, Jerome H., *Honor and Shame in the Gospel of Matthew* (Louisville, KY: Westminster John Knox Press, 1998), 62.

218. Nida, Eugene, *Customs and Cultures* (New York: Harper, 1954), 150.

219. 'Individual people have a person-ality, cultural groups share a group-ality', Georges, Jayson, *The 3D Gospel*, Kindle loc. 135.

220. Key names in this field are Witherington, Jewitt, Malina, Neyrey, DaSilva, Woo.

221. Muller, Mischke, Georges.

222. Mischke, Werner, *The Global Gospel: Achieving Missional Impact in our Multicultural World* (Scottsdale, AZ: Mission ONE, 2016), Kindle loc. 6109.

223. Adeney, *Strange Virtues*, 66.

224. Malina, *The New Testament World*, 40.

225. deSilva, David A., *Seeing Things John's Way: The Rhetoric of the Book of Revelation* (Louisville, KY: Westminster John Knox Press, 2000), 292.

226. Jacquet, Jennifer, *Is Shame Necessary?: New Uses for an Old Tool*, Kindle Edition (London: Penguin, 2017), 181.

Chapter 14
Multisense

Having considered that different cultures *reason* differently, *relate* differently and are *motivated* differently, we now turn to explore the idea that different cultures *feel* differently.

One of the great cultural variations between Eastern and Western Christianity is in the use of the senses. Protestant worship today, particularly in newer churches, is almost entirely built around one sense, the sense of hearing. The majority of our input as Western Christians is through preaching and music, both of which enter our souls via our auditory canal.

The Orthodox Church, conversely, has traditionally claimed that liturgy should engage all five senses. Andrew Walker, himself Orthodox, writes:

> Holistic worship should enable us to engage God as the embodied creatures that we are. As such it should be multi-sensory, appealing not merely to the ears – through songs and sermons – but to the eyes, to touch, to taste, to smell ... Christian liturgical practices are a 'socially mediated, bodily enacted, sensually attuned' means of knowing Christ.[227]

When we first rented a building in order to launch public worship in Istanbul, we decorated it to be as non-churchy and as modern-looking as possible, as we would have done in the UK. We wanted the building to say, loud and clear, 'We are not religious!' About a year in, though, the local believers began to complain, 'It is hard to encounter God here because it doesn't look, and therefore doesn't feel, like a church.' We encouraged them to have the meeting hall decorated as they felt appropriate, and ended up with dim lighting, deep carpets, a large cross on the wall, a big picture of Jesus, candles, and silver trays for the Lord's Supper!

In the UK, our emphasis had been on being relational, non-formal, family, and decidedly non-religious. In the Middle East, you can't say something important in scruffy clothes, or in a dirty building. Why? Because the medium *is* the message. Your untucked shirt is creating such loud static that the listener cannot hear what you are saying. Rather than dismissing this as 'religious formalism' (sometimes, of course, it is), we need to think about the difference between high and low context cultures.

High and low context

This distinction was originally highlighted by anthropologist Edward T. Hall,[228] talking about differences in communication. Low-context cultures are more direct and explicit, they 'spell it all out'. High-context cultures are more indirect, they take so many cues from context that less actually needs saying. In a low context, *what* is said is important; in a higher context, *how* it is said is more important. Voice tone, body language and many other social cues come into play. These are almost impossible for outsiders to the culture to spot and to decode.

On one occasion a local believer from another fellowship visited our church several Sundays in a row. We felt a little uncertain about him, so the next Sunday I met him as he came through the door, greeted him, and politely asked him if he had talked to his pastor about the fact that he was visiting our church so often. He took offence, stormed out angrily, and later I heard through the grapevine that I had 'thrown him out of the church'. Amazed, I asked a local friend to help me understand how I had offended him so much. It turns out that although my words never said so explicitly, all the contextual cues said, 'We don't want you here, get out!' My voice tone and body language. Where we were standing. The fact I had spoken to him before, not after the worship service. All the vibes he had picked up from me were negative, even though my words had been measured.

A high-context communication is one in which little has to be said or written because most of the information is either in the physical environment or supposed to be known by the persons involved, while very little is in the coded, explicit part of the message. This type of communication is common in collectivist cultures. A low-context communication is one in which the mass of information is vested in the explicit code, which is typical in individualist cultures.[229]

The medium *is* the message

The context of your message is as important as your message. If we want to communicate Christ clearly, we need to think not just about our words, but our body language, our location, our physical appearance. Those from high-context cultures are highly attuned to these things, and will not differentiate them from the message itself. Those from lower contexts don't really care!

A Brazilian friend of mine told me about a certain hand gesture that is very rude in Brazil. He spent a year in a church in South Africa, where the pastor used to make this hand gesture regularly whilst preaching. My friend says he could not hear what was being preached because the hand gesture 'drowned it out'. This action was, for my friend and unbeknown to the preacher, louder than the words that were being spoken.

I have seen too many blonde college-age girls wearing sleeveless tops on short-term evangelism teams giving out evangelistic literature on the streets in Middle Eastern cities. They may feel that they are giving out 'the message' as written on the leaflets, but what is being 'heard' by the local men is a very different kind of invitation.

All five senses

On one visit to Armenia I was fascinated to visit a Pentecostal church that was keen to pull away from the ritualism of the traditional Armenian Apostolic Church. For example, they only celebrate Communion three times a year because they want to undo the ritualistic background from which most have come. Yet they had robed choirs, a lighting rack, and a smoke machine on stage. They've escaped incense and yet got a smoke machine! Why? Because they want their people to fully encounter God via their meetings, and understand that this needs to be multisensory.

Understanding that Christ can be met through our other senses makes sense of the Lord's Supper, baptism and the laying on of hands as tangible theology: can the Spirit not work through these 'sacraments'?

There are times when biblical writers warn against empty ritualism. As Protestants we are comfortable with these scriptures; in a sense the Protestant Reformation came about in reaction to empty ritualism, formalism and sacramentalism. 'You leave the commandment of God and hold to the tradition of men.'[230] 'This people draw near with their mouth and honour me with their lips, while their hearts are far from me.'[231]

However, if we discount all form and ritual, then we are making informality a gospel essential, when it is only a cultural preference. We must learn to contextualise to high-context cultures!

At our baptism ceremonies we now serve a certain dessert, *helva*, that is only served in Turkey at funerals. It always gets a laugh, 'I congratulate you on your funeral and hope you enjoyed eating your own *helva*,' but it makes a powerful, multisensory theological point: you felt yourself buried in the water and then raised, you tasted your own funeral dessert, you experienced the absoluteness of this break with your old life!

> It is not just who says what to whom, but how the message is channelled to the respondent that determines how the message will be decoded. Language is basic to communication, but language does not stand alone. As we have said, words are augmented by pictures, actions, sounds, silence, smells and objects.[232]

Using touch, props, gestures, dramatised examples will make the gospel you are sharing come alive. In our church building we have little pot plants everywhere. Countless times I have sat with an enquirer, reached for a pot plant, and started, 'Well it all began in the garden.' Jesus took hold of a child, pointed at the lilies, sat to read the scroll, lifted his hands to heaven, broke the bread. We say, 'Actions speak louder than words.' In communication to high-context people, this is tangibly true.

In many group-orientated cultures, where you are sitting determines the content of the conversation. Sitting in a public café, for example, some people spend their whole time tuning into and observing all the other conversations going on. If you are sensitive to context, you won't be able to help it! People can be concerned about security or being recognised. All of these considerations could be 'louder' than what you are trying to talk about.

Even your identity affects how you will be received. Roland Muller observes that many successful evangelists to Muslims have developed an identity for themselves as 'religious teachers'. They are received as those with authority and listened to differently.[233] This is obviously not possible or even desirable everywhere, but the observation is sound: context determines how a message is understood. Sometimes, this can give foreign evangelists from 'Christian' nations a tacit advantage; people expect you to know the Bible because you are Western. However much we might choose to disagree with the premise, it can serve the preaching of the gospel.

Concessions to high-context cultures

There are key times when Bible heroes make concessions to high-context culture.

The story of Naaman and Elisha in 2 Kings 5 relates a world view clash between the two men. Naaman expects a dramatic, magical, high-context healing ritual, while Elisha calls him to a simple act of obedient faith.

> *2 Kings 5:11:* But Naaman was angry and went away, saying, 'Behold, I thought that he would surely come out to me and stand and call upon the name of the LORD his God, and wave his hand over the place and cure the leper.

Later, however, when Naaman wants to take some Israelite soil back home so he can worship appropriately, Elisha assents. He knows that there is nothing sacred in the soil itself, but he acknowledges Naaman's desire to worship, and makes the concession.

In cross-cultural evangelism and discipleship, you need to pick your battles. On the healing, Elisha stood firm and challenged an almost-magical view of healing. On the issue of soil, Elisha chose to let Naaman go ahead. How do we know when to challenge and when to concede? By the leadership of the Holy Spirit. There is no other way.

It could even be argued that the giving of the Lord's Prayer was a concession to high-context disciples who wanted a prayer to memorise and recite. Jesus spent lots of time fighting for the deformalisation and deritualisation of prayer, but then gave his disciples a prayer which was open to the danger of becoming a gathering-point for empty religion. Totally extemporising prayer may be too great a step for many from more formal religious backgrounds, and a gradual approach with some guide-rails may be necessary.

> To enter another culture means to allow yourself to feel the pull of another way of seeing the world.[234]

Being aware that I don't naturally think about context, but that many of the people to whom I am ministering are powerfully distracted or impacted by it, has really helped me in sharing Christ cross-culturally. Thinking about what you wear, what you are doing with your hands and voice tone, venue décor and sacraments may seem irrelevant or even a waste of time. I have at times caught myself candle-shopping or shining my shoes and smiled to myself at how far I have come from a dirty school hall and a guitar in London, but if our business is to remove all stumbling blocks except the cross of Christ, then let us press on to make him known, to reduce the static, to make sure that what we are saying is what they are hearing, to seek to get truth into people's hearts via any of the five senses created by God for human encounter with him.

> I had heard of you by the hearing of the ear, but now my eye sees you …
> *Job 42:5*

Endnotes

227. Walker, Andrew G. and Parry, Robin A., *Deep Church Rising: Rediscovering the Roots of Christian Orthodoxy* (London: SPCK, 2014), Kindle loc. 2181.
228. Hall, Edward T., *Beyond Culture* (Waterlooville: Anchor Books, 1976).
229. Hostede, Geert, *Cultures and Organizations: Software of the Mind* (London: McGraw-Hill, 1991), 212.
230. Mark 7:8.
231. Isaiah 29:13.
232. Hesselgrave, David J., *Communicating Christ Cross-Culturally: An Introduction to Missionary Communication* (Grand Rapids, MI: Zondervan, 1991), 537.
233. Muller, *The Message, The Messenger, The Community*, 25.
234. Adeney, *Strange Virtues*, 73.

Incarnational Humility:
Thinking About Leadership

Entering a new culture is like dying.

Jesus, speaking of his own death, said 'unless a [seed] falls into the earth and dies, it remains alone; but if it dies, it bears much fruit.'[235] When you enter a new culture it can feel like death (if you do it well!). Particularly in our recommended initial few years, where possible, of focusing on learning the language and the culture. You go from being competent and successful in your home culture to dependent and babyish in the new. You go from being able to express yourself to utter inarticulacy. You go from being respected to being misunderstood and unable to defend yourself. You go from feeling 'useful' to God to feeling the total opposite.

It's like dying! Dying to what you knew, dying to the right to comment, dying to things that you had assumed to be absolutes. It hurts.

The hymn-fragment in Philippians 2:6-11 summarising Jesus' career has often been taken as a great model for cross-cultural life and ministry. The V-shaped progression from his pre-incarnate glory in heaven, down to earth and death, and then up through resurrection to exaltation is a pattern for all Christians, although in crossing cultures it must be remembered that you are not leaving a better (higher) culture for a worse (lower) one as Jesus did. You are moving from one fallen culture to another. The pain is in leaving your preferences, assumptions, given world view and natural habitat behind and *that* is like dying.

The wonderful thing about a seed if it is buried properly and deeply is that it will take root, grow, and in time produce something. When Jesus' killers buried him they gloated, they did not realise they were burying God's long-promised 'seed' (which is traceable through Scripture all the way from

Genesis 3:15), through which the new creation would be brought to birth as the fruit of resurrection burst from the ground. In the fairy tale, Jack's mother threw away good-for-nothing beans and they became a mighty beanstalk. The stone the builders rejected became the capstone.[236]

Likewise, every time we as foreigners feel buried under incompetence, shame, uselessness, illiteracy, we must remember that we are being buried deeply into a soil where we shall take root, we shall bear fruit, and the more deeply we are planted, the more thoroughly we die to our former cultural preferences, the more locally and lastingly will our fruit be rooted.

Entering a new culture is like falling into a hole in the ground and choosing not to grab hold of the familiar to save yourself. There were so many familiar routines and comforts we could have grabbed hold of in the early, dark, chaotic days of relocating. A bit of English TV. Some time with foreign friends. Of course, you've got to keep some carefully crafted fixed points for the sake of your family's well-being. We kept pizza and a movie on Friday nights. But the more of your old shape that you hang onto, even in family life, the less deeply you will enter.

A British soldier can live anywhere in the world, keep his discipline, shave every morning, drink gin and tonic every evening, and stay habitual and presentable. But he does not enter the culture, he camps upon it.

If you are falling into a black hole of chaos, if all your family routines are shot to pieces, if you are choosing not to hang onto the familiar, then take heart, you are entering the culture.

Entering a new culture is like scuba diving. I've only done this once and they put such a heavy weighted belt on me that I sank to the bottom and kicked along in the mud, panicking... until I stood up in the three feet of water we were practising in! The weighted belt is to keep you down, otherwise you have a natural buoyancy that brings you back up again. We will all naturally default back towards our sending culture, our inbred tendencies. We don't stay as deep as we would like. Therefore, we need to dive as deep as possible at the beginning, knowing that with time we will default back to a level slightly above. Deeper than feels comfortable or sustainable. And we need to weight our belts with disciplines that will keep us down.

Incarnational Humility understands that entering a new culture is like dying. It's like falling through a hole. It's like diving deep. It hurts, it's shameful and no one understands. It rips your once-orderly family life and inner world to pieces. It strips you of dignity and competence. Much like Jesus did as he entered our culture and went right down to death. You are being buried, my friend. It's a baptism. It's cruciform. It's heroic. It's apostolic. It's sacrificial. It hurts.

This section, *Incarnational Humility,* develops the idea that our mission is a continuation of Jesus' mission to make the Invisible One tangible and visible, to ground Universal Truth in the local and the particular. Vital to this is a rethinking of the role of cross-cultural leadership. What kind of leadership should foreigners bring in planting churches that are to become local expressions of the body of Christ?

Endnotes

235. John 12:24
236. See Matthew 21:42.

Chapter 15
Contextualise Yourself!

All authentic mission is incarnational mission.
John Stott[237]

Entering another culture is choosing to be a slave to that culture.

Imagine that you were captured through war and sold as a slave to a foreign family. You would quickly learn their language, adopt their schedules, live in their way as a matter of course. In New Testament times, a slave in a Roman household was expected to adapt to Roman ways, a slave in a wealthy Jewish household likewise to Jewish customs. What they ate, how they dressed would all be different. A slave 'was an outsider who brought no rights with him from the society he came from, and had no claims on the society which maintained him'.[238]

Remember Joseph diving into Potiphar's household and becoming to all intents and purposes Egyptian? Or Daniel and his friends learning the language and literature of the Babylonians? Even Naaman's wife's slave girl in 2 Kings 5:2-3? They maintained a distinctiveness, a witness, they never forgot who they were, and they were used by God amongst the nations. Yet their success was in large part due to their obedience in getting stuck into the cultures where God had sovereignly placed them.

This is the language Paul employs in 1 Corinthians 9:19-23:

1 Corinthians 9:19: For though I am free from all, I have made myself a servant [slave] to all, that I might win more of them.
1 Corinthians 9:20: To the Jews I became as a Jew, in order to win Jews. To those under the law I became as one under the law (though not

being myself under the law) that I might win those under the law.

1 Corinthians 9:21: To those outside the law I became as one outside the law (not being outside the law of God but under the law of Christ) that I might win those outside the law.

1 Corinthians 9:22: To the weak I became weak, that I might win the weak. I have become all things to all people, that by all means I might save some.

1 Corinthians 9:23: I do it all for the sake of the gospel, that I may share with them in its blessings.

I enter any new household, any new nation, not as a know-it-all, not as an internationally acclaimed speaker, not as an answer-carrier – I enter as a slave, says Paul. I bind myself to their customs, their food, their rhythm of life, I constrain myself to their constraints, I limit myself within their limitations.

We call this contextualisation, or inculturation, or incarnation. But let's be clear. In these verses Paul is not primarily referring to contextualisation of the *message* (although Paul was a master at this). Paul is primarily talking about contextualisation of the *messenger*.

If you are concerned about reaching new nations for Christ, then you are concerned with contextualisation. We must seek to identify as closely and deeply as we can with the people we are reaching. But why?

1. Because God contextualised himself in Christ

Jesus didn't bring a message, he was the message.

When God wanted to communicate salvation to us, he didn't give us a book, or an angel, or a prophet, he gave us a life, lived at a certain time in a certain place in a specific culture and language. Born of a woman, born under the law, to redeem those under the law (Galatians 4:4-5). With my Muslim friends I am constantly debating this – Jesus didn't bring a book, Jesus is the book. He makes the invisible God visible. He earths the principles of the gospel in a real life that could be touched and asked questions of and accepted or rejected.

The gospel was incarnated, inculturated, *in Jesus*. René Padilla puts it like this: 'In the incarnation, God contextualised himself.'[239] The Eternal was made local, the Intangible, tangible, the Transcendent was made present in Christ.

God is not a Middle Eastern first-century man, but he lived on earth as one. God is not under the Mosaic Law, but he chose to be. 'The incarnation meant the deliberate self-limiting of a divine being in order to be truly and fully human.'[240]

The gospel isn't the sermon on the mount, it is Jesus' actions in life and death and resurrection. As Tim Chester writes: 'this is how Luke describes Jesus's mission strategy: "The Son of Man came eating and drinking."'[241]

So with us – preaching will take up a very small part of your time; living, eating, relating, commuting, parenting will take up most of it. The message is you. Your life. The Son of God had to incarnate. So do you.

2. To communicate effectively

Communication theory states that you have only communicated effectively if the listener has understood. Timothy Keller writes:

> Contextualisation is not – as is often argued – 'giving people what they want to hear.' Rather, it is giving people the Bible's answers, which they may not at all want to hear, to questions about life that people in their particular time and place are asking, in language and forms they can comprehend, and through appeals and arguments with force they can feel, even if they reject them.[242]

To communicate effectively you have to be close enough to people to know what questions they are asking. How can you give answers if you don't know what the questions are? You have to listen. Communication is a two-way bridge; we cannot just expect to traffic our message over to them, without first allowing traffic from them over to our side.

> Even Jesus didn't start off by telling people who he was – but listening to who they were.
> *Bob Roberts*[243]

We become slaves to the culture we are entering in order to get close enough to people to hear their stories, their fears, their heart-questions. And we take on as many of the cultural forms as is feasible because *the medium is the message.*

3. To empathise

Jesus didn't just suffer *for* us, he suffered *with* us. Hence, he is a sympathetic High Priest (Hebrews 2:17-18). He had to draw grace from the Father and comfort from the Spirit in the wilderness, and in Gethsemane.

When I sit in the traffic on a four-hour daily commute, or am struck by a virus that has emptied half the schools in the city, people will listen to me *because I live here too!* I am vulnerable to the same limitations, temptations and frustrations and need to learn how to draw on grace, and when I preach on these things people nod their heads because I speak with empathy.

When a foreign worker does something for the good of the city it is both missional and empathetic, because if he genuinely lives in the city, then 'in its welfare you will find your welfare'[244] is authentically true for him. If I work to make my neighbourhood safer, or cleaner, I benefit too because I live here!

Empathy cannot be faked. Only one who has suffered can comfort one who suffers. Although it is rare for cross-cultural workers to genuinely 'become' local, the effort that you make to expose yourself to the same lifestyle as those you are seeking to reach – your schooling options, accommodation, work hours, food – will go a long way to communicating the compassion of Christ who lived among Jewish men as a Jewish man.

4. To earth the gospel into the culture you are reaching

If a Westerner communicates the gospel to an Easterner, the immediate assumption is that the gospel is Western. So as far as possible we inculturate our lives, as the gospel is communicated not just with words, but with lifestyle. We show what the good news about Christ looks like, feels like. It is different in every culture. There is no such thing as Christian culture, as there is a Muslim culture from Indonesia to Morocco. We communicate Christian values by 'fleshing them out' in the culture that we are serving. That is what Jesus did.

In London, we used to throw parties intentionally inviting a wide range of people who we knew. So when we first arrived in Istanbul we did the same thing; we threw a party and invited a whole raft of friends, including the local shopkeeper. In an honour-shame culture status is a huge deal – 'you are a teacher, I am a lawyer… I am higher-status than you'. Our friends were nonplussed, even appalled that we had invited 'the market man'. They took me into the kitchen to rebuke me.

This then becomes an enactment of the gospel, the God who accepts all regardless of social status, the new community where inclusivity trumps exclusivity – much as the parties that Jesus attended 'fleshed out' his message of grace, hope and new community.

Living cross-culturally, we have a unique opportunity to proclaim the gospel *through how we live* from within the culture.

> It is not merely the preaching of the gospel per se that is important, but the preaching of the gospel through a messenger who incarnates its message such that the hearers can both understand it clearly from one who obviously empathises with them and can see what it would look like if it took root in them.[245]

5. We get inside the culture in order to challenge the culture

Part of mission must be to confront sin, but this is best done after taking time to enter. For your first few years in a new place you bite your tongue, you refuse to judge, you choose, instead of saying 'that is wrong' to say, 'That is… different!' As a guest, you do not have the right to judge your host.

I am currently entering a new place (again). The leader of the church we are attending keeps asking me to comment on how they do things as a church; he is genuinely interested in how I would assess the church's style and ministry. I am keeping my mouth shut. Until I have entered, and understood, and belonged, who am I to judge or comment or correct?

Anthony Gittins, picking up the language of 'host' and 'guest', asks:

> Do we show adequate and genuine deference to our hosts? Do we willingly acknowledge their authority in the situation, and their rights and duties as hosts? Do we allow ourselves to be adequately positioned

as strangers, according to the legitimate needs of the hosts? Or do we try to seize initiatives, show them clearly what our expectations are, make demands on them, and thus effectively refuse the role of stranger, thereby impeding them from being adequate hosts?[246]

Adeney, on this issue, comments:

> Strangers have no inherent right to credibility or trust. These must be earned. Legitimation is a gift from the host ... One of the worst things a guest can do is to take away the rights of a host to be the host.[247]

Some foreigners seem to always be on the outside, are always treated with suspicion, and may never earn the right to challenge. Others seem to gain acceptance or legitimisation by their local friends. This has always been true. Colonials used to accuse some of 'going native', meaning that they ate or fraternised or lived in a way that overly identified with local people. It is only these who ever gain the relational authority to challenge, with a view to changing, some aspects of cultural sin.

Timothy Keller uses an apt example from the world of demolition to illustrate the importance of 'getting inside' the culture we are seeking to reach.

> Say you are building a highway and want to remove a giant boulder. First, you drill a small shaft down into the center of the rock. Then you put explosives down the shaft into the core of the stone and detonate them. If you drill the shaft but never ignite the blast, you obviously will never move the boulder. But the same is true if you only blast and fail to drill – putting the explosives directly against the surface of the rock. You will simply shear off the face of it, and the boulder will remain. All drilling with no blasting, or all blasting with no drilling, leads to failure. But if you do both of these, you will remove the rock. To contextualize with balance and successfully reach people in a culture, we must both enter the culture sympathetically and respectfully (similar to drilling) and confront the culture where it contradicts biblical truth (similar to blasting).[248]

If you are not in a culture deeply enough to feel the power of and be tempted to sin by a prevalent cultural stronghold, you will probably not be able to demolish it. All you will do is stand in judgement over it.

Those going to a place where fear is prevalent will often themselves come under the power of fear. This is good – they will have to learn how to resist it 'from underneath'; otherwise there would be a danger of merely judging others for being fearful. I have a friend working in Mongolia who posted, 'Just found out that Mongolia has the highest rate of anti-depressant useage in the world, so I'm off to the pharmacy!' He was joking, but the point is good. If I live here, who is to say I should be immune? To smell the rose you need to get close enough to feel the thorn.

You can't bomb a culture from the outside. But on the journey to the inside you will learn and be changed so much that you'll find the target is very different to what you originally assumed. You can only confront a culture from within the culture.

6. To upset hierarchical cultural apple-carts

Paul's Corinthian readers would be appalled at his comparing himself to a slave. 'One does not usually think of slavery as a position of influence.'[249]

The kingdom of God turns the status-hungry world principle upside down. This is expressed differently in every culture, but is common to all. It started with Satan's upward ambition. In the Kingdom we have a downwardly mobile principle, modelled by the Lord. This will offend every culture – the offence (*skandalon*) of the cross (1 Corinthians 1:23). But the cross will only offend the heart if it is understood in the heart.

A huge amount of Jesus' teaching, and of Paul's letters, address the issue of status. Neither Jesus nor Paul, however, did this by critiquing from a distance. They lived out a relevant example of servanthood.

7. To be an example

'You yourselves know how I lived among you the whole time', Paul is able to say in Acts 20:18. He was not just close but transparent, weak and vulnerable. In 2 Corinthians he appeals to his weakness, shame and pain as proof of his apostleship (as opposed to the super-apostles who just flew in, preached and flew out again). How else can the grace of God be displayed than through the struggles of our everyday lives?

Our family's example has certainly been one of weakness: struggles with our boys' special needs, with my wife's health, with fear and uncertainty. This weakness, rather than disqualifying us, earths and models the grace of God in the local church.

I believe that the apostle's understanding was this: I so intentionally study and humble myself to enter the culture that I can represent Christ and embody the gospel in a way that will be received. I don't just contextualise my message, I contextualise myself, because the message is in my life. And when the gospel seed bears fruit in the gathering of a local church community, cultural forms can be adopted and cultural strongholds demolished, and the gospel will find its own local expression.

Endnotes

237. Stott, John R.W., *The Contemporary Christian: Applying God's Word to Today's World* (Downers Grove, IL: IVP, 1992), 35.

238. Wiedemann, T., *Greek and Roman Slavery* (London: Routledge, 1981), 15.

239. Padilla, C. René, *Mission Between the Times* (Grand Rapids, MI: Eerdmans, 1985), 83.

240. Witherington III, Ben, *The New Testament Story* (Grand Rapids, MI: Eerdmans, 2004), Kindle loc. 2693.

241. Chester, Tim, *A Meal with Jesus: Discovering Grace, Community and Mission Around the Table*, Kindle Edition (UK: IVP, 2013), Kindle loc. 151-152.

242. Keller, *Center Church*, 89.

243. Roberts, Bob in an unpublished talk in 2012.

244. Jeremiah 29:7.

245. Ciampa, Roy, E. and Rosner, Brian S., *The First Letter to the Corinthians* (Grand Rapids: Eerdmans, 2010), 431.

246. Gittins, Anthony J., *Gifts and Strangers: Meeting the Challenge of Inculturation* (Mahwah, NJ: Paulist Press, 1989), 117.

247. Adeney, *Strange Virtues*, 132.

248. Keller, *Center Church*, 119.

249. Ciampa and Rosner, *The First Letter to the Corinthians*, 422.

Chapter 16
Sent Like Jesus

Christmas is a celebration of meekness. Son of God became Son of Man in fragility, in nakedness. The parable of the tenants[250] is Jesus' reflection on his sent-ness. In Luke 20:13 we are privy to God's soliloquy, 'What shall I do? I'll send my beloved son! Perhaps they will honour him.' God sends his son, unarmed and defenceless, into a violent, rebellious world, with not much more than a 'perhaps'![251] And the result is rejection and suffering, even death.

We live on the other side of this story, where Jesus has said, 'As the Father has sent me ... I am sending you.'[252] From his going we understand our going. We are servants of the Sent One! Jesus' incarnation is the model for our incarnation. His vulnerability is the template for our vulnerability. His humility, the prototype for our humility. His pain, the pattern for our pain.

> This incarnation principle at the heart of the faith itself has, perforce, to characterise the Church which serves it, as participatory in the living world, incurring, not eluding, its burdens.[253]

Undressing

Jesus' first step in taking flesh was to lay aside his heavenly garments. In John 13, Jesus' enactment of the incarnation, we read: 'He laid aside his outer garments, and taking a towel, tied it round his waist' (John 13:4). Before clothing himself as a slave in the new culture he was entering, he removed his former garments. Paul called this Jesus' *kenosis*, or self-emptying (Philippians 2:7).

There is a sense in which, when we enter a new culture for the gospel, we too must self-limit, self-empty, or undress. Always bearing in mind that Jesus crossed from a perfect culture into a fallen one, whilst we are crossing from one fallen culture to another, nevertheless those who take seriously the entering of another culture for the sake of the gospel must consider the need to undress.

Hudson Taylor literally cast off his English garments in order to wear Chinese dress. This was not only pragmatic, allowing him to travel unmolested in the inner provinces, it also symbolised his decision not to rely on the long arm of the British Empire, a decision which was tested and proven many times during his career.

Those who cross cultures must unlearn many things before they can learn new things, must de-Westernise as they Easternise, must be emptied before they can be filled. This is all part of undressing.

In the 2009 movie *Avatar*, Jake Sully is trying to enter the indigenous culture. The high priestess, Moat, tells him it will be impossible, because if your cup is already full, it is hard to add anything to it. Sully, who has already lost everything, is able to reply that his cup is empty. This dialogue beautifully illustrates the priority of undressing. If your cup is already full, what need have you of learning a new culture? Incarnation starts with a choice to be emptied, to be unclothed, to be vulnerable.

Vulnerability

In the parable, the son is sent into a dangerous, violent situation, alone and unarmed. This seems like a terrible strategy, yet it is how the disciples were sent by Jesus: 'Behold, I am sending you out as lambs in the midst of wolves.'[254] Defencelessness characterises cross-cultural Christian mission.

> Authentic evangelism involves being vulnerable, following the example of Christ by carrying the cross and emptying oneself.[255]

Living cross-culturally exposes our vulnerability. We are failures every day. We spend all our energy trying to be 'good' ambassadors for Christ; good at speaking the language, good with people, good with our families, good with the gospel. And we feel that our weakness makes us less effective communicators of Jesus. 'If only I wasn't so weak, I would embody him better,' we think.

In fact, the vulnerability of humans is what makes them beautiful, and what makes them uniquely fitted to make the Invisible One visible.

We often think that our weakness is as a result of the Fall, but what if it is essentially human? What if it is part of the image of God in us? What if God put vulnerability into us when he made us, even before the Fall?

And if the image of God in us is essentially missional; if we represent him and embody him in the world, then this vulnerability is missional. 'God has chosen the weak' through whom to make himself known. If vulnerability is intrinsic to human personhood, then it is intrinsic to divine mission, because divine mission is via human personhood. The 'treasure in jars of clay'[256] is then not incidental or unfortunate, it is ordained.

This is most fully seen in Jesus, sent to make the Invisible visible as the man of sorrows, essentially frail. Jesus does what we failed to do in making God known through the faltering medium of human dust.

Kenneth Cragg develops this line of thinking in the context of engagement with Islam: 'In this sense, and in this sense alone, we have to conclude that there is vulnerability in the being of God.'[257] His argument is that openness to betrayal, meekness, pathos are intrinsic to God, therefore to the incarnation, therefore to Christianity and therefore to Christian mission. There were no invulnerable prophets. There are no un-clay jars. And it is God's design to reveal himself in spite of, in fact because of, our frailty.

Suffering

Isaiah's commission is often preached in recruitment for cross-cultural mission.

Isaiah 6:8: And I heard the voice of the Lord saying, 'Whom shall I send, and who will go for us?' Then I said, 'Here am I! Send me.'

What follows, however, in verses 9-13, is not always given to new missionary recruits as a promise! Isaiah is promised rejection and hardness of heart. And this, in fact, was his experience. Isaiah spent almost his entire life prophesying to bad kings in dark days, with the exception of a short window under King Hezekiah. He died during the reign of Manasseh by being sawn in half.

The call to bear the gospel is a call to suffer. Of Adoniram Judson it was written:

> There began a life-long battle in the 108-degree heat with cholera, malaria, dysentery and unknown miseries that would take two of Judson's wives and seven of his 13 children, and colleague after colleague in death.[258]

David Livingstone wrote in his journal:

> It is a venture to take wife and children into a country where fever prevails. But who that knows Jesus would refuse to make a venture for such a captain? ... It seems my duty to go. And were I alone it would not cost me a thought. But O, my children. Am I sacrificing them?[259]

The call to suffer has always been part of the missionary call to the unreached. It is naïve to think otherwise.

On one occasion I met a pastor from a Central Asian country. He had just been released after ten years in prison for preaching the gospel. 'All the new arrivals in prison had to line up and explain who had put them in prison,' he told me, 'whether it was the Drug Enforcement Agency or the National Security Bureau. I stood up and said, "*God* has sent me to prison – so that I can preach to you all!" I was regularly beaten, and at one point I had such a damaged back that I could hardly walk. I was praying for healing. One day the warden made me do push-ups, and as I was doing push-ups he kicked me. As his foot crashed into my back, I felt the Holy Spirit come upon me and I was instantly healed!'

For years afterwards, whenever I would tell this story, I would declare, 'Does anyone here have a bad back? Well line up, we will kick you, and God is going to heal you!'

Another family working in a violent and dangerous country would often come and stay with us in Istanbul for a little respite. Most nights, their young daughter would wake up screaming. One evening fireworks went off in our neighbourhood, and she ran inside and hid under the table, so accustomed was she to gunfire. The call to bear the gospel is a call to suffer, and the price our families pay is very high. It is in *this* context that we hear the voice of the Lord calling, 'Who will go?'

Success-less-ness

The sending of the son to the vineyard looked like a poor investment. Humankind had shamed and killed the prophets and was in rebellion – earth wasn't 'open to the gospel' – it was a lost, dark place that Jesus came to, and it resisted him. The logic of only sending people to 'open' countries and not 'closed' ones, 'easy' places not 'hard' ones, does not stand up to the scrutiny of the incarnation of Jesus Christ. Expediency is not part of this decision-making process. When the tenants were in their most advanced state of rebellion against the landowner, he sent his son!

Samuel Zwemer, the 'Apostle to Islam', wrote, at the end of his faithful life, 'I am now in my 81st year and have spent sixty years thinking of the Moslem [sic] World and its problems ... *Never have I regretted choosing a hard field and an impossible task*.'

New measures of success are required in evaluating the 'fruitfulness' of cross-cultural ministry into hard places. Jesus spent thirty years 'entering', living amongst people, working as a carpenter, and only three years preaching. The thirty years' entering made the three years preaching pretty effective! Imagine Jesus sending prayer letters home to his 'support base' in heaven during those thirty years – pretty uneventful! Our prayer letters home are not always stories of miraculous conversions. Sometimes they are 'I learned a new verb' or 'My son made a new friend'. The incarnation requires us to evaluate success through a different lens. Serious missionaries from the last few centuries have well understood that reaching the unreached is a slow, life-long commitment:

> You like tales of success which I cannot give you. These stories you send me to pronounce on are hopeful, but I do not trust spectacular things; give me the seed growing secretly every time.[261]

I have seen the beginning, middle and end of several limited term missionaries. They are all good for nothing. They come out for a few years, with the view of acquiring a stock of credit on which they may vegetate the rest of their days ... The motto of every missionary ought to be 'Devoted for life.'[262]

Eustace, if after my removal any one should think it worth his while to write my Life, I will give you a criterion by which you may judge of its correctness. If he give me credit for being a plodder he will describe me justly. Anything beyond this will be too much. I can plod. I can persevere in any definite pursuit. To this I owe everything.[263]

Incarnation is inefficient. Reaching the unreached is often expensive, slow, difficult and 'unsuccessful'.

It was seven years
...before Carey baptised his first convert in India.
...before Judson won his first disciple in Burma.
...that Morrison toiled before the first Chinaman was brought to Christ.
...declares Moffatt, that he waited to see the first evident moving of the Holy Spirit upon his Bechuanas of Africa.
...before Henry Richards wrought the first convert, gained at Banza Manteka.[264]

A friend of mine wrote the following, after having been 'in country' in an unreached nation for four months.

Well, we have been here for almost four months and a lot of that time has been spent in offices, courts and police stations trying to sort out visas, residencies, etc. Unless you have lived in a country with this system you would probably find the amount of time we have spent doing this unbelievable but it literally has been never-ending and is still ongoing. A highlight was at one point having to make an oath that I was married but they only had a Qur'an to swear on, so they got me to hold my hands up to the sky and swear to my God that I was telling the truth. Repeating the man's broken English, I think I dramatically, with my hands in the air, looking up to the sky said something like, 'My God I will the truth speak.'

Risk

Grace is a high-risk endeavour. Sending (or being sent) is an act of grace in which both sender and sendee leave themselves vulnerable to exploitation and rejection. I am from a risk-averse culture, but to reach the unreached will be impossible without a degree – often a high degree – of risk.

Dr Anna Hampton, who after having lived in Afghanistan for ten years published her PhD on cross-cultural risk, poses the problem: 'The risk-adverse culture of North America does not lend itself to producing a generation of cross-cultural staff able to be resilient and withstand extreme danger.'[265]

In the parable under consideration, verse 13, '*perhaps* they will feel shame in his presence' is also fraught with danger. The landowner sends his unarmed and defenceless son in amongst violent rebels – a lamb amongst wolves. The potential gain and potential loss are both increased. Perhaps they will respect him and repent. Conversely, the land owner risks the death of his beloved son, and the loss of his inheritance.[266] Land is honour in the Middle East. To lose one's heir and one's land is to lose everything – his name will disappear, his entire world will be jeopardised. Grace is a high-risk strategy. In England we say, 'Never bet the farm', yet that is literally what the landowner was doing here!

There are many aspects to cross-cultural risk. There are many things which are gambled and potentially lost. As families, we risk physical and mental health, our children's security and education. As sending churches and movements, we invest money and people with no guarantee of reward. It is perfectly possible to pour hundreds of thousands of dollars into a cross-cultural enterprise which never bears fruit. Reaching the unreached requires sending precious people on a 'perhaps' – for which Luke 20:13 gives us good precedent.

Terry and Payne, in their now classic *Developing a Strategy for Missions*, observe that sending churches and mission agencies need to take into account the potential 'success-less-ness' of investing money into reaching the unreached.

> Whether we work with faith goals or with measurable objectives, we need to be especially clear and biblical in how we ultimately assess missionary effectiveness. We – the missionaries, agencies, and boards; the sponsoring, sending, and supporting churches; and the sacrificially giving believers – must exercise great caution. We should all fear the paradigm shift that places supreme value on getting the most return for our missionary dollars ('getting the most ministry bang for your missionary buck'). This attitude puts significant and at times inappropriate pressure on the missionary to 'produce' in terms more suitable to a corporate venture than to a spiritual undertaking.[267]

Death and vindication

The parable ends with the son being killed. What was the point? What a tragic loss! Yet, there is a prophetic note of vindication, 'The stone that the builders rejected has become the [capstone]'.[268]

God sowed him into the earth. Jesus himself said, 'Unless a grain of wheat falls into the earth and dies, it remains alone; but if it dies, it bears much fruit' (John 12:24). As mentioned earlier, like Jack's mother in the fairy tale *Jack and the Beanstalk*, the seed that was thrown away proved to be the one that would grow. When Jesus was being buried, the Seed of the kingdom was being planted in planet Earth.

In like vein, Jesus spoke of sowing his disciples into the world (Matthew 13:38: 'the good seed is the sons of the kingdom'). Entering a new culture is like dying. Maybe really dying. We would do well to think deeply on the following from Johan Ludwig Krapf of East Africa:

> Our God bids us first build a cemetery before we build a church or dwelling house, showing that the resurrection of East Africa must be affected by our own destruction. Our sanguine expectations and hopes of immediate success may be laid in the grave like Lazarus, yet they shall have a resurrection and our eyes shall see the glory of the Lord at last.[269]

Build a cemetery before you build a church – that is good advice. Turkish evangelist Hakan Tastan, whom I have watched bearing false accusations and court cases for years with dignity and courage, puts it somewhat more bluntly: 'Everyone wants to go to heaven, but no one wants to die.'

Likewise, sent ones, every time you feel buried under incompetence, shame, uselessness, pain, loneliness, fruitlessness, just remember that you are being buried deeply into a soil where you will take root, you will bear fruit, and the more deeply you are planted, the more locally and lastingly will your fruit be rooted.

Vulnerability, struggle, death, rejection, risk; this is the story immemorial of cross-cultural gospel preachers. Not that they are possible side-effects, they are in the core, at the very heart of Christian witness. God sent Jesus *to die*. To embody divine non-retaliation. To showcase frailty. Our weakness reveals his glory. If they rejected him, they will reject us too. And if God vindicated him, brought the kingdom through his suffering, will he not avenge us also?

> Out of the anguish of his soul he shall see and be satisfied …
> *Isaiah 53:11*

Endnotes

250. Luke 20:9-18.
251. Bailey, *Jesus Through Middle Eastern Eyes*, 417.
252. John 20:21.
253. Cragg, Kenneth, *The Order of the Wounded Hands: Schooled in the East* (London: Melisende, 2006), 155.
254. Luke 10:3.
255. Commission on World Mission and Evangelism, *Together Towards Life: Mission and Evangelism in Changing Landscapes*, 2012, Section 92.
256. 2 Corinthians 4:7.
257. Cragg, *The Order of the Wounded Hands*, 82.
258. Piper, John, *Adoniram Judson: How Few There Are Who Die So Hard!* (2012). http://www.desiringgod.org/articles/adoniram-judson-biography-free-ebook (accessed 6.10.17).
259. Tompkins, Stephen, *David Livingstone: The Unexplored Story* (Oxford: Lion Books, 2013), Kindle loc. 1115.

260. Benge, Janet and Geoff, *Samuel Zwemer: The Burden of Arabia (Christian Heroes: Then and Now)* (Seattle, WA: YWAM Publishing, 2013), Kindle loc. 1921, emphasis mine.

261. Allen, *The Ministry of the Spirit*, Kindle loc. 425.

262. Judson, Adoniram, cited in Anderson, Courtney, *To the Golden Shore: The Life of Adoniram Judson* (Prussia, PA: The Judson Press, 1987), 409.

263. Carey, William, cited in Smith, George, *The Life of William Carey, Shoemaker and Missionary*, Kindle Edition (Harrington, DE: Delmarva Publications, 2014; first printed 1909), 4, Kindle loc. 18.

264. Gordon, A.J., cited in Ravenhill, Leonard, *Why Revival Tarries* (Carlisle: Send the Light, 1972), 31.

265. Hampton, Dr Anna E., *Facing Danger: A Guide Through Risk*, Kindle Edition (New Prague, MN: Zendagi Press, 2016), Kindle loc. 452-453.

266. The Mishnah ruled that there was a form of 'squatters rights' for renters who remained over three years, hence 'Let us kill him, so that the inheritance may be ours' (Luke 20:14). Bailey, *Jesus Through Middle Eastern Eyes*, 420.

267. Terry, John Mark and Payne, J.D., *Developing a Strategy for Missions,* 39.

268. Matthew 21:42.

269. Krapf, Johan Ludwig cited in Benge, *Samuel Zwemer*, Kindle loc. 1483.

Chapter 17
Scaffolding

I look on foreign missionaries as the scaffolding round a rising building; the sooner it can be dispensed with the better – or rather, the sooner it can be transferred to other places, to serve the same temporary purpose.

Hudson Taylor[270]

Church planters need to be told, *know that your role is temporary*. Hudson Taylor called missionaries the 'scaffolding'. We are there to help the building get up and get strong, but at some point we will be dismantled and needed again elsewhere. We are not the building. Our whole attitude should be '[they] must become greater; I must become less'.[271] We should be working ourselves out of a job. We should be actively making space for local responsibility and expression. We should be laying a foundation upon which others can build. This is, and always has been, the task of the cross-cultural preacher.

Barnabas

In this regard, I think Barnabas is an underappreciated cross-cultural apostle. His gift, the ability to recognise and foster the grace of God at work in the lives of others, is the gift we need. When everyone else was afraid and suspicious of the newly converted Saul, Barnabas brought him in, vouched for him, was his sponsor.[272] He saw something that no one else could see. Later, when he went to Antioch, we read that he 'saw the grace of God'.[273] Despite a different cultural expression, ways of doing things that would have been difficult, even impossible for most Jerusalem Jews to swallow,

Barnabas was able to see through surface issues and discern the grace of God at work.

Barnabas then immediately decides he can't do it alone, and goes in search of Saul. Where so many would have said, 'Finally, it's my chance to lead something,' Barnabas says, 'This important church needs various gifts to serve it, Saul already has extensive cross-cultural experience amongst the Nabatean Arabs in Arabia, I'll partner with him.' Later we see that Peter visits Antioch, and James sends men too. Reaching the unreached requires collaboration between different apostolic spheres, open-handedness and a non-possessive approach. Barnabas understood that he was scaffolding. He understood that his role was 'temporary, secondary and advisory',[274] that if the church in Antioch was going to become genuinely Antiochene, yes, there were things to teach and a foundation to help lay, but there would also be a time to move on.

In moving on from Antioch, it is clear that Barnabas is leading and Saul is with him. Yet during chapter 13 of Acts we observe a transition from 'Barnabas and Saul' to 'Paul and Barnabas', where Paul (Saul) is the prominent figure and Barnabas beginning to take a back seat. This is the genius of Barnabas, that he brings through others who then surpass and replace him. He later did the same with Mark. This is the kind of role that cross-cultural leadership must play.

Underleading

In order to ensure that local leaders emerge, we must create space for people to take responsibility by leaving undone things that would otherwise need to get done. We call this *underleading*. Roland Allen, writing a century ago, understood that 'the besetting sin of European missionaries is the love of administration'.[275] This is profound! Many Europeans find it hard to sacrifice the love of administration on the altar of contextual leadership, and would rather hold on to detail than give it away. 'They may not administer it at all to our satisfaction, but I fail to see what our satisfaction has to do with the matter.'[276]

In another book, *The Ministry of the Spirit*, Allen unpacks this idea some more:

The continued presence of a foreigner seems to produce an evil effect. The native genius is cramped by his presence, and cannot work with him. The Christians tend to sit still and let him do everything for them and to deny all responsibility ... A visit of two or three months stirs up the Church, long continued residence stifles it.[277]

The apostle Paul saw church planting in terms of two metaphors – seed-sowing and foundation-laying. He described himself as a seed sower. 'I planted, Apollos watered, but God gave the growth. So neither he who plants nor he who waters is anything, but only God who gives the growth.'[278] Seed-sowing is risky, there is no control. You make your contribution and move on. After all, the work belongs to God and not to you!

Paul also saw himself as a foundation-layer. Yet even here, there is a laying of the foundation, and then a moving on. Paul told the church in Corinth, where he had spent eighteen months doing just that, 'According to the grace of God given to me, like a skilled master builder I laid a foundation, and someone else is building upon it.'[279]

When the same leader sows then waters, or when the same leader lays a foundation then builds on it, do we miss something of the diversity of gifts witnessed in 1 Corinthians 3? Moving on creates space for other leaders to contribute to God's garden and God's temple.

There *is* ongoing apostolic involvement. Paul writes letters to the Corinthians. He visits them. He corrects and rebukes them. David Devenish, from whom I have learned so much, in his ground-breaking book on apostolic ministry today, adds this caution:

I would not go so far as to say, as some do, 'Leave it all to the nationals,' i.e. Westerners should not presume to apply biblical principles to a different culture. I believe that this denies the gifting and benefit of apostolic wisdom, as well as the objectivity that someone from outside can bring.[280]

If there were no role for the foreign church-planting agent, this book you are reading would be redundant! The call is to remember that if foreigners do not see their role as specific and temporary, then there will be no emerging local leadership, no indigenisation, no reproducibility and no local responsibility. The task of the outsider is to set a direction, but the local believers will run in it, to lay a foundation, but the local believers will build on it, to trace an outline, but the local believers will colour in the detail.

> He should remember that he is the least permanent element in the church. He may fall sick and go home, or he may die, or he may be called elsewhere. He disappears, the church remains. The native Christians are the permanent element. The permanence of the church depends on them.[281]

Local elders as soon as possible

One of the primary ways for the Church to become locally rooted is by appointing local elders. At the same time, this is one of the most difficult aspects of cross-cultural church planting. Paul and Barnabas seemed to appoint local leaders relatively quickly, for example in Acts 14:23, they have only just been through Galatia evangelising, and now they are returning and appointing elders within the churches.

There is a major contextual difference between the list of eldership requirements in 1 Timothy 3 and the list in Titus 1. In Titus 1, two conditions of eldership are absent: 'not … a recent convert' and 'able to teach'. This is because the Timothy letter was written to the church in Ephesus which was an established, metropolitan, large community, where it really would be inappropriate for a new believer to be part of the eldership team. Titus, however, was written to Crete, *where everyone was a new believer!*

The contextual nature of eldership is vital to our cause. Elders should be from within the community and recognised by the community, not imposed from outside. Someone who is an elder to one group of people may not be received by another group. I was appointed as an elder aged twenty-five in our church plant in London, but at the same age would probably not have been able to lead in a larger, more mature church. The biblical standard for eldership is contextual not universal, and the appropriate leaders for a community will be supplied by the Holy Spirit.

In one context, we appointed a brother who had been a believer for three years into eldership, but in a church where the majority of the believers were even newer than him! We must avoid the tendency to hold appropriate leaders to an impossible global standard. Sometimes we do this ethically, expecting an expression of morality or marriage that looks the same as ours. Sometimes we do this in our expectation of the task of leadership, where we have not learned how to de-Westernise our conception of an effective leader. And sometimes we do this in our view of the requirement of theological training and knowledge. Oh, for the eyes of Barnabas to see, 'Is the grace of God at work in this person?'

One friend of mine who is planting many churches in a Muslim nation speaks of initially investing all of his time into promising, young, charismatic guys, and being frequently disappointed. 'Then I realised,' he says, 'they don't need to be gifted. They just need to be faithful. I stopped looking for gifted guys and started looking for steady guys. Now I am, with these guys, planting churches all over the region.' Many of his church planters are relatively new converts, former addicts who have come to Christ through their rehabilitation centre, but there is a characteristic humility, simplicity and steadiness to them.

A British journalist once asked Mother Teresa her secret. She replied, 'I'm not called to be successful, I'm called to be faithful.' Kenneth Bailey warns against the danger of reading the parable of the talents[282] through a capitalistic lens. 'Is the focus of the story on *profits*, or is it *faithfulness* to an unseen master in a hostile environment?'[283] Leadership should not be evaluated by productivity but by steadfastness.

Bringing through local leaders from amongst unreached peoples is always a major spiritual battle. I do believe, however, that often our standard is too high. Or maybe not too high, perhaps just wrong. Not that we must compromise on a biblical standard, but that with our Western lens we read into the biblical standard that which was never there. Have we filled the word 'leadership' with extra-biblical definition and made it impossible to translate culturally? This question is explored in the next chapter.

Taking down the scaffolding

When is a church ready for the cross-cultural church-planters to move on and entrust it to local leaders and the Holy Spirit? Answer: As soon as possible.

In Acts 20, Paul tells the Ephesian elders that they will never see him again. He warns them that 'after my departure fierce wolves will come in among you, not sparing the flock; and from among your own selves will arise men speaking twisted things, to draw away the disciples after them'.[284] Devenish comments on this verse:

> What a way to leave these Ephesian elders! Surely Paul should have stayed to support them against the 'savage wolves' who would attempt to wreak havoc in the church. Yet Paul was confident in the maturity of the Ephesian elders; while they needed his warning and encouragement, they didn't need him to sort out the problem.[285]

In the book of Acts (which starts with the 'moving on' of Jesus even though his disciples were less than ready), the moving on of leaders is an ever-present theme. Sometimes through persecution or crisis, sometimes sent on by the Holy Spirit, whatever the reason, the cross-cultural church planting process is not complete until the scaffolding is removed and the building is seen for all its glory! Only in this way will there be local expression. Also, the church planters can move on and plant again!

> Within a short time, the new believers coming to Christ in Church Planting Movements may not even know that a foreigner was ever involved in the work. In their eyes, the movement looks, acts and feels home-grown.[286]

Henry Venn, whom later generations would remember primarily as the father of the 'three-selfs' formula (the indigenous church should be self-supporting, self-governing and self-propagating), was also famous for his use of the phrase 'the euthanasia of a mission' in a speech in 1851:

> The 'euthanasia of a mission' takes place when a missionary, surrounded by well-trained native congregations, under native pastors, is able to resign pastoral work into their hands.[287]

Venn's concern was that the foreign Christian worker perform the apostolic functions of evangelism and foundation-laying, not the settled work of pastoring. This had to be the responsibility of local brothers. In fact, Venn's thought became so popular with emerging indigenous churches that he is credited with a significant contribution to the emergence of nationalism in West Africa, so hard did he fight against the racism and paternalism that had kept local Christians supressed. The Chinese church, wanting to be free of foreign influence, has repeatedly affirmed its 'three-self' status since 1949.[288]

Half a century later, Roland Allen developed and popularised Venn's ideas, demonstrating that the apostle Paul's method had been precisely this.

> Paul established the church and intentionally moved on to repeat the process. The apostle understood any new church to be just as legitimate as any well-established local church. Paul's retirement was done to help the church exercise 'the powers which they possessed in Christ. He warned them of dangers, but he did not provide an elaborate machinery to prevent them from succumbing to the dangers.' Paul had confidence in the Holy Spirit who had baptised the infant believers.[289]

Sow the seed and entrust it to the Master Gardener. Lay the foundation and entrust it to the Master Builder. There is a place for evangelising and teaching, discipling and pastoring. There are initial battles to be fought and won. There are leaders to be trained and an example to be lived. It is a fierce battle to see the church planted, her foundation strong, her core gathered and her leaders leading. In some unreached contexts, this could take a generation. In church planting movements, the catalytic agents are very quickly in a peripheral coaching role. The point here is not to rush, neither to overstay. The church planter must know when they have laid the foundation, when they have sown well the seed, and must not overstay. We entrust local communities to the grace of God, to the Holy Spirit, and to local leaders. Paradoxically, with cross-cultural leadership the saying 'less is more' definitely seems to be true. Paul stayed a shorter time than we often do, and the churches he planted lasted longer. If your arriving was important, your departing is even more so!

Endnotes

270. Taylor, Dr and Mrs Howard, *The Spiritual Secret of Hudson Taylor* (New Kensington, PA: Whitaker House, 1997), 299.

271. John 3:30, NIV.

272. Acts 9:27.

273. Acts 11:23.

274. Fleming, Daniel cited in Hutchison, William R., *Errand to the World: American Protestant Missionary Thought and Foreign Missions* (Chicago, IL: University of Chicago Press, 1987), 151.

275. Allen, Roland, *Missionary Methods: St. Paul's or Ours?* (Cambridge, UK: Lutterworth Press, 1912; Kindle Edition 2006), Kindle loc. 2404.

276. Ibid. Kindle loc. 1284.

277. Allen, *The Ministry of the Spirit,* Kindle loc. 345.

278. 1 Corinthians 3:6-7.

279. 1 Corinthians 3:10.

280. Devenish, David, *Fathering Leaders, Motivating Mission: Restoring the Role of the Apostle in Today's Church* (Milton Keynes: Authentic Media, 2011), 251.

281. Allen, *Missionary Methods*, Kindle loc. 3034.

282. Luke 19:11-27

283. Bailey, *Jesus Through Middle Eastern Eyes*, 403.

284. Acts 20:29-30.

285. Devenish, *Fathering Leaders, Motivating Mission*, 267.

286. Garrison, David, *Church Planting Movements: How God is Redeeming a Lost World* (Bangalore: WigTake Resources, 2007), Kindle loc. 271.

287. Knight, W., *The Missionary Secretariat of the Rev. Henry Venn* (London: Longmans, Green & Co., 1880), 307.

288. Shenk, Wilbert, 'Henry Venn and Mission Thought', *Anvil*, vol. 2, No.1, 1985, 36.

289. Payne, J.D., paraphrasing Roland Allen, in Payne, J.D., *Roland Allen: Pioneer of Spontaneous Expansion* (J.D. Payne, 2012), Kindle loc. 338.

Chapter 18
Leadership is Not Like Riding a Bicycle

Professionalism is not supernatural. The heart of ministry is.
John Piper[290]

Leadership is not like riding a bicycle. I have ridden bikes in many different countries, and although the bikes are different and the roads are different, the skill-set is the same (yes – in India it was admittedly a little scarier!). Leadership is not a context-independent bundle of abilities. One cannot simply take a leader, parachute them into the jungle, and ask them to lead the tribespeople. One cannot simply look at an individual and say, 'Here is a leader.' Leadership is relative to and in respect of a community – a leader is a leader *amongst* or a leader *of*. Leadership is not an absolute function.

The twenty-first century equivalent of 'dressing the native converts in European clothing' is the teaching of 'leadership principles'. A hundred years ago our sin was exporting 'cultural righteousness'. Today, it could be exporting 'expedient Christianity'. I fear that we do this just like the Men from James: 'This helped us in Jerusalem, it will help you here in Antioch', oblivious to the cultural insularity of most leadership material, or just naïvely assuming that training leaders is like training people to ride a bike – the same everywhere. The science of leadership is one of the most prevalent forms of neo-colonialism around in the Church today.

'Leadership' itself is a relatively new term. It scarcely appeared in American discourse before the Second World War, and gradually made its way into the churches from the 1960s onwards.[291] It is a particularly American term,[292] and its language is soaked in US world view vocabulary, especially the 'Success narrative'.[293] To say this is to take nothing away from the phenomenal men and women of God who through their writing and teaching and ministries have served the Church of Jesus Christ, but just to ask that we not blindly assume that what is true in one culture is automatically true, or at all beneficial, when transferred into a different context.

I learned to lead in a London church, where Hybels and Maxwell and Covey had much to teach us. People in UK churches at the current time expect to be strongly led, expect clear articulation of vision and values, speed of communication and a high degree of organisation. This is a cultural reality, and church leaders will do well to be cognisant of this in order to serve their people well. However, if I had relocated to Istanbul thinking, 'I can lead in London, therefore I can lead in Turkey. I will pack my bike and ride it when I get there,' I would have been sadly mistaken.

In fact, the opposite is true. Many of the skills I learned in London had to be unlearned in order to lead in Turkey. This is one of the reasons why crossing cultures throws up so many surprises. Those who could lead in their home culture suddenly find they cannot lead in the new, or vice versa. I have heard many sending church pastors tell me over the years, 'You know, she didn't really amount to much in our church here, but when she moved to China she seemed to come alive!'

One Russian missionary reaching Muslims in the Caucasus region put it this way: 'Churches in Russia would only send us people they could not use or did not value; largely former drug addicts. Many of these have become our best church planters.'[294] The stone the builders rejected has become the capstone!

Analysing the world view underlying much leadership teaching

Stephen Pattison, who has written much to help us think biblically about leadership/management, highlights some unspoken assumptions of much literature on the subject, including:

- Everything that is significant can and should be measured objectively
- Clear goals and objectives can be set for the future and they can and will be attained
- A trivialisation of the chaotic and unpredictable nature of the world

His point is that many of these are components of a modern American world view, but not necessarily of a biblical one. 'There is a real need for Christians to be critical of management words and practices, not necessarily with a view to dismissing or discarding them, but with a view to using them judiciously and with full awareness of their implications.'[295]

As Richards and O'Brien have written, 'the things that go without being said are some of the most important parts of culture.'[296] World view is invisible, but we need to work hard to understand the suppositions that underlie any teaching, otherwise we will just transfer them unquestioningly into a new context.

De-Westernising leadership

What follows is an attempt to *deconstruct* some of the commonest assumptions in leadership material doing the rounds in the Church. These are explicit or implicit qualities of leaders which make leadership 'work' in a Western context, but which may be culturally insular. After that, I will make some suggestions towards *constructing* a contextual view of leadership. In order to teach biblical leadership cross-culturally, bodies of teaching need to be 'undressed' and then 're-dressed' in appropriate cultural forms. Here are some common presuppositions which will inevitably burn up on entry into foreign orbits:

Homogenisation of leadership personality type (the extrovert ideal)

Susan Cain in her popular book, *Quiet*, critiques the American obsession with extroversion.

> Introversion – along with its cousins sensitivity, seriousness, and shyness – is now a second-class personality trait, somewhere between a disappointment and a pathology. Introverts living under the Extrovert Ideal are like women in a man's world, discounted because of a trait that goes to the core of who they are. Extroversion is an enormously appealing personality style, but we've turned it into an oppressive standard to which most of us feel we must conform.[297]

Many Mediterraneans may not assess personality in terms of introversion/ extroversion, but in terms of temperature. Is this person warm or cold? This is appraised almost intuitively by the relational vibes given off. Body language, voice tone, people orientation, emotional intelligence and 'expansiveness' all seem to be part of someone's temperature.

Efficiency and expediency

So much of leadership seems to be about making better use of time or resources. For example: build a system of small groups in order to care for people more efficiently. However, in many places pastoring through a system does not work! In fear-power cultures where leadership is about presence, or in highly relational cultures where influence comes from knowing everything that is going on in someone's extended family, relationship cannot be delegated to others. If this limits the numerical growth of the church then so be it; perhaps relationships are more important than efficiency and instead of one large church, several smaller churches should be planted! Bernard Adeney says it straight: 'If peak efficiency and productivity are your goals, it is probably better not to enter another culture.'[298]

This came home to me at a time when I was struggling to keep up with home visits, hospital visits and phoning everyone every day. In Istanbul, frequency of communication is incredibly high; friends and family members are in touch constantly. I was listening to a radio programme where listeners phoned in to talk about their plans for New Year's Eve. One listener phoned in and said, 'We are having an enormous party in our home – seventeen people!' All the presenters oohed and aahed, and I realised, people here have very small friendship circles – that's how they can maintain the intensity of commitment! Perhaps churches in Turkey are small, not because of a lack of leadership, but because relational intensity is so high.

Efficiency is not, of course, unique to the West. There are many wonderful, highly organised churches in Asia. Faith Community Baptist Church in Singapore, led by Lawrence Khong, has been influential in the development of the cell church model. The Abba Love network of churches led by Eddy Leo in Indonesia combines deep values and an amazing degree of organisation. Korea and Japan and China are extraordinarily efficient countries. However, if leading in a place where organisation is not a high value, should it be expected from leadership candidates?

Task orientation

One of the strengths of Western culture is a focus on the task at hand. Many, however, would argue that task-orientation has no place in the Church, which is primarily a relational context. For example, Maxwell's Law of Connection, 'Leaders touch a heart before they ask for a hand' is implicitly task-orientated. And a Middle Easterner (who are often highly emotionally intelligent and tuned into social cues) will instantly understand that you are just being nice to them because you want something, that you are building a functional relationship. Task-orientated Christianity will not succeed in the Majority World, and probably is not appropriate anywhere.

In one instance, a church member's sister was employed to clean the church building. The foreign-led church-planting team felt that this was poor stewardship of church funds, that a better job could be done at lower cost. Their sense of stewardship (of funds) had a task-bias. As they were working in a strongly relational culture, the very fact that this issue was being discussed resulted in a breakdown of trust. For the local believers, leadership should have been about stewardship of the relationship rather than achievement of the task.

Generalising principles

When I was learning to lead in London there were plenty of principles floating around that were assumed to have universal application, for example, 'If your venue is 80 per cent full you are hostile to a visitor.' That may have been true in London, but in some cities it is the opposite, where personal space and crowdedness feel very different. Just look at the public transport – the fuller the better!

Many leadership texts (Maxwell's *Indisputable Laws*, Hybels' *Axiom*, Covey's *Habits*) presuppose a view of the world wherein there are universal or general principles, rules, laws that are always true. But this too is a uniquely Western perspective: there are many cultures where this is not how the world is perceived.

Paul had a rule about not circumcising Gentile converts,[299] but then broke his own rule in circumcising Timothy.[300] Why would he break his own principle? Isn't that inconsistent? Luke tells us that it was 'Because of the Jews who were in those places'.[301] For Paul, as a Middle Eastern man, relationships were more important than hard and fast principles. Relationships trumped rules.[302]

Obsession with measurability and performativity[303]

Wherever there is a scoreboard there is the potential for envy and competition. There is potential for pride in achieving goals or a sense of failure in not achieving them. Newer church networks often seem to appeal to measures of success to legitimate authority because they lack the traditional mechanisms of ordination and legitimisation. We believe in charismatic authority, that God calls and anoints leaders, but we look for measurable manifestation of that anointing, so we ask, 'What has he built?' or 'How many churches have they planted?' When leadership is seen as a function, then we seek to evaluate it according to outcomes.

Twenty years after having left, I visited Cyprus together with my parents. On the Sunday, we attended a Greek evangelical church which we had known when I was growing up. As we walked in to the meeting, I could hardly believe my eyes! In the room were the same small handful of families, the same hymnbooks, the same pastor (preaching the same sermon)! All my leadership instinct about growth and development was appalled – twenty years later and no change! Then I remembered the difficulty of the context, the pressure on these believers from their Greek Orthodox families, and I realised that in their context, success is keeping going. Attendance numbers would be an inappropriate scoreboard to assess their faithfulness, their resilience, their Christianity. Some things just are not quantitative.

Failure to equip for leadership in persecution

Leadership in winter (where the church is a persecuted minority) requires different, even contrary skills to leadership in summer (where the church is peaking in popularity).[304] Andrey Bondarenko in Ukraine commented with sadness about their churches during the 2015 crisis, 'some who were great leaders in peacetime couldn't lead in time of war'.[305] Sri Lankan Ajith

Fernando, in his book on church leadership, *The Call to Joy and Pain* (what a name for a leadership book!), writes: 'One of the glaring omissions in modern church-growth studies is the key part that suffering has played in the growth of the Church.'[306]

Towards a contextual understanding of leadership

It is all very well to deconstruct, but we are concerned with reaching the unreached, planting churches, and encouraging local leadership. We have seen that merely translating books about leadership will not help in many local contexts. Even the word 'leadership' itself is simply transliterated into many other languages; the concept it embodies is so alien that there is often no word for it! How, then, should we approach the task of understanding and developing leadership cross-culturally?

Biblical terminology

The New Testament terms for church leadership are diverse and specific: elder, overseer, shepherd, deacon, apostle. There is a wonderful colour and diversity and a depth of biblical meaning to these words. This creates all kinds of difficulties in Bible translation, because many languages lack this degree of specificity, and all over the world we find a hotchpotch of loan words in the church, whether from Greek (presbyter, episcopal), from Latin (pastor, missionary), or from English (leader). It can often be important, when laying foundations into the church in emerging contexts, to return to the biblical languages, teach thoroughly, and look for local vocabulary or cultural cues to emerge with time.

One of the things that I have loved about Newfrontiers over the years is a commitment to fight for New Testament terms, such as elder or apostle, rather than taking the lazy route and speaking generically of *leadership*. The word *leader* is a catch-all, a non-specific word that often gets chosen instead of doing the due diligence of digging through the biblical language:[307] 'like a blank square in a game of Scrabble [it] can be filled with whatever the organisation's agenda *du jour* might be.'[308]

We must continue to work hard with the biblical vocabulary.

Which metaphor for Church?

The metaphors for Church that we choose will lead into the metaphors for leadership. If the Church is an organisation, then leaders will organise and strategise. If the Church is a flock, then leaders are shepherds. We all make choices about which metaphors we employ, and which ones we ignore; as did the biblical writers. Each picture of the Church has strengths and weaknesses.

For example, Laurenti Magesa, writing in his East African context, chooses to prioritise 'church as clan'. The elders, therefore, are obliged 'to do whatever is in [their] power to protect and prolong the life of the clan-community'.[309] A positive outcome of this view is a commitment to strong relational health, a negative outcome will be that the leaders feel threatened by other 'clans'. Deciding what the Church is will determine what her leaders are.

Culture

It is essential to explore how leadership is viewed in a culture, and what are the values that are esteemed. Not that leadership in the Church should necessarily conform to leadership in the culture, but there will always be a default to the underlying cultural norms. The unseen and unspoken aspects of culture are the most powerful, and the gaps that we leave will be filled by cultural defaults.

In his study of the Malawian concept of *umunthu* ('I am because we are') and its impact on Christian leadership in the Malawian Church, Harvey Kwiyani emphasises that the most prized traits in a leader are communality and generosity. '*Umunthu* is the most celebrated leadership philosophy in Africa. Without it, leaders lose their following and end up dictators.'[310] Leadership is less through command and control than through invisibility; the ability to promote the well-being of the group without people even knowing that you are doing so. The groupality of Malawian culture demands a totally different kind of leader.

At the wedding in Cana,[311] Jesus transforms the situation and saves the face of the groom (and the whole village) without anyone knowing that there had been a problem or that it had been resolved. The bridegroom takes the credit for Jesus' intervention. This expresses the heart of *umunthu* beautifully. What a refreshing paradigm of leadership!

Susie Howe, the founder of Bethany Children's Trust, was invited by a government minister to provide care for AIDS orphans in the Zvishavane District of Zimbabwe. She was told that there were 2,000 orphans in the district, and a piece of land was available on which an orphanage could be built which could house twenty orphans. 'What about the 1,980 other children who need care?' Susie wondered. She then devised a programme utilising local churches and volunteer 'uncles and aunties' in which orphans could be cared for holistically within their communities rather than through an institution. 'Remember the African saying, "It takes a village to raise a child"', Susie proposed. 'We'll be going back to the traditional ways of *ubuntu*[312] where all are for one and one is for all, and where there is an interconnectedness that means that no man or woman will allow any child around them to be an orphan ... this way, we'll be able to mobilise care and support for thousands of children.'[313] By tapping into a local cultural value, Susie was able to multiply local responsibility to provide a sustainable, indigenous solution, rather than by imposing a foreign organisational culture.

Simon Cozens has shown that in Japanese house churches, the main function of leaders is to ensure group cohesion. He calls this 'leadership as relationship management'. In a culture where uniformity and maintaining face are the most treasured values, the goal of Christian leaders is not to develop or expand the Church, but to ensure unity. Hospitality becomes an essential task of pastoral ministry (not unlike 1 Timothy 3:2).

Cozens quotes from the authoritative work on Japanese leadership, Nakane (1972), who says, 'Japanese soil cannot grow a charismatic leader'.

She is not, as some have suggested, making a negative statement, but a positive one. She is essentially stipulating that within a culture oriented around personal and emotional ties, a dominating leader is undesirable. The effect of charisma is limited to the immediate personal relations, rather than the influence directed towards the organisation at large.[314]

Isn't that interesting? In group-orientated cultures, strong visionary charismatic leadership is not healthy or even desirable. Where the culture is different, leadership must look different!

Measuring success

Finally, there is a need to get away from quantitative measurability of leadership performance. Particularly for leaders amongst the unreached, continually asking for hard outcomes or 'How many are you gathering?' is totally inappropriate.

> I am convinced that we must engage in a thorough critique of our church planting thinking if we are to break the 'quantitative fallacy' which measures success by numbers rather than the transformative mission of God.[315]

I was powerfully impacted by David Devenish's 2001 sermon, 'The Plumbline not the Measuring Rod'.[316] In Zechariah 2:1-5 the young man is rebuked for trying to measure Jerusalem. Instead, in Zechariah 4:8-10 we see a plumbline in the hand of Zerubbabel.

Wherever there is a scoreboard there is competition. There are winners and losers. Saul heard the maidens singing about thousands and tens of thousands, and it awakened envy in him, which led to anger, paranoia, attempted murder and demonisation.[317] There is something in human nature which responds dangerously to quantitative measurement. We need to throw away our measuring sticks!

Instead, grab a plumbline! Where measuring sticks evaluate quantity, plumblines observe quality. Measuring sticks measure the external, plumblines the internal. Measuring sticks give temporary and ever-changing numbers, plumblines evaluate the overall direction. Measuring sticks are concerned with size, plumblines with health.

1 Corinthians 3 is a chapter about leadership legacy, and Paul is very clear in verse 13 that what will be tested by fire is the *quality* (NIV), or *value* (NLT) of each person's work – not the quantity or size. Passing the eschatological leadership test will be like passing any other exam; you need

to answer the right questions. If the question is about *quality* not *quantity*, then let's pour our energies into the right place!

Anyone involved in cross-cultural ministry needs to interrogate, de-Westernise and then reconceive areas of teaching and of church life appropriate to their new context, 'undress' and 're-dress'. Only in this way will the Church be free to wrestle with the Scriptures in her own *situ* without being beholden to a foreign standard.

Endnotes

290. Piper, John, *Brothers, We Are Not Professionals* (Nashville, TN: B&H Publishing Group, 2013), Kindle loc. 80.
291. Frank, Thomas Edward, *Clergy Journal 85*, No. 3 (Jan/Feb 2009), 52-55.
292. Ibid.
293. Frank, Thomas Edward, 'Leadership and Administration: An Emerging Field in Practical Theology', *International Journal of Practical Theology*, 10, No. 1, July 2006, 113–136.
294. In a private conversation.
295. Pattison, Stephen, 'Management and Pastoral Theology' in *Pastoral and Practical Theology* (Wiley Blackwell Readings in Modern Theology), Woodward, James and Pattison, Stephen (eds.) (Oxford: Blackwell Publishers, 2000), 290.
296. Richards and O'Brien, *Misreading Scripture With Western Eyes*, 12.
297. Cain, Susan, *Quiet: The Power of Introverts in a World that Can't Stop Talking* (London: Penguin Books, 2013), 4.
298. Adeney, *Strange Virtues*, 131.
299. Galatians 5:2; 1 Corinthians 7:18.
300. Acts 16:3.
301. Ibid.
302. Richards and O'Brien, *Misreading Scripture With Western Eyes*, 167.
303. Frank, 'Leadership and Administration'.
304. See discussion in Chapter Six, 'Whose Story?'
305. In a private conversation.
306. Fernando, Ajith, *The Call to Joy and Pain: Embracing Suffering in Your Ministry* (Nottingham: IVP, 2008), 75.
307. Wilson, Andrew, 'Brothers, We Are Not Managers', *Christianity Today*, June 2015.
308. Frank, 'Leadership and Administration'.
309. Georges, Titre Ande, *Leadership and Authority: Bula Matari and Life-Community Ecclesiology in Congo* (Oxford: Regnum Books International, 2010), 115.
310. Kwiyani, Harvey C., 'Umunthu and the Spirituality of Leadership: Leadership

Lessons from Malawi', *Journal of Religious Leadership*, 12, No. 2 (Fall 2013), 39-59.

311. John 2.

312. *Umunthu* in Malawi and *ubuntu* in Zimbabwe seem to be broadly similar concepts.

313. Howe, Susie, *Resistance Fighter: God's Heart for the Broken* (Nottingham: IVP, 2011), 74.

314. Cozens, Simon, *Leadership in Japanese House Churches* (Gloucester: Wide Margin) 2010, 59.

315. Memory, Jim, 'How Can We Measure the Effectiveness of Church Planting?' in Van de Poll and Appleton (eds.), *Church Planting in Europe: Connecting to Society, Learning from Experience*, Kindle loc. 3761.

316. Devenish Sunday a.m. Stoneleigh 2001 main session, also referenced in Devenish, *Fathering Leaders, Motivating Mission*, 271.

317. 1 Samuel 18:7-12.

Theological Humility:
Thinking About Thinking

The apostle Peter underwent a massive emotional and theological journey, some would even say a conversion, from being a Torah-abiding Galilean Jew to someone who could 'eat with the Gentiles' in Antioch.[318] Peter's key crisis moment was the Cornelius event narrated in Acts 10-11, starting with his vision of the sheet whilst on the rooftop. We are told, in Acts 10:19, that Peter 'pondered' this vision; a very gentle translation of *enthymoumenou*, which could be better translated 'fumed'! When God touches something you hold dearly, it can make you angry!

> He was angry because the vision overthrew his long-held opinions. It pressed Peter to change his entire perspective on how God works in the world. Was he suddenly expected to overthrow the understandings of centuries?[319]

Pioneering involves personal world view change. You can't break new ground externally unless you are breaking new ground internally. It is God's prerogative to call us to do things which we had previously considered to be wrong, like calling Abraham to sacrifice Isaac, or calling Joseph to marry pregnant Mary. For Peter, eating with Gentiles was wrong. And yet here he was!

Acts 12 – 14 then picks up the story with Barnabas and Paul taking the lead in carrying the gospel to the Gentiles. Acts 15 is then a massive theological reflection moment; for Barnabas and Paul, for Peter, indeed for all the early believers. It is a moment to gather and consider, if God is working in this way, what are the implications for our theology?

This section, *Theological Humility*, might be the most controversial section of this book. Indeed, as I have taught some of this material around the UK over the last few years, I have learned that touching the way people do theology always elicits quite strong reactions! At its most basic, *Theological Humility* argues that because Christianity is a diverse, global phenomenon, we should approach varieties of interpretation, even varieties of methodology, with mutual respect and a desire to learn. As the apostles and elders came together to listen to each other in Jerusalem, so should we. Because, depending on where you are standing, your perspective will be different.

The reason that this upsets some people is because it can be seen, particularly in a purely Western context, as opening the door to relativism, as denying that there is one truth or one orthodoxy, as taking away from the universal need for salvation in Christ. This is never my intention. The point is a global one. Given that, as we have seen, cultures and languages and histories are *different*, this will inevitably lend itself to theological difference, because theology is necessarily culture- and language-embedded. And for the cross-cultural church planter, for those whose passion is to plant indigenous, self-governing, self-funding, self-replicating and self-theologising communities of Christ-followers, if the gospel is to be translated not just transliterated, then we must learn to think in terms of theological difference.

The Newfrontiers family of churches of which I have been a member for many years has grown from an Anglo-centric movement in its first generation, to a now more fully multi-centric movement, with apostolic centres and spheres in many different nations, expressed in different languages and styles. They are therefore experiencing something of an Acts 15 moment. What does it mean to be relationally connected, mutually honouring, able to see the grace of God at work in each other?[320] The need is for theology that is robust and yet agile. If our theology is too brittle, it will not cope with the constant change that missional expansion brings. Perhaps, with Dr Paul Davies' neatly coined use of language, we need to find contours for our theology that are 'consciously contextualised', 'process not product', 'occasional not systematic', and 'coherent and vital'.[321]

May it '[seem pleasing] to the Holy Spirit and to us'[322] to explore these themes together.

Endnotes

318. Galatians 2:12.
319. Bailey, *Jesus Through Middle Eastern Eyes*, 45.
320. Galatians 2:9.
321. Paul Davies, in a private conversation.
322. Acts 15:28

Chapter 19
Narrative

To focus on the narrative character of the Bible not only does justice to the character of the Bible; it also makes possible a hermeneutic that connects with the character of people's experience. Stories come naturally to people. The human world, it has been said, is story-shaped.

Richard Bauckham[323]

The goal of missions is indigenous expression of ancient truth. The danger for missionaries is bringing the gospel *plus* something additional. Part of evangelism is confronting cultural narratives, and part of church planting is laying a foundation. So there is a need for teaching, but *how* should we teach? There is a place for preaching, but *what* should we preach? The answer, to a certain extent, is *narrative*.

Bible storying and narrative preaching are growing areas of interest in missions circles. It is understood that oral cultures learn better from narrative whilst literate cultures learn better from abstract principle. Where people are illiterate, they get their Bible through chronological Bible storying. Even in the West, we are increasingly aware of the power of narrative to shape world view. In the 60s and 70s every ideology had a theory. Now ideologies have stories. Terrorist groups use stories to recruit. We live in a more storied world now.

Apostolic preaching isn't, however, just the telling of Sunday school stories round a campfire in the jungle. It isn't just real theology's simplistic cousin. There is a power and rigour to narrative theology that has its roots in the nature of revelation itself. In this chapter, we will examine some of the 'why' of narrative gospel communication.

God has revealed himself through narrative

The Bible is a big story, made up of many smaller stories. God chose the medium of narrative to communicate who he is and what he is like.

> The Bible, in the sense of truth communicated from a spiritual source, is a narrative of God's self-revelation through history, in the midst of a multiplicity of persons and cultures. It is a revelation of God's being in the context of life's reality.[324]

> Narrative theology is based on the observation that the Bible tells stories about God, just as much as it makes doctrinal or theological statements.[325]

Hans Frei in *The Eclipse of Biblical Narrative* pointed out how the Enlightenment's drive to reduce theology to general rational concepts led to a disregard for the narrative quality of the biblical writings.[326] We can become so used to abstracting principles from the story that we miss the fact that the inspired revelation from heaven *is* the story we are reading.

If our concern is to bring revelation, rather than our interpretation of revelation, then telling the story has its own intrinsic power. Whenever we move from narrative preaching into interpretation or application, we need to be aware that we have stepped onto different ground. Not that this should never be done, but our desire is to ensure that the Church is being built on Jesus as revealed through the narrative Scriptures.

One practice we have used to good effect is to have the foreign preacher declare the story, then have a local believer step in to help to ground it in application. It is often when we move from what is written in the Scripture into application that our culturally conditioned biases kick in.

Jesus was a narrative theologian

Story is not confined to the Old Testament and the Acts. Jesus answered questions with stories. He taught with stories. Many of Jesus' parables have a high Christology, a profound eschatology, and are retelling the story of the world, not through propositional truth but through metaphor.

This way of teaching was memorable and repeatable, so that the Christian tradition spread on an oral basis and was only later committed to writing.

> When we are telling the story of the New Testament, we are telling the story of a second-order phenomenon, the story of a literary residue of a largely oral movement which grew on the basis of preaching and teaching, praying and praising, and other forms of oral communication. It was not mainly, in the earliest period of Christian history, the texts that spread the Word, but rather the oral proclamation.[327]

This way of teaching earthed divine truths in everyday realities; it was, if you like, narrative contextualisation.

Jesus' birth, life, death and resurrection are a historical narrative event, and are the gospel

The heart of the Christian faith is the story of Jesus. Our argument with Muslims is that Jesus did not come with a book, he *is* the book. His life reveals God. 'Whoever has seen me has seen the Father.'[328] Jesus makes the invisible God visible. The story of his life is therefore pure theology. Telling the stories of Jesus' actions shows people what God is like.

Paul's gospel was the story of Jesus Christ

There is growing scholarly appreciation for Paul's underlying narrative thought world.[329] N.T. Wright, for example: 'Having begun (a long time ago) with exegesis, I have been driven to world view models to try to understand what early Christianity was all about.'[330] If asked, 'What is the irreducible essence of the gospel Paul preached?' the Reformers may well have answered 'justification by faith'. However, we only encounter justification by faith in Romans, Galatians and Philippians. To other churches Paul writes using his many other metaphors of salvation; such as redemption, reconciliation, adoption, choosing the appropriate term for the appropriate context.

Flemming writes: 'I believe that when we recognise that Paul's gospel has a narrative framework, we best capture the heart of his thought.'[331] Paul's gospel is consistent; there is one narrative, one Christ-event, one incarnation and crucifixion and resurrection, but he is able to write different letters into different contexts explaining this event in different, context-specific ways. Paul was an extraordinary contextualiser of the gospel, and it was his narrative understanding that made this possible. The story is unchanged, but the illustration and application of the story varies with context.

World view is a story, and we must undermine it and replace it with a better story

World view is a story. If the Bible is to change world view, it must be able to subvert and reshape the baseline narrative of a culture.

> It would be quite clearly wrong to see [Jesus'] stories as mere illustrations of truths that could be articulated in purer, more abstract forms. They were ways of breaking open the world view of Jesus' hearers, so that it could be remoulded into the world view which he, Jesus, was commending.[332]

We have to retell the story of humankind: where we came from, what the problem is and how to fix it. This is what Jesus was doing with the good Samaritan, the prodigal son, the workers in the vineyard. This is what Paul does with Abraham and with Adam. These are eschatological, Christological, salvation-historical teachings in storied form.

> It is striking, then, to see how Paul applies the gospel to confront and complete each society's baseline cultural narrative.[333]

Bible stories are often open-ended

The real work of translation begins when the story stops and the application begins. Did the older brother in Luke 15 repent? Did the bridegroom in John 2 take the credit for what Jesus had done? Storying that challenges world view and then leaves the application open allows for respondents to make their own decision and application in a culturally appropriate way, rather than imposing our idea of how they should respond. Asking questions, drawing people out and allowing them to make their own decisions avoids the soft control of application.

Jesus, the master story-teller, often did this. 'Which of the two did the will of his father?';[334] 'Which is easier, to say, "Your sins are forgiven," or to say, "Rise and walk"?';[335] 'Which of these three, do you think, proved to be a neighbour …?'[336]

When local believers are equipped with a grasp of the grand plan of Scripture, they are able to apply this to their context. The work of theologising becomes theirs.

Western theology zooms in. Oral learners zoom out

The Bible tells big stories – we must allow them to be big. Sometimes they are messy stories – we must allow them to be messy. Jacob's story resolves and unresolves several times (much like a Turkish soap opera). We are used to a neat Hollywood packaging and ending, half an hour on a Sunday morning. We need to allow these big stories to carry over several tellings; hence the growing appreciation for Chronological Bible Storying.

Oral learners can carry a great deal of backstory in their heads; in fact, they need the backstory to make sense of the current story. We need to know where we came from to understand where we are. One of our relatively new believers was invited to preach on a psalm; he spent twenty minutes on the backstory and fifteen minutes on exposition!

I remember trying to story 2 Samuel 6, about the Ark being brought to Jerusalem, with a small group. The group didn't let me get past verse 2. 'David arose and went with all the people who were with him from Baale-judah.' Why was the Ark in Baale-judah? Because Saul had neglected it. Why did Saul neglect it? Why did God allow Saul forty years of kingship whilst neglecting his Presence? Why do humans always try to do things their own way without acknowledging God? We never got to the main story, instead we kept going backwards… all the way to Eden! But we had a profound time with the Scriptures.

Stories are multi-sensory: with stories we feel and are drawn in

The imagination is more important than knowledge.
Einstein

We engage with a story with more of our being. We identify with the characters. We find ourselves inside the story, and find the story inside us. While we could reject a proposition, a story tends to invade our imagination and win our hearts. It is much harder to reject the premise once the story has got to us via our emotions.

> Metaphor, symbol, ritual, sign, myth, long maligned by those interested in 'exact' expressions of rationality, are today being rehabilitated; they create forms that synthesise and evoke the integration of mind and will; they not only touch the mind and its conceptions, and evoke action with a purpose, but compel the heart. So we see an upsurge of interest, especially in Third-World churches, in 'narrative theology', 'theology as story', and other non-conceptual forms of theologising. It is important to recognise that these modes of thinking and expression are not irrational or antirational.[337]

Shouldn't truth be encountered by the whole person, by feelings and imagination as well as by logic? A psychologist friend of mine, explaining to me the importance of dopamine, put it like this: 'When people are depressed, they produce less dopamine. They know cerebrally the right thing to do (e.g. get out of bed), but because they cannot *feel* much, they don't do it. Cerebral knowledge is not compelling enough. People need to *feel* truth. That is where dopamine comes in.'

With story, there is beauty, or sadness, or anger, or joy, and these have morally compelling power. Emotion creates motion! Never underestimate the power of story.

Declare the whole counsel of God

When laying a foundation into churches, the apostle Paul declared 'the whole counsel of God'. This is God's great plan from Genesis to Revelation, his plan for the planet, his plan for people, and the central role of Christ within this story.

> The foundation of truth we lay, according to New Testament practice, is essentially a story and not just an analysis of theology. When

people understand the overall story and their part in it, they are on a good foundation. The world views of many cultures are essentially narratives, and the only way of replacing one world view is by taking on another narrative.[339]

What about systematic theology?

What we are proposing is that theology that crosses cultures must be narrative, not systematic. Theology comes from the questions we are asking, and the questions in different contexts and at different times are different. 'Systematic theology … is by definition static. It takes a still-life picture, a single photograph of what is essentially a moving film.'[340]

The idea of systematic knowledge is a Greek concept and not specifically a biblical one.[341] It belongs more to the culture of Linear-Active thinkers than to Multi-Actives. An African studying Grudem or Calvin will not find answers to some of his most burning questions: polygamy, ancestors, tribalism. If he is well-grounded in the narrative of Scripture, however, he will be well-positioned to dig for these answers himself.

There is teaching to be done cross-culturally. This is inescapably New Testament and a major part of making disciples. Apostolic preaching was narrative. Let's get better at telling stories!

Endnotes

323. Bauckham, Richard, *Bible and Mission: Christian Witness in a Postmodern World* (Milton Keynes: Paternoster, 2003), 12.

324. Shaw and Van Engen, *Communicating God's Word in a Complex World*, 29.

325. McGrath, *Christian Theology*, 167.

326. Ibid. 168.

327. Witherington, *The New Testament Story*, Kindle loc. 66.

328. John 14:9.

329. Phrase from Witherington III, Ben, *Paul's Narrative Thought World: The Tapestry of Tragedy and Triumph* (Louisville, KY: Westminster John Knox Press, 2004).

330. Wright, N.T., *Paul and the Faithfulness of God* (London: SPCK, 2013), 474.

331. Flemming, Dean, *Contextualization in the New Testament: Patterns for Theology and Mission* (Leicester: Apollos, 2005), 95.

332. Wright, N.T., *The New Testament and the People of God* (London: SPCK, 1992), 77.

333. Keller, *Center Church*, 112.

334. Matthew 21:31.

335. Matthew 9:5.

336. Luke 10:36.

337. Bosch, *Transforming Mission*, 353.

338. Acts 20:27.

339. Devenish, *Fathering Leaders, Motivating Mission*, 102.

340. Parratt, *A Guide to Doing Theology*, 95.

341. Ibid. 93.

Chapter 20
Parable

The true parable is not an illustration to help one through a theological discussion; it is rather a mode of religious experience. It belongs to the same order of things as altar and sacrifice, prayer, the prophetic vision, and the like. It is a *datum* for theology, not a by-product.

T.W. Manson[342]

A parable is like a Trojan horse. It sneaks past the defences and invades the heart. The Greeks under Agamemnon pounded the walls of Troy for two years with no success. The ruse of the giant wooden horse led to the gates being opened, the horse welcomed in, and with it the soldiers hidden inside who would sack the city.

Often in evangelism direct argument gets nowhere. This is particularly true with Muslims living in the West, who can be inured to the classic arguments of the gospel, and only rarely does direct 'attack' breach the well-established defences. A parable, however, a story, a metaphor, an indirect approach can conceal 'the cunning of the serpent within the innocence of the dove.'[343]

A parable is like a Tardis. On the outside, a small, insignificant story, but once you get inside it, a vast landscape. Jesus' parables were often small, a few verses long, yet consider how much ink has been spent in exposition, in commentary. Metaphor is a compact, dense way of retelling the story of the world. Kenneth Bailey says that a parable is like a house – the reader is invited to sit within and experience the perspective on offer.[344]

Many parables have a long history of Christological interpretation, they are stories about who Jesus is. The limiting of parables to 'one point per parable' is a relatively recent, Western, development that simply cannot be accepted in many parts of the global Church.

Cranfield, commenting on Mark 4, agrees that

> Julicher's attack on the long-established custom of treating the parables as allegories to be interpreted detail by detail marked a real step forward. It effected a liberation from much that was fantastic, for which we must be thankful ... *But it is a mistake to make this into a hard and fast rule. To maintain a rigid distinction between parable and allegory is quite impossible in dealing with material originating in Hebrew or Aramaic, languages which have only one word to denote both things.*[345]

Parable is a category that makes lots of sense in many parts of the world today. It was said of Rabbi Meir that he spoke one-third in legal decisions, one-third in exposition and one-third in parables.[346] Languages such as Arabic and Farsi are rich with indirect, metaphorical turns of phrase. High-Context communication prefers non-literal speech. As Bailey said, 'The average Middle Easterner does not "illustrate ideas"; he or she "thinks in pictures".[347] Parable, then, is more than a way of illustrating or simplifying conceptual truth, it is an appropriate medium in which truth can live. It is a grounding of truth in the thought-world of the listener. As Barclay wrote, 'There is a sense in which *every* word must become flesh.'[348]

If parable was good enough for Jesus, the Master Communicator of truth, then we ought to consider the reasons why, and perhaps be persuaded that parable can still be a powerful medium for cross-cultural gospel-proclamation today.

Parable is powerful for indirect confrontation

In honour-shame cultures, confrontation is complex. To face-off with someone older or higher status than you is an elaborate dance, and even to rebuke a peer can result in a loss of face. You may win the argument, but you will lose the relationship. When Nathan approached King David about his adultery with Bathsheba and murder of Uriah, he was taking his life in his hands. He resorted to parable.

Parable in this context enables the teacher to say hard truths in a soft way. It puts the ball in the court of the hearer, and allows them to accept the truth, even to repent, without a public loss of face.

Part of the role of the cross-cultural disciple-maker is to confront cultural strongholds, to 'uproot and tear down'.[349] Jesus employed parable to good effect to achieve this purpose. Often, he would teach his disciples obliquely by arguing with others directly, whilst his disciples listened on. Mark 7 is the longest conflict speech in this gospel, and Jesus is arguing with the Pharisees and scribes. In verse 17, when everyone has gone, his disciples ask him about the teaching:

> *Mark 7:17:* And when he had entered the house and left the people, his disciples asked him about the parable.

Jesus has been rebuking and correcting the Pharisees, but for the benefit of his disciples' world view change. They would have had the same misunderstanding as the Pharisees, but could ask about it without loss of face.

I have often seen this 'indirect discipleship' work effectively. In one shop that I visit, a lady was often present sitting quietly in the corner listening to our discussions. I usually tell a Bible story and then we debate it. There are always loud, assertive Muslims present who, like the Pharisees and scribes above, are looking for a good argument. This lady, however, after sitting quietly and listening for several months, came to see me and requested prayer and a Bible. She had not been directly involved in the arguments and could show interest without loss of face, something which would have been much more difficult to do for those who had been seen to publicly argue against the gospel.

Parable is an interface between evangelism and the sovereignty of God

Jesus told the parable of the sower, and then announced:

Mark 4:9: And he said, 'He who has ears to hear, let him hear.'
Mark 4:10: And when he was alone, those around him with the twelve asked him about the parables.
Mark 4:11: And he said to them, 'To you has been given the secret of the kingdom of God, but for those outside everything is in parables,
Mark 4:12: so that 'they may indeed see but not perceive, and may indeed hear but not understand, lest they should turn and be forgiven.'

A parable, then, is a double-edged sword. For those whose hearts are being opened to the gospel, there is the opportunity to believe and to engage with the truth. Many will have the experience of Lydia: 'The Lord opened her heart to pay attention to what was said'.[350] For others, the function of this 'hiddenness' is to bring a tacit judgement, a sign that they are under condemnation.

> The parabolic teaching was at once a judgement pronounced upon their unpreparedness for the kingdom of God and also an expression of divine mercy that desires to spare and save.[351]

Staying faithful to the truth under fire

The apocalyptic genre – which, like parable, is symbolic, coded, metaphorical – comes especially into its own when believers are a persecuted minority. The 'ears to hear' phrase appears once again in the book of Revelation. This genre enables believers to speak truth to one another whilst announcing the inevitable destruction of the persecuting authorities, using coded speech. So Revelation condemns the Emperor Cult, for those with ears to hear. The Roman secret police would have needed considerable hermeneutical skill to pin a specific accusation on John!

> Apocalyptic rises in periods of persecution to stir the hopes of the people of God ... Apocalyptic declares the judgement of God ... Apocalyptic is the moment of truth and justice ... Apocalyptic is the hope of the oppressed.[352]

Likewise, Jesus used parables to criticise the Jewish authorities, whilst avoiding arrest until his time had come. The people delighted in his scathing attacks, but the powerful could pin nothing on him. Even at his eventual trial, they found it hard to accuse him of an exact blasphemy or insurrectionist sentiment.

> A parable is art harnessed for service and conflict … in its most characteristic use the parable is a weapon of controversy, not shaped like a sonnet in undisturbed concentration but improvised in conflict to meet the unpremeditated situation.[353]

In countries where the Church is a persecuted minority, parable gives the opportunity for believers to declare truth in ways that are not strictly illegal.

Kenya's former Anglican leader, David Gitari, spent most of his episcopal career under Kenya's authoritarian and sometimes brutal leader Daniel arap Moi. Gitari was a master at employing metaphor and parable in his preaching, in ways that would comfort the flock and declare God's judgement on unrighteous leadership. For example, during the political crisis of 1990 and 1991 he often returned to Ezekiel 34, contrasting righteous and unrighteous shepherds. 'How wonderful it is to know that God cannot leave his sheep to be exploited forever, because the sheep belong to him', he preached.[354]

Professor N.T. Wright, speaking about the role of Christians in arts and the media in post-Christian Europe, draws parallels with the apocalyptic genre:

> This is part of the task of early Christian 'apocalyptic': to create a glorious, poetically imagined world in which people are able to glimpse what it might mean to say that on the cross Jesus defeated all the powers of the world, and then to live from within that newly imagined world.[355]

Media and the arts have a creative, parabolic power to hold a mirror to society, to speak of judgement and hope, but in non-direct ways which engage the imagination in a society which does not accept the authority of the Bible *prima facie*.

Metaphor is an appropriate way to articulate mystery

Human language is always insufficient to bear divine mystery. Very few of our words are ontologically specific. Much more of our understanding of God is metaphorical than we at first sight realise. 'The hand of the Lord', 'The face of God' are anthropomorphic metaphors. Jesus was unafraid to say 'the kingdom of heaven is like...' In fact, he knew that the only way our tiny human brains could conceive of the divine was through the medium of comparison to the material, everyday world. When explaining why he used parables, Jesus used the word 'secret' or 'mystery'.

> *Mark 4:11:* And he said to them, 'To you has been given the secret of the kingdom of God, but for those outside everything is in parables ...

Avery Dulles writes that mysteries 'are realities of which we cannot speak directly. If we wish to talk about them at all we must draw on analogies afforded by our experience of the world'.[356] Parable is the only way to talk about invisible reality. What is the Church? It is a mystery[357] which we only understand through metaphor: body, bride, family, army. There are more than 100 metaphors for the Church in the New Testament, because only through this variegated perspective can we grasp what is the wonder that is the called-out people of God.

Avis, in his excellent book, *God and the Creative Imagination*, makes this point at length:

> Like the true fundamentalist, the conservative evangelical believes that the Bible makes explicit claims for itself and sets forth divine revelation accordingly in factual statements or propositions. He is uncomfortable with the notion that Scripture reveals the truth of God indirectly, obliquely, through images and similitudes, and in a manner constrained by its historical and cultural context. Augustine's hint that God communicates with us in a poetic mode and Blake's tenet that Jesus and the Apostles were artists would seem to conservative evangelicals to make divine revelation rest on the shifting sands of subjective, arrogant human subjectivity. A recent major study concludes that an obsession with factual accuracy, a penchant for

literal interpretation and a predictable tendency to arrive at maximally conservative conclusions – whatever arguments are considered along the way – mark (and mar) the conservative evangelical approach to biblical interpretation and serve to stake out common ground with fundamentalism.[358]

In fact, there is a danger wherein materialistic Westerners read literally things which were written symbolically. Classic examples from both ends of the Bible would be reading symbolic numbers in Revelation as literal numbers (such as the 1,000 years), and many aspects of the Adam and Eve story in Genesis 1 – 3. Walton, commenting on the symbolic nature of 'dust' and 'rib' in the composition of woman, writes:

> If the text chooses to use metaphorical symbols, it is free to do so, and we would be remiss to read them any other way.[359]

Parable is essential in making known divine mystery. Often times the limitations of language give us no choice.

Parable and metaphorical Christology

This brings us to an area of heated controversy today in contextualisation amongst Muslims, the issue of Christ as 'Son of God'. 'Son' is considered offensive to Muslims as it conjures up a biological even sexual trajectory, like the Greek and Roman gods who had sex and produced offspring. Because of this, in some newer, contextual, translations of the Bible, 'Son' is softened or replaced. For example, in the *Al Kalima* Arabic translation Matthew 28:19 becomes, 'Cleanse them by water in the name of Allah, his Messiah and his Holy Spirit.'

The debate is large and convoluted, but one of the key considerations is that 'Son' is used in many different ways in Scripture, some of which are strictly biological, others more metaphorical, and it is very difficult to know which is which.[360] 'Son' can mean *representative*, which is more metaphorical in meaning, or *offspring*, which has a strictly biological meaning. Certainly, it is OK and even prudent, when sharing the good news with people of Muslim faith, to focus on Jesus as a representative of God, the one who makes the invisible one visible,[361] rather than to argue endlessly about Jesus being God's son in a biological or literal sense. Why start your evangelistic relationship with a word that is so profoundly anathema and indigestible for your Muslim friend? To explain Jesus as the one who fulfils the Old Testament Messianic title 'Son' can be compelling.[362] To depict Jesus as the second Adam, who was called 'Son of God' in the sense of image-bearer and corporate head of the human race, can add clarification.[363] Even demonstrating that Jesus is God himself in the flesh can be clearer than trying to explain what is not meant by the word 'Son'.

The problem is that you cannot do this with Bible translation, because 'Son' is used in so many different ways, and it is difficult to discern when it is meant ontologically and when it is meant symbolically. Additionally, softening a potentially offensive phrase at the evangelistic interface is one thing, but the same Bible will then be used to build the Church and construct theology, hence Carson:

> Once Bible Translations are adopted, they become the standard for the rising Christian community that would then be saddled with translations that fail to preserve these biblical trajectories which make sense of the pattern of the New Testament use of the Old.[364]

What we must understand, however, is that Jesus was a metaphorical theologian, and taught much of his Christology through parable and metaphor. The 'I am' statements of John and many of Jesus' parables are reappropriations of Old Testament understandings of God, but with Jesus at the centre. All the way through the Old Testament the shepherd is God, so when Jesus says, 'I am the good shepherd',[365] he is claiming to be God, in a way that the Jews would have clearly understood.

We must pay close attention to Kenneth Bailey's prophetic insight:

> In the inevitable coming theological interface with Islam, *Christology from the mouth of Jesus* has the potential to bypass centuries-old roadblocks to understanding and authentically communicate afresh, without compromise of meaning, the biblical understanding of who Jesus affirmed himself to be.[366]

Conclusion: parables are powerful

The restaurant owner said to me, 'You are a Christian, aren't you?'

'Yes.'

'Tell me, we accept your prophet but you don't accept ours. Why is that?'

'Can I tell you a story? Jesus had just insulted the temple and the religious leaders were upset. They asked him, "Where do you get your authority from?" and he answered with this story…

'A man planted a vineyard with great care and love. Then he rented it to some men, but these tenants were dishonouring and arrogant. When harvest-time came, they did not pay their rent. The owner sent some messengers to ask for the rent. They beat them. He sent some more. They beat them worse. Then the owner was in a dilemma. "What shall I do? They have shamed me and made me look weak. They have claimed for themselves what is actually mine. They are acting like owners when in fact they are renters. What shall I do? I know, I will send my son. Maybe they will respect him." So he sent his son, unarmed and defenceless, to ask for the rent. They killed him. Jesus told this story one week before he was killed by the religious leaders.'

I turned to look the man in the eye.

'In the story, who do you think is the vineyard owner?'

'God, of course.'

'And the vineyard?'

'The world that he has made.'

'And the renters?'

'Mankind, who is ungrateful and does not give God the honour and worship he is due.'

'That is true. And who are the messengers?'

'The prophets, whom God sent to warn mankind.'

'Yes, my brother, I agree. And tell me, who then is the son?'

The man dropped his eyes, mumbled an excuse, and returned to the kitchen.

You see, this parable, like many of Jesus' parables, is small but powerful. It retells the story of the world, creation, Fall, the prophets and eventually the son. It shows Jesus' self-awareness as standing in the line of the prophets and yet superior to the prophets. It shows subtly why Christians cannot accept another prophet after Christ; prophet – prophet – prophet – Son. Another prophet would be an anti-climax. It speaks of the gracious choice of God to send his Son into a rebellious world. It calls for individual response to Christ. It does not offend, and yet it is filled with offence.

Parables are powerful. We must get better at understanding and teaching via metaphor, that the gospel may invade hearts and imaginations, bringing salvation to those with ears to hear.

Endnotes

342. Manson, T.W., *The Teaching of Jesus: Studies in its Form and Content* (Cambridge: University Press, 1935), 73.

343. Wright, N.T., *The New Testament and the People of God* (London: SPCK, 1992), 40.

344. Bailey, *Jesus Through Middle Eastern Eyes*, 280.

345. Cranfield, C.E.B., *The Gospel According to St. Mark* (Cambridge, UK: Cambridge University Press, 1959), 159, emphasis mine.

346. Barclay, William, *The Gospel of Mark* (Third Printing) (Edinburgh: St Andrew Press, 2009), 98.

347. Bailey, Kenneth E., *The Good Shepherd: A Thousand-Year Journey from Psalm 23 to the New Testament* (Downers Grove, IL: IVP, 2014), 272.

348. Barclay, *The Gospel of Mark*, 100.

349. Jeremiah 1:10, NIV.

350. Acts 16:14.

351. Cranfield, *The Gospel According to St. Mark*, 157.

352. Richard, Pablo, cited in Jenkins, *The New Faces of Christianity*, 151.

353. Cadoux, C.J., cited in Barclay, *The Gospel of Mark*, 102.

354. Gitari, David, *In Season and Out of Season* (Carlisle: Regnum, 1996), 111-114.

355. Wright, N.T., *Church, Media and Public Life in a Post-Rational World*. Notes to a speech delivered at the Church and Media Conference 2016. http://themedianet. org/professor-nt-wright-church-media-public-life-post-rational-world/ (accessed 9.10.17).

356. Dulles, Avery, *Models of the Church* (Garden City, NY: Doubleday, 1974), 7.

357. Ephesians 3:6.

358. Avis, Paul, *God and the Creative Imagination: Metaphor, Symbol and Myth in Religion and Theology* (London: Routledge, 1999), 4.

359. Walton, John H., *The Lost World of Adam and Eve: Genesis 2 – 3 and the Human Origins Debate* (Downers Grove, IL: IVP, 2015), 138.

360. Carson, D.A., *Jesus the Son of God: A Christological Title Often Overlooked,*

Sometimes Misunderstood, and Currently Disputed (Wheaton, IL: Crossway, 2012), Kindle loc. 1336.

361. John 14:9.

362. Psalm 2:12.

363. Genesis 5:1-3; Luke 3:38.

364. Carson, *Jesus the Son of God*, Kindle loc. 1336.

365. John 10:11,14.

366. Bailey, *The Good Shepherd*, 273, emphasis mine.

Chapter 21
Theology as a Verb

Theology should be taught as a verb and not as a noun. To theolog-ise. Especially cross-culturally. We must teach people *how* to think, not *what* to think. As my friend Andy Martin, when teaching cross-cultural hermeneutics says, 'Plant seeds, not trees.' Parratt writes: 'Theology should be done, not regurgitated.'[367]

By implication, this means that cross-cultural workers, in their training, should be taught to do theology, not just to know doctrine. For those reaching the unreached, there is likely no systematic compendium available in the context to which they are going, and very few available books or resources (even technical Christian vocabulary) in the local language. So there will be nothing to regurgitate; which is actually a good thing! The cross-cultural worker is thrown upon the Bible and the Spirit in his task of making disciples and planting churches.

Theology comes from the questions that are being asked. And different cultures are asking different questions. I remember the first man who came to faith in our church asking, 'If I become a Christian, where will you bury me?' To which I replied, 'In England we burn people!' – which didn't satisfy him; in the Middle East burial is important, but in many places there are no Christian graveyards! I have never sat in a class on burial ethics and had no box for this question!

Many of the questions that we are coming across in the Middle East have no obvious answer in theology grown in the West. So theology needs to be done in context. Mishcke, writing about the African context, makes the same point.

The truth is that Western models of theology are too small for Africa. Most of them reflect the world view of the Enlightenment, and that is a small-scale world view, one cut and shaved to fit a small-scale universe ... They have nothing useful to say on issues involving such things as witchcraft or sorcery, since these do not exist in an Enlightenment universe. Nor can Western theology usefully discuss ancestors, since the West does not have the family structures that raise the questions.[368]

Theology as reflection on the Scriptures in the light of what God is doing

At the end of John's Gospel, Peter and John at the empty tomb: 'saw and believed; for as yet they did not understand the Scripture, that he must rise from the dead.'[369]

Resurrection had not been in their world view. It was in the Scripture, but they had not seen it before. They saw the empty tomb and the risen Christ (experience), and then went back to reflect upon the Scripture with their lenses adjusted, and found something that had been there all along.

Similarly, later on the same day Thomas calls Jesus, 'My Lord and my God!'[370] No one has understood that Jesus is God yet, although he has been dropping hints that they would later understand. When Thomas sees the risen Christ, however, his Christology is changed.

In both these instances, something happens, the disciples then reflectively apply hindsight, and what they could not see earlier they are able to see now. John Wimber used to say, 'Experience changes theology.' His point was, if you are cessationist and then a miracle happens to you, then you will go back and look at the Scriptures through fresh eyes and see things that had previously been in your blind spot. Miracles were promised all along, you just didn't see them! Experience does not change the Scripture, but it changes the way we read the Scripture. That is why theology changes as cultures are crossed.

The classic New Testament example is Peter at Cornelius' house, in Acts 10. Many have called this story 'Peter's conversion', arguing that we need a similar conversion when crossing cultures. Until the vision of the sheet and then the outpouring of the Spirit on Cornelius' household,

Peter's prejudice was theologically embedded. In the lens with which he read the scripture, it would have been impossible for God to accept Gentiles as they were. It would have been *against* Scripture. It would have been *wrong*. So when the Spirit came indisputably and manifestly upon these Romans, Peter had a choice; either to deny the experience somehow, because it didn't fit his box, or to go back and look at the Scripture through the new lens of 'maybe God does accept Gentiles', and see if it had been there all along!

Dunn writes:

> The development of Christianity was shifted on to a new track by the manifest work of the Spirit. Christianity might have remained a Jewish messianic sect had it not been for the unexpected and Scripture-breaking, tradition-breaking initiative of the Spirit. The Spirit opened up a whole new vista for the first Christians, and they were brave and bold enough to follow where the Spirit showed the way.[371]

The Council of Jerusalem convened (Acts 15) in order to reflect on this question. New and unexpected things were happening, and this 'hermeneutic community' would now reflect on the Scripture in the light of these new developments – perhaps it was in the Scripture all along, but we could not see it!

In this context, James read from Amos 9:11-12, but from the Greek Septuagint translation, not from the Hebrew. The Hebrew version focused on the benefit to Israel, 'in order that they may possess the remnant of Edom …', so it is no wonder that the inclusion of Gentiles was obscured! The Septuagint, however, had a different nuance: 'in order that those remaining of humans and all the nations upon whom my name has been called might seek me out …' These translators had phrased the focus of this verse as benefit to the Gentiles.[372]

Remember the vital importance of the translatability of Christianity! A scripture that had been read thousands of times, read in a new context, studied in a different translation, in response to new questions being raised by the breakthrough of the Spirit, yields an answer to a question that had not been asked before. Theologising on mission should look something like this.

Culture is always changing, and with it theology changes; becomes more nuanced, answers questions which had not been raised previously. This is a gradual, and sometimes imperceptible process. But when there is a jump into a very different culture, there is something of an epistemological break, a more obvious and instantaneous disruption. This is what happened in Acts 10-11.

Study of the doctrine did not lead to the wider activity; enlarged activity led them to understand the doctrine.[373]

The account of Peter and Cornelius in Acts 10 is a powerful example of the way in which mission experience impacts biblical interpretation.[374]

The Bible is supposed to help us understand the way in which God works in the world, and reinterpretations in the light of Holy Spirit breakthrough are not disloyalty to Scripture, but rather loyalty to the living God.

Theology as art not science

If it is true that our cultural lenses make us less objective than we would like, and if it is true that the same Scriptures can be read over and over yet not understood because of blind spots, then it follows that we must be more humble about our theology. Which is the purpose of this book! Avis proposes that 'because the Church is not generally infallible, doctrines are not irreformable'.[375]

Biblical interpretation as a 'science' assumes that if we do certain things and apply certain principles, then we will discover the 'real' meaning of a text. And there is no doubt that some sciences have massively enhanced our understanding of the Scriptures: archaeology, the study of ancient languages, the study of history, to name but a few.

If, however, it is true that objectivity is limited because of our cultural biases, then it follows that biblical interpretation cannot, and never should have been, a science, because it cannot, and never should have been, objective.

The contrast between the West and the non-West is never between culture-free Christianity and culturally-embedded Christianity, but between varieties of culturally embedded Christianity.[376]

The best hermeneuts and the best historians are well aware of this. They are alert to many dimensions of bias and the endless (and therefore endlessly discussable) significance of their own horizons and presuppositions.[377]

In other words, an objective and universally applicable hermeneutic is itself a post-Enlightenment Western assumption. This isn't just a postmodern claim, let's be careful here. Postmodernism cannot accept just one meta-narrative. We believe there *is* one big story, one God, one Truth, one Gospel. But in a globalised world and a multicentric church we have to understand that there is not only one way of interpreting this one narrative. And to assume that one's hermeneutic is more objective than someone else's is to miss the point; perhaps interpretation is supposed to be more art than science. What if beauty had as much value in theology as logic? Surely the preference for one over the other is a cultural preference anyhow? Stone and Duke put it like this: 'Theological reflection is a creative, craft-like enterprise.'[378]

Shaw and Van Engen, thinking about the history of interpretative approaches with different cultural emphases, write:

As the church moves through history, it deepens its understanding of the Gospel. It does not rewrite or change the Scriptures, but it does deepen its understanding and interpretation of them. That means that what is true is not unchangeable. It can be true at that moment, in that historical context, yet be understood differently later. Without this kind of critical thinking about historical development, there can be no multicultural evangelism. Without the development of theology through history, there can be little communication from one era to another or from one culture to another.[379]

Even the great scholar N.T. Wright, reflecting on a generation of Pauline studies, albeit limited to the Anglophone world, makes explicit that the direction Pauline studies is taking, indeed needs to be taking, is more art, and less science, than had previously been thought.

> In that work, precisely because it is an art as well as a science, and because it exemplifies the point that ultimately the two need to be held together, we can no longer pretend to a detached, fly-on-the-wall 'objectivity'. At the very moment when we are most aware that the culture we are studying is significantly different from our own, we are also aware that we are still looking at it through our own eyes, and that the cultural spectacles we ourselves wear will have an effect on how we see the object, and how we then see differently those objects that are closer to home. It may be as well, therefore, to make all this more explicit.[380]

The hard science of interpretation is still there: texts, inscriptions, historical evidence, lexicography. We need the rich heritage of scholarship and are grateful to God for its existence. Equally, however, much scholarship, as we have seen above, humbly understands its limitations, its agenda-drivenness, the impossibility of impartiality. The holding up of hands and the voicing of this reality is true scholarship.

Theology as doing, not just knowing

James 1:22: But be doers of the word, and not hearers only, deceiving yourselves.
James 1:23: For if anyone is a hearer of the word and not a doer, he is like a man who looks intently at his natural face in a mirror.
James 1:24: For he looks at himself and goes away and at once forgets what he was like.
James 1:25: But the one who looks into the perfect law, the law of liberty, and perseveres, being no hearer who forgets but a doer who acts, he will be blessed in his doing.

Now, these verses from James tell us something more, that we are supposed to read the Scripture subjectively. That the Bible is a mirror in which we are supposed to see ourselves. That to examine the frame of the mirror – oh, how beautifully carved it is! – or the glass – oh, how smooth and clear! – without seeing our own reflection is entirely to miss the point.

> While reading God's Word you must incessantly say to yourself: It is I to whom it is speaking: it is I about whom it is speaking.[381]

Kierkegaard felt that not only is objective reading of Scripture impossible, it is undesirable. David Cain makes this comment of Kierkegaard's 'engaged hermeneutic'; '*How* one reads is decisive in determining *what* one reads.'[382]

> There is a temptation, both for scholars and those who read their books: the temptation to substitute study for faith and action.[383]

The advantage of teaching people to theologise, rather than importing theology, is that the very process of digging into the Scriptures prayerfully and with reference to the context in which one finds oneself precipitates action. It necessarily engages head, heart and hands. It necessarily puts us in the frame and commits us to what we are reading.

In 1976 a group of Third World theologians met at Dar es Salaam, Tanzania, and in their concluding statement wrote the following hard-hitting words:

> We reject as irrelevant an academic type of theology that is divorced from action. We are prepared for a radical break in epistemology which makes commitment the first act of theology and engages in critical reflection on praxis of the reality of the Third World.[384]

Knowing without doing is not really knowing!

This mini-metaphor, Bible as Mirror, proposes that if you do not apply, then you have not read properly. There should not be a large gap between what you know and how you live. If that gap is growing, stop reading and start doing.

I wonder if the person who knows one verse will be judged on what they did with that one verse, and the person who has read 1,000 books will be judged accordingly. It is, after all, Jesus the Judge who declared, 'Everyone to whom much was given, of him much will be required.' [385]

Finally, let's just enjoy for a moment the word 'Gaze; in verse 25 of James 1. *Parakupto* means to bend over, to stoop down and peer within.

We meet this same word in John 20:11. Mary, weeping, leans over to peer into the empty tomb. She is hopeless, bereft, and as she looks within, wonder and amazement begin to dawn. Could it be?

We find this word again in 1 Peter 1:12. Angels stoop down to look at the Church in wonder. The promised heirs, God's great plan, these frail people? Could it be?

That's how we should look in the mirror. As a weeping woman gazes into an empty tomb. As angels gaze at us. Could it be?

That's how we should read the Bible. With humility. With hope. With wonder. With head and heart and hands. The blessing in verse 25 is on your doing, not on your reading. Keep the gap small between what you know and what you do. Don't read anything else today until you have done what you last read. Don't forget who you are!

The book of James makes this connection between orthodoxy (right belief) and orthopraxy (right action) more explicitly than any other New Testament document. Isn't it interesting how James is well-loved in the Global South, while under-appreciated in the North? In the West we can have a disconnect between knowing and doing, and on this subject at least we need to learn from our brothers and sisters in other places!

Endnotes

367. Parratt, *A Guide to Doing Theology*, 95.

368. Mischke, *The Global Gospel*, Kindle loc. 911.

369. John 20:8-9.

370. John 20:28.

371. Dunn, James D.G., *Jesus, Paul and the Gospels* (Grand Rapids, MI: Eerdmans, 2011), 159.

372. Law, Timothy Michael, *When God Spoke Greek: The Septuagint and the Making of the Christian Bible* (New York: Oxford University Press, 2013), Kindle loc. 2004.

373. Allen, *The Ministry of the Spirit*, Kindle loc. 1214

374. Redford, Shawn B., *Missiological Hermeneutics: Biblical Interpretation for the Global Church* (American Society of Missiology Monograph Series) (Eugene, OR: Pickwick, 2012), 237.

375. Avis, *God and the Creative Imagination*, 6.

376. Mark Knoll, cited by Andy Martin, Middle East Bible School 2016.

377. Ford, David, *Theology: A Very Short Introduction* (New York: Oxford University Press, 1999), 154.

378. Stone, Howard W. and Duke, James O., *How to Think Theologically* (Minneapolis, MN: Fortress Press, 1996), 63.

379. Shaw and Van Engen, *Communicating God's Word in a Complex World*, 61.

380. Wright, *Paul and His Recent Interpreters*, 285.

381. Kierkegaard, S., *For Self-Examination; Judge for Yourself!* Kierkegaard's Writings 21 (Ed. and trans. Hong, H.V. and E.H.) (Princeton, NJ: Princeton University Press, 1990), 43-44.

382. Cain, D., "'Death Comes In Between": Reflections on Kierkegaard's For Self-Examination', *Kierkegaardiana* 15 (1991), 71.

383. Bauckham, Richard, James: *Wisdom of James, Disciple of Jesus the Sage (New Testament Readings)* (London: Taylor & Francis, 1999), 5.

384. Bevans, Stephen B., *Models of Contextual Theology, Revised and Expanded Edition* (Maryknoll, NY: Orbis, 2008), 73.

385. Luke 12:48.

Chapter 22
De-Westernising Your Eschatology

One of the surprises that confronts Christians when they cross cultures is in the area of eschatology. Many get into missions because of a desire to 'speed the Lord's coming', or to tick off one more unreached people group from a decreasing list. There can often be a hope for the 'gradual Christianisation' of the world, colouring in one more Christian country on the map. Or sometimes Christians have a 'rescue as many souls as possible' view; the time is short so let's get as many souls off this sinking planet into heaven as we can!

How we see the story of the world has a massive impact on world view; in fact, world view is a story within which we live and through which we define everything. When we cross cultures, either through encountering different world views, or through experiencing setbacks and disappointments, our eschatology begins to become unstuck. We realise that like so many other aspects of our understanding, our eschatological expectation is culturally embedded and must be de-Westernised. Firstly, if we are going to understand for ourselves, and secondly, if we are going to teach others.

The dogma of progress

Lesslie Newbigin, in *Signs Amid the Rubble*, came back from India arguing that what most Western Christians believe resembles Hegel-Marx-Darwin (i.e. that history is *developmental*) much more than it does the Scripture. We do not interrogate, but assume the baseline 'dogma of progress', which then becomes the lens through which we read Scripture.[386]

So we love scriptures that affirm this world view, such as:

Matthew 24:14: And this gospel of the *kingdom* will be proclaimed throughout the whole world as a testimony to all nations, and then the end will come.[387]

– a verse which we often read progressively or developmentally, and we struggle with scriptures such as:

Matthew 24:9: Then they will deliver you up to *tribulation* and put you to death, and you will be hated by all nations for my name's sake.[388]

– which comes only a few verses earlier!

Presumably, Christians in Mosul, Iraq would more readily relate to verse 9 than verse 14. The cathedral in Mosul recently (due to ISIS) had to stop celebrating Mass which it had celebrated virtually every Sunday for the last 1,800 years. In their eyes, Christianity is not a growing influence in the world, but a declining one. Remember, where Christianity in some nations is moving towards summer, in others it is moving into winter.[389]

Old Testament prophecy anticipated two distinct promised figures who seemed mutually exclusive. There was Messiah, an anointed, powerful king like David who would extend his rule and make his enemies a footstool for his feet. And there was Isaiah's 'suffering servant', who would experience pain and rejection. These two figures are never linked in the Old Testament; indeed, they could not be. A suffering servant could never gain a following, and a powerful Messiah could not be killed. Only at the baptism of Jesus are these two connected by the heavenly voice, 'You are my beloved Son' (referencing Psalm 2, a Messianic psalm), 'with you I am well pleased' (from Isaiah 42, one of the 'suffering servant songs').[390]

We know that through the cross, Jesus is both Victorious King and Suffering Servant. That his victory is through suffering. Yet somehow, when we come to eschatology, we tend to de-couple these two again, with our focus being either on victory (Matthew 24:14) or on difficulty (Matthew 24:9). With Jesus, it is always both!

I was once in some meetings with Eddie Leo, a church leader from Indonesia. He was telling stories from his nation, showing photos on the projector. Some stories were amazing: deliverance, raising of the dead, whole village conversions. Other stories were devastating: martyrdoms, imprisonment, pain. All accompanied by graphic photos! It was at once stomach-churning and exhilarating. Yet the point was clear: where the kingdom is coming, good stories get more good and bad stories get more bad.

In Revelation 1:9 we see both.

Revelation 1:9: I, John, your brother and partner in the *tribulation* and the *kingdom* and the *patient endurance* that are in Jesus, was on the island called Patmos on account of the word of God and the testimony of Jesus.[391]

According to this verse we are, and have been for 2,000 years, 'in the kingdom' of Matthew 24:14. We are, and have been for 2,000 years, 'in the tribulation' of Matthew 24:9. The kingdom is now and the tribulation is now. Therefore, what is demanded is 'patient endurance'.

When we view the kingdom of God as a Hollywood movie or the American dream – a humble beginning, a struggle, gradual growth, then worldwide success – what are we missing? Is that really the story that Jesus and the apostles were telling?

Many Bible stories repeatedly resolve and then unresolve again: just follow Jacob's life, or the book of Judges. Walking with God often more resembles a Turkish soap opera than a Hollywood movie. Lesslie Newbigin:

History is a growth of good and evil side-by-side, a real growth of good – a real attainment of progressively higher goods, but along with this an equally real growth of evil – a growth in the power and range of evil forces.[392]

David Devenish, teaching on the parable of the wheat and the tares (Matthew 13:24-30), agreed with Newbigin: 'Good and evil will grow side by side in the field of the world.'[393] If there is any development chronologically, it is that both wheat and tares are growing! N.T. Wright:

All time since the resurrection of Jesus is 'messianic time'. Might that not raise other disturbing questions, either about the two thousand years which have rolled along since then, or about the elevation of events in eighteenth-century Europe (and America?) to the status of a messianic moment? Might a grandiose and self-congratulatory reading of the Enlightenment not be part of the problem, part of the pride which Paul's gospel would undermine?[394]

Context is key

Eschatology is often defined in terms of a spectrum. Between 'now' and 'not yet'. Between the new creation being 'continuous' or 'discontinuous' with this life. Between 'resisting' this present age or 'transforming' it. Or, as I have suggested above, between 'victory' and 'suffering'. The problem is that different parts of the New Testament emphasise different points on these spectra according to context. Context, as ever, is key!

The apostle Paul raises different emphases according to the needs of the churches to which he is writing. In 1 Thessalonians his eschatology is very 'not yet'; they need to hear that they are still awaiting the Day of the Lord.[395] In Galatians, however, Paul's eschatology is very 'realised'. The whole emphasis of this letter is that ethnic boundary markers like circumcision are no longer needed because new creation has come![396] His eschatology is not inconsistent, he is merely bringing different emphases into different contexts where needed to correct and encourage.[397]

Different apostles, writing into different contexts and at different times, also bring different emphases. Try reconciling Romans 13 with Revelation 13. In Romans 13, Paul is encouraging Christians to submit to the Roman authorities, whilst in Revelation 13, John is calling Rome demonic and urging believers not to bow down to her!

If New Testament eschatology presents different emphases according to context, then it is unsurprising that different believers at different times and in different places have seen these emphases... you guessed it... differently. That is why it is so important to de-Westernise one's eschatology as part of the cross-cultural journey. Your new context will demand a new emphasis. In fact, eschatology is one area where Western Evangelicals tend to hold an anti-logical, 'both-and' perspective. The kingdom is 'now' and 'not yet'. Praise God, we are happy, it seems, in this area of thinking to throw out the law of contradiction and, more like Easterners, to hold two mutually exclusive truths together.

Redefining terms

When we cross cultures we take on the local words for most eschatological terms: 'heaven', 'hell' and 'salvation' for starters! If adopting these words, we must understand that they come pre-packaged with meaning, and not necessarily meaning that we would choose. Refilling terms with biblical (not Western) meaning is a key part of the task of missions.

Jesus often did this in dialogue. If he found the terms of the question inadequate, he would rephrase it as part of his answer. In Matthew 19:16 he is asked '… what good deed must I do to have eternal life?' 'Eternal life' is quite an escapist phrase; 'pie in the sky when you die', and as Jesus answers he replaces it with various terms which he prefers.

First, he says, 'If you would enter life' (19:17). Then, 'If you would be perfect' (19:21). He speaks of entering the 'kingdom of heaven' (19:23) and entering the 'kingdom of God' (19:24). Finally, he speaks of a 'new world', or 'new genesis' (19:28).[398] He is redefining expectation of what 'eternal life' means.

The general Muslim conception of salvation is escapist. Death leads to a new life in a heavenly paradise. I have found it necessary to speak constantly of our hope as life with Christ in the renewed heavens and the renewed earth. I would say this in almost every sermon or conversation. I want to emphasise the 'continuous' nature of new life, because the 'discontinuous' aspect is assumed anyway.

Imagine a narrow path with a ditch on each side. If someone is walking too far on the left, we will call them to veer right. If they are too far right, to veer left. Handling eschatology cross-culturally is like this.

The New Testament presents eschatology as spectra between various positions for precisely this reason; we teach the whole council of God, but we adjust the emphasis viz-a-viz the context we are in. The story of Christ ought to bring correction to the baseline narrative of whichever culture we are addressing.

The book of Revelation

One of the reasons that Westerners can misrepresent eschatology is because they misunderstand Revelation. 'Many of us would rather look away and pretend as if the apocalyptic Jesus never existed.'[399]

The Reformers did not love this book. Calvin wrote a commentary on every book of the Bible except Revelation, and when asked why reportedly answered, 'Because I don't understand it.' Luther, famously, said, 'Everyone imparts to this book what his own spirit desires.'

If we are honest, Western culture is not best positioned to interpret or appreciate apocalyptic literature. Revelation's symbols appeal more to imaginative cultures than analytical ones. We struggle with the symbolic, rather than literal, portrayal of reality. Our Western understanding of time makes us want to force Revelation into a sequence whilst its view is more like several CCTV cameras all viewing the same events from various perspectives, and our lack of experience of persecution virtually closes the genre to us, as apocalyptic literature has always been the language of persecuted minorities.

Apocalyptic literature is more for feeling than for understanding cerebrally. P. Claude once said that our primary concern should not be to understand the book of Revelation but rather to walk inside it like one would walk in a cathedral and fall on one's knees in awe and wonder and worship God.[400]

Revelation is understandable, but to read it right requires all your senses: read this book looking out for smells and sounds and tastes and colours and its impact on you will be much greater! Reading passages from Revelation out loud in high-context congregations I have seen people shudder, even weep, because of the way the scenes wrap around you, engaging all the senses. Even in the UK, I have seen that preaching passages from Revelation interactively, with the congregation reading aloud, the elders falling face down, and so on, can have enormous dramatic effect. Revelation is supposed to be more felt than analysed, and must be allowed to exercise its power in this way.

Eurocentrism is rarely more evident in Bible interpretation than in the history of the interpretation of Revelation. Beale writes in the introduction to his monumental commentary on Revelation, 'The historicist view … limits the prophecies of the Apocalypse to Western church history, leaving aside the worldwide church.'[401] Historicist interpreters generally see Revelation as predicting the major movements of Christian history up to their own time.

And so, just as history and geography are always read ethnocentrically,[402] so then is this book!

And yet, the Global South loves the book of Revelation! Fidon Mwombeki, the Tanzanian Lutheran leader, writes of Africans loving Revelation for these reasons: the dead are still living in the other world and influencing this world; visions, dreams and revelations; the Lamb, the throne, blood and animals are common in African religious symbolism; sacrificial blood and blood crying out from the ground correspond to present-day African beliefs.[403] An African reading Revelation feels at home in its symbolic world! The Chinese Church also loves Revelation:

> The theology of the Lamb as One who suffers and the One who controls history speaks to the Chinese Christians as the assured victory of the faithful despite the apparent domination of the evil power. It is the hope portrayed in the Book of Revelation that sustains Chinese Christians to endure to the end.[404]

If we are struggling to accept that 'our way' of reading the Bible could be inadequate, wrestling with the idea of 'theological humility' as presented in these chapters, at the very least the book of Revelation, and the area of eschatology more generally, should cause us to throw up our hands and say, 'Please help me understand this!' Revelation is more about feeling than thinking, so why can't we expect more 'feeling' cultures to teach us how to read this book? We all need a witness from outside ourselves to help us overcome our blind spots. Developing humility should help us to reach out, explore other points of view, travel to learn not just to teach, even to ask for help.

Theological humility tells us that what we don't know is much greater than what we do know. And stirs us to press on to know more.

Endnotes

386. Newbigin, *Signs Amid the Rubble*, 11.
387. Emphasis mine.
388. Emphasis mine.
389. Chapter 6.

390. Mark 1:11.

391. Emphasis mine.

392. Newbigin, *Signs Amid the Rubble*, 44.

393. Devenish, David (Catalyst Festival 2015 Main Session).

394. Wright, *Paul and His Recent Interpreters*, 321.

395. 1 Thessalonians 4:13 – 5:11.

396. Galatians 5:1-13; 6:12-15.

397. Flemming, *Contextualization in the New Testament*, 115.

398. Goldsmith, Martyn, *Matthew & Mission: The Gospel Through Jewish Eyes* (Carlisle: Paternoster, 2001), 146.

399. Capes, David B., Reeves, Rodney and Richards, E. Randolph, *Rediscovering Jesus: An Introduction to Biblical, Religious and Cultural Perspectives on Christ* (Downers Grove, IL: IVP, 2015), 139.

400. Claude, P., *Ouvres Completes*, vol. 26, 1965 (Paris Editions Gallimard, 1955-65), 11-12.

401. Beale, G.K., *The Book of Revelation* (The New International Greek Testament Commentary) (Grand Rapids, MI: Eerdmans, 1999), 46.

402. Chapter Six: Whose Story?

403. Mwombeki, Fidon R., 'The Book of Revelation in Africa', *Word and World* 15, No. 2 (1995), 145-50.

404. Khiok-khng, Yeo, *What Has Jerusalem to Do with Beijing? Biblical Interpretation from a Chinese Perspective* (Harrisburg, PA: Trinity Press International, 1998), 234.

Chapter 23
Apostolic Plurality

The move to understand all theology as contextual is also a move to recognise the complex reality of theological pluralism.
Stephen Bevans[405]

Does contextual theology mean that there must be plurality of meaning? If an Indian reads a verse one way, and an Inuit reads it another way, because of cultural lenses affecting their reading, who is right? Who is wrong? And how can these be reconciled? How different should a Middle Eastern theology be from a North American theology? I know this is a mind-boggling question, but we have to have the courage to ask it.

Evangelicals tend to think of there being only one orthodoxy (their own), which means that a 'fresh' reading of Scripture must either inform and change the centre, or else fall down under scrutiny. What cannot be acceptable, it is argued, is for a verse to mean different things in different places. Surely the author could only have meant one thing when he wrote the verse, so there must be one meaning, and therefore one theology.

A contextual reading of Scripture that has been in vogue in recent years comes from the late Kenneth Bailey. Kenneth was a friend of my parents and I grew up listening to him teach on summer retreats for missionaries in the mountains of Cyprus. After a formidable forty years in the Middle East, grasp of half a dozen languages (including the biblical ones), and access to early Arabic and Syriac translations of and commentaries on the Scriptures, Dr Bailey was able to speak back to the 'centre' of Evangelicalism in a way that meets the necessary criteria for scholarly rigour. His work on Luke 15, for example, has in turn affected 'centre' men like Timothy Keller[406] and, it could be argued, has changed the perspective within Evangelical Christianity on the parable of the prodigal son. The margins have, in some small way, changed the centre. Bailey has helped Westerners see Jesus 'through Middle Eastern eyes'. Many would be happy with this model of contextual theology – a passage can only mean one thing, and so a fresh reading in a new context helps to shape and inform what this one meaning is.

But what about all the things that people in non-Western, non-academic contexts see in Scripture that never gain acceptance at the centre? Because they are not published in English. Because they do not meet the standards of rigour in the twenty-first century. We are forced back to the question of plurality of meaning.

Orthodoxy cannot be intrinsically unitary. Christianity is so diverse! Must we really believe that of all the positions on a certain issue within the massive 'movement of movements' that is global Christianity,[407] we are right and everyone else is wrong? The sad thing is, many think exactly that.

Interpretive plurality

Augustine lived in a world (much like ours) where the rapid spread of Christianity had led to many divergent, contextual readings of Scripture. He wrote in the *Confessions*:

> Accordingly, when anyone claims 'Moses meant what I say', and another retorts, 'No, rather what I find there', I think that I will be answering in a more religious spirit if I say, 'Why not both, if both are true?' And if there is a third possibility, and a fourth, and of someone else sees an entirely different meaning in these words, why should we not think that he was aware of all of them?[408]

Augustine was comfortable with a degree of plurality of interpretation. His contemporary, Ephrem the Syrian, rather more poetically, expresses a similar perspective.

> Anyone who encounters Scripture should not suppose that the single one of its riches that he has found is the only one to exist, rather he should realise that he himself is only capable of discovering that one

out of the many riches which exist in it ... A thirsty person rejoices because he has drunk: he is not grieved because he proved incapable of drinking the fountain dry.[409]

These Church fathers at the end of the fourth century were working out what it meant for interpreters to live as part of a multicentric religion, in a way that we are beginning to grapple with again in the twenty-first. I wonder if the fascination with singularity of meaning is a 'distinctly modern anxiety'.[410]

Apostolic plurality

Even the writers of the New Testament did not always agree with each other! Famously, the difference between Paul and James on justification by faith has used up a lot of ink over the years. Do they contradict each other? Was James writing to get back at Paul for his anti-law stance? Surely only one of them can be right? But which one?

Those with Western-type, systematic brains feel the need to systematise or homogenise the teaching of Scripture, meaning that one perspective gets prioritised, and others marginalised. There has been a long tradition of attempts to harmonise the four Gospels, which is done by prioritising the schema or chronology of one and relegating the others. But why did the Holy Spirit inspire four perspectives and not just one? To understand the Gospels, we must allow each to speak with its own voice. Instead of the differences between the Gospels being an embarrassment, we affirm the fact that 'the four gospels are four "contextualisations" of the one story [and] form an important piece of the total picture of how the Christian message is re-expressed for new audiences in the New Testament'.[411]

The challenge in the Paul-James debate is that so often priority is given to Paul, perhaps due to canonical order, perhaps due to volume, perhaps because our Western minds understand Paul's rhetoric but struggle with James' aphoristic style. So James only gets interpreted in the light of Paul, rather than being allowed to speak in his own voice. Luke Timothy Johnson, quite strongly, on the fact that most commentary on James is taken up with 2:17 in reference to Paul, writes:

Although it is a historical fallacy of the plainest sort to infer from Paul's canonical importance data relevant to his historical importance, scholars continue to read whatever is different from Paul with reference to Paul, rather than allow it to stand as simply different.[412]

Richard Bauckham, after a persuasive discussion of James and Paul, arrives at a conclusion which is relevant to our discussion here.

We can speak of 'apostolic pluralism' in the canon, provided the term 'apostolic' carries its Irenaean and canonical sense of fundamental agreement in a common message.[413]

James' context was different to Paul's. He was in a different place, writing to different people, answering different questions, dealing with different concerns, in a different style. A study of the theology of James in its own right is what yields fruit. A comparison of James with Paul brings us, as it did Luther, unfortunately to have to relegate one to semi-canonical status. European Protestants have struggled with James ever since Luther. Yet in many parts of the Global South it is one of the best-loved, best-understood New Testament books.[414] Why? Because James speaks to different questions, questions that many in the Global South are asking today!

Do you see why it is important, in a global world, to talk about the difficult issue of plurality of meaning? It doesn't make us liberal, or postmodern, but rather humble.

In another place, Bauckham expands this idea of 'apostolic pluralism'. Just because we are talking about 'particular meaning' this is not a postmodern denial of 'universal meaning'.

The particular has its own integrity that should not be suppressed for the sake of a too readily comprehensible universal. The Bible does, in some sense, tell an overall story that encompasses all its other contents, but this story is not a sort of straitjacket that reduces all else to a narrowly defined uniformity. It is a story that is hospitable to considerable diversity.[415]

The call to embrace plurality in this chapter comes from an observation that Western Evangelical missionaries on the whole can be too inflexible. Hence this emphasis. If this is not your context, and pluralism is rife where you are, then perhaps you need to veer the other way, towards what Bauckham calls above an 'Irenaen and canonical sense of fundamental agreement in a common message'.

We accept that there are many millions across the world reading the same Scriptures and arriving at different conclusions. We desire to engage in robust theological debate (like Paul and James did), but are happy to conclude that different apostolic spheres require different approaches. We are humble towards scholarship, towards catholic and orthodox (small c, small o) tradition, towards historic interpretation. But we are also aware that culture plays a role in interpretation. That no one theology is truly objective. That Christianity is multicentric. That local elderships and not external hierarchies are responsible for doctrine in local churches. That different people's thought processes work in different ways. That many in the world would have no problem saying, like the infuriating Nasreddin Hodja in the anecdotal story in Chapter Eleven, 'You are right. You are also right,' to two seemingly mutually exclusive positions. Raimon Pannikar, for example, maintains that Indians cannot really accept the principle that might be called the backbone of Western philosophical thinking, the principle of contradiction. For Indians, Pannikar insists, things can indeed be and not be at the same time.[416]

Newbigin, writing about the plurality of Christology in the New Testament, can answer this more densely and eloquently than I.

It is important for a faithful doing of Christian theology that we should affirm and insist that the New Testament contains not one Christology but several. This is not an unfortunate defect to be regretted or concealed. It is, on the contrary, of the essence of the matter because it will make clear the fact that Christology is always to be done *in via*, at the interface between the gospel and the cultures that it meets on its missionary journey … The variety of Christologies actually to be found in the New Testament is part of the fundamental witness to the nature of the gospel; it points to the destination of the gospel in all the cultures of mankind.[417]

Ability to handle an apostolic plurality is requisite for individuals going across cultures. Instead of black and white, right and wrong, in and out, it will enable the practitioner to handle different, even divergent or seemingly contradictory truths. Without this ability, individuals will either mindlessly condemn, or else have the bottom fall out of their faith.

Ability to handle an apostolic diversity is also vital for movements seeking to plant churches in other nations. There is every possibility that the church planted in a new context will come up with new readings, new perspectives... new theology. At least, if it is planted with the goal of indigenisation, release not control, seeking to raise sons not slaves, converts not proselytes. A global movement that has the breadth and courage to handle differences of interpretation and contextual variants, to trust the Holy Spirit, even actively to encourage local expression, is a movement that understands the truly contextual nature of revelation that is unique to Christianity's claims.

Apostolic spheres

Within Newfrontiers, this is being worked out based upon the biblical concept of 'apostolic spheres'. The Greek word *kanon* from which this language derives appears three times within 2 Corinthians 10:13-16 and is variously translated as 'sphere' (NASB, NEB), 'area of influence' (ESV), 'rule' (KJV), 'line of duty' and 'sphere of action' (JBP), and 'field', 'area of activity' and 'territory' in the NIV.

> The idea is clear: Paul and his team (note the plural 'us' in these verses) had been assigned a sphere for apostolic ministry which consisted of the churches they had planted ... the biblical concept for these new groups of churches would be 'apostolic spheres' or 'apostolic fields.'[418]

There were different apostolic spheres of churches within the first century, and each approached cultural contextualisation in different ways, with different emphases. This explains the differences between the Gospels, or between Paul and James and Peter. This is never outside of fundamental agreement in a common message, the treasures of Church history and scholarship, and ongoing lively, robust, loving debate. Within Newfrontiers, apostolic leaders of the various spheres meet regularly to debate issues and to learn from one another. It is still too early to say how diverse the movement will end up becoming, but the current trajectory suggests that this way of working is a flexible and expansive wineskin allowing each sphere to contextualise in its own way depending upon its own cultural contexts.

> A plurality of cultures presupposes a plurality of theologies and therefore, for Third-World churches, a farewell to a Eurocentric approach. The Christian faith must be rethought, reformulated and lived anew in each human culture, and this must be done in a vital way, in depth and right to the culture's roots.[419]

Friends, mission is full of surprises. The world is full of beauty, but it is also fallen. Sin has wreaked havoc and humankind is enslaved. The calling of Abraham and Israel, fulfilled and perfected in the advent of Jesus Christ, teaches us that God loves to take the universal and make it particular, to ground the global in the local, to redeem from within not impose from without, to identity and empathise and suffer alongside. As the new creation is both *apocalyptic* – breaking in upon history in Christ's resurrection from the dead – and *continuous* with and within the old creation – the kingdom is now and not yet – so too when we carry the gospel to a previously unreached people. There is a breaking-in, a work of the Spirit, a sovereign salvation *from above*. But there is also an incarnation, an embodiment, a salvation *from amongst*. The story of cross-cultural mission is a story of considered, strategic sacrifice, of immersion and anonymity and success-less-ness. It is the story of the Spirit's leading and the Church's obedience. It is a story that is still being written…

Endnotes

405. Bevans, *Models of Contextual Theology*, 140.
406. Keller, Timothy, *The Prodigal God: Rediscovering the Heart of the Christian Faith* (London: Hodder & Stoughton, 2000), 136.
407. Addison, *Movements That Change the World*, Kindle loc. 254.
408. Augustine, *Confessions* 12.31.42.

409. Ephrem, *Commentary on the Diatesseron*, 1.18-19

410. Law, *When God Spoke Greek*, 168.

411. Flemming, *Contextualization in the New Testament*, 235.

412. Johnson, Luke Timothy, *Brother of Jesus, Friend of God: Studies in the Letter of James* (Grand Rapids, MI: Eerdmans, 2004), Kindle loc. 1924.

413. Bauckham, James, 144.

414. Jenkins, *New Faces of Christianity*, 60.

415. Bauckham, Richard, *Bible and Mission: Christian Witness in a Postmodern World* (Paternoster, Milton Keynes: 2003), 93.

416. Bevans, *Models of Contextual Theology*, 10.

417. Newbigin, Lesslie, *The Open Secret: An Introduction to the Theology of Mission*, Revised Edition (Grand Rapids: Eerdmans, 1995), 156.

418. Devenish, *Fathering Leaders, Motivating Mission*, 197-198.

419. Bosch, *Transforming Mission*, 452.

Bibliography

Achebe, Chinua, *Hopes and Impediments: Selected Essays*, New York: Doubleday, Anchor 1989.

Addison, S., *Movements That Change the World*, Smyrna, DE: Missional Press, 2009.

Adeney, Bernard T., *Strange Virtues: Ethics in a Multicultural World*, Leicester: Apollos, 1995.

Allen, Roland, *The Ministry of the Spirit: Selected Writings*, David M. Paton (ed.), Cambridge, UK: Lutterworth Press, 2011.

Allen, Roland, *Missionary Methods: St. Paul's or Ours?*, Cambridge, UK: Lutterworth Press, 2006, Kindle.

Alter, Robert, *The Art of Biblical Narrative*, New York: Basic Books, 1981.

Ande Georges, Titre, *Leadership and Authority: Bula Matari and Life-Community Ecclesiology in Congo*, Oxford: Regnum Books International, 2010.

Anderson, Bernhard W., *From Creation to New Creation: Old Testament Perspectives*, Minneapolis, MN: Fortress Press, 1994.

Anderson, Courtney, *To the Golden Shore: The Life of Adoniram Judson*, Prussia, PA: The Judson Press, 1987.

Ansaray, Tamim, *Destiny Disrupted: A History of the World through Islamic Eyes* (New York: PublicAffairs, 2009.

Arnold, Bill T., *Genesis (The New Cambridge Bible Commentary)*, Cambridge, UK: Cambridge University Press, 2009.

Asad, Talal, *Formations of the Secular: Christianity, Islam, Modernity*, Redwood City, CA: Stanford University Press, 2003.

Aulen, Gustav, *Christus Victor: An Historical Study of the Three Main Types of the Idea of Atonement*, London: SPCK, reissued 2010.

Avis, Paul, *God and the Creative Imagination: Metaphor, Symbol and Myth in Religion and Theology*, London: Routledge, 1999.

Bailey, Kenneth E., *Jesus Through Middle Eastern Eyes: Cultural Studies in the Gospels*, London: SPCK, 2008.

Bailey, Kenneth E., *The Good Shepherd: A Thousand-Year Journey from Psalm 23 to the New Testament*, Downers Grove, IL: IVP, 2014.

Barclay, William, *The Gospel of Mark (Third Printing)*, Edinburgh: St Andrew Press, 2009.

Barr, James, *A Line in the Sand: Britain, France and the Struggle that Shaped the Middle East*, London: Simon & Schuster, 2001.

Bartholomew, Craig, Greene, Colin J. D. and Möller, Karl (eds.), *After Pentecost: Language and Biblical Interpretation*, Carlisle: Paternoster Press, 2001.

Bauckham, Richard, *Bible and Mission: Christian Witness in a Postmodern World*, Milton Keynes: Paternoster, 2003.

Bauckham, Richard, *Gospel of Glory: Major Themes in Johannine Theology*, Grand Rapids, MI: Baker Academic, 2015.

Bauckham, Richard, James: *Wisdom of James, Disciple of Jesus the Sage (New Testament Readings)*, London: Taylor & Francis, 1999.

Beale, G.K., *The Book of Revelation (The New International Greek Testament Commentary)*, Grand Rapids, MI: Eerdmans, 1999.

Benge, Janet and Geoff, *Samuel Zwemer: The Burden of Arabia (Christian Heroes: Then and Now)*, Seattle, WA: YWAM Publishing, 2013

Bevans, Stephen B., *Models of Contextual Theology, Revised and Expanded Edition*, Maryknoll, NY: Orbis, 2008.

Boman, Thorleif, *Hebrew Thought Compared with Greek*, London: Norton, 1970.

Bonino, Jose Miguez, 'Genesis 11:1-9: A Latin American Perspective', Levison, John R. and Pope-Levison, Priscilla (eds.), *Return to Babel: Global Perspectives on the Bible*, Louisville, KY: Westminster John Knox Press, 1999.

Bosch, D.J., *Transforming Mission: Paradigm Shifts in Theology of Mission*, Revised Edition, Maryknoll, NY: Orbis, 2011.

Bosch, David J., 'Reflections on Biblical Models of Mission', in Gallagher, Robert L. and Hertig, Paul (eds.), *Landmark Essays in Mission and World Christianity*, Maryknoll, NY: Orbis Books, 2009.

Bruce, F.F., *Paul: Apostle of the Heart Set Free*, Grand Rapids, MI: Eerdmans, 1977.

Brueggemann, Walter, *Genesis: Interpretation, A Bible Commentary for Teaching and Preaching*, Atlanta, GA: John Knox Press, 1982.

Caiger, Stephen L., *Lives of the Prophets: A Thousand Years of Hebrew Prophecy Reviewed in its Historical Context*, London: SPCK 1949.

Cain, D., '"Death Comes In Between": Reflections on Kierkegaard's For Self-Examination', *Kierkegaardiana* 15 (1991), 69–81.

Cain, Susan, *Quiet: The Power of Introverts in a World that Can't Stop Talking*, London: Penguin Books, 2013.

Capes, David B., Reeves, Rodney and Richards, E. Randolph, *Rediscovering Jesus: An Introduction to Biblical, Religious and Cultural Perspectives on Christ*, Downers Grove, IL: IVP, 2015.

Carson, D.A., *Jesus the Son of God: A Christological Title Often Overlooked, Sometimes Misunderstood, and Currently Disputed*, Wheaton, IL: Crossway, 2012.

Carson, D.A., *The Gospel According to John* (Pillar New Testament Commentary), Leicester: Apollos, 1991.

Carson, D.A., France, R.T., Motyer, J.A. and Wenham, G.J. (eds.), *New Bible Commentary, Fourth Edition*, Nottingham: IVP, 1994.

Chester, Tim, *A Meal with Jesus: Discovering Grace, Community and Mission Around the Table*, Kindle Edition, UK: IVP, 2013.

Church, Rev. Leslie F. (ed.), *Matthew Henry's Commentary in One Volume*, (Grand Rapids, MI: Zondervan, 1960.

Churchill, Winston S., *Painting as a Pastime*, Electronic Edition, New York: RosettaBooks, 2014.

Ciampa, Roy, E. and Rosner, Brian S., *The First Letter to the Corinthians*, Grand Rapids: Eerdmans, 2010.

Claude, P., *Ouvres Completes*, vol. 26, 1965, Paris Editions Gallimard, 1955-65.

Clements, E.A. *Mothers on the Margin? The Significance of the Women in Matthew's Genealogy*, Eugene, OR: Pickwick Publications, 2014.

Commission on World Mission and Evangelism, *Together Towards Life: Mission and Evangelism in Changing Landscapes*, 2012.

Cozens, Simon, *Leadership in Japanese House Churches* (Gloucester: Wide Margin) 2010.

Cragg, Kenneth, *The Order of the Wounded Hands: Schooled in the East*, London: Melisende, 2006.

Cranfield, C.E.B., *The Gospel According to St. Mark*, Cambridge, UK: Cambridge University Press, 1959.

Crossman, Eileen, *Mountain Rain: A New Biography of James O. Fraser*, Littleton CO: OMF International, 2011.

Crystal, David, *English as a Global Language*, Second Edition, 1997; Cambridge, UK: Cambridge University Press, 2003.

Dalrymple, William, 'One Sure Way for Britain to Get Ahead: Stop Airbrushing Our Colonial History', *The Guardian*, Wednesday, 2 September 2015. https://www.theguardian.com/commentisfree/2015/sep/02/britain-colonial-history-islam-white-mughals (accessed 5.10.17).

daSilva, David A., *Seeing Things John's Way: The Rhetoric of the Book of Revelation*, Louisville, KY: Westminster John Knox Press, 2000.

De Armendi, Nicole, 'The Map as Political Agent: Destabilizing the North-South Model and Redefining Identity in Twentieth-Century Latin American Art', *St Andrews Journal of Art History and Museum Studies*: 2009, 5-17.

Devenish, David, *Fathering Leaders, Motivating Mission: Restoring the Role of the Apostle in Today's Church*, Milton Keynes: Authentic Media, 2011, 251.

Dulles, Avery, *Models of the Church*, Garden City, NY: Doubleday, 1974.

Dunn, James D.G., *Jesus, Paul and the Gospels*, Grand Rapids, MI: Eerdmans, 2011.

Duvall, J. Scott and Hays, J. Daniel, *Grasping God's Word (Second Edition)*, Grand Rapids, MI: Zondervan, 2005.

Endo, Shusaku, *The Samurai* (trans. Van C. Gessel), New York: New Directions Books, 1982.

Ephrem the Syrian: Hymns (trans. Kathleen McVey), New York: Paulist Press, 1989.

Fernando, Ajith, *The Call to Joy and Pain: Embracing Suffering in Your Ministry*, Nottingham: IVP, 2008.

Flemming, Dean, *Contextualization in the New Testament: Patterns for Theology and Mission*, Leicester: Apollos, 2005.

Ford, David, *Theology: A Very Short Introduction*, New York: Oxford University Press, 1999.

Foster, George M., 'Peasant Society and the Image of Limited Good', *American Anthropologist*, April 1965, 67, No. 2: 293–315.

Frank, Thomas Edward, *Clergy Journal 85*, No. 3 (Jan/Feb 2009), 52-55.

Frank, Thomas Edward, 'Leadership and Administration: An Emerging Field in Practical Theology', *International Journal of Practical Theology*, 10, No. 1, July 2006: 113–136.

Gairdner, W.H.T., *Brotherhood – Islam's and Christ's*, London: Edinburgh House Press, 1923.

Gallagher, Robert L. and Hertig, Paul (eds.), *Landmark Essays in Mission and World Christianity*, Maryknoll, NY: Orbis Books, 2009.

Garrison, David, *Church Planting Movements: How God is Redeeming a Lost World*, Bangalore: WigTake Resources, 2007.

Georges, Jayson, *The 3D Gospel: Ministry in Guilt, Shame and Fear Cultures* (Jayson Georges, 2014).

Gitari, David, *In Season and Out of Season*, Carlisle: Regnum, 1996.

Gittins, Anthony J., *Gifts and Strangers: Meeting the Challenge of Inculturation*, Mahwah, NJ: Paulist Press, 1989.

Goldsmith, Martyn, *Matthew & Mission: The Gospel Through Jewish Eyes*, Carlisle: Paternoster, 2001.

Greenlee, David, 'Missiological Contributions from the Middle East' in Taylor, William D. (ed.), *Global Missiology for the 21st Century*, Grand Rapids, MI: Baker, 2000.

Greenman, Jeffrey, P. and Green, Gene, L., *Global Theology in Evangelical Perspective: Exploring the Contextual Nature of Theology and Mission*, Downers Grove, IL: IVP Academic, 2012.

Hall, Edward T., *Beyond Culture*, Waterlooville: Anchor Books, 1976.

Hampton, Dr Anna E., *Facing Danger: A Guide Through Risk*, Kindle Edition, New Prague, MN: Zendagi Press, 2016.

Hesselgrave, David J., *Communicating Christ Cross-Culturally: An Introduction to Missionary Communication*, Grand Rapids, MI: Zondervan, 1991.

Hiebert, Theodore, 'The Tower of Babel and the Origin of the World's Cultures', *Journal of Biblical Literature* 126, No. 1 (Spring 2007): 29-58.

Hostede, Geert, *Cultures and Organizations: Software of the Mind*, London: McGraw-Hill, 1991.

Howe, Susie, *Resistance Fighter: God's Heart for the Broken*, Nottingham: IVP, 2011.

Hutchison, William R., *Errand to the World: American Protestant Missionary Thought and Foreign Missions*, Chicago, IL: University of Chicago Press, 1987.

Ibn Ezra, Abraham, *Ibn Ezra's Commentary on the Pentateuch* (trans. H. Norman Strickman and Arthur M. Silver), New York: Menorah, 1988.

Iqbal, Muhammad, *Armaghan-i Hijaz* 851:3 in Iqbal, Muhammad (trans. Mustansir Mir), *Tulip in the Desert*, London: C. Hurst & Co., 2000.

Jacquet, Jennifer, *Is Shame Necessary?: New Uses for an Old Tool*, Kindle Edition, London: Penguin, 2017).

Jenkins, Philip, *The New Faces of Christianity: Believing the Bible in the Global South* (New York: Oxford University Press, 2006.

Jeremias, J., *Jesus and the Message of the New Testament*, Minneapolis, MN: Fortress Press, 2002.

Jewett, Robert, *Romans: A Commentary*, Minneapolis, MN: Fortress Press, 2007.

Johnson, Ros, 'Cutting out the Middleman: Mission and the local church in a globalised postmodern world' in Tiplady, R. (ed.), *One World or Many: The Impact of Globalisation on Mission* (Pasadena, CA: William Carey Library, 2003.

Johnson, Todd M., *World Christian Encyclopaedia, Second Edition*, New York: Oxford University Press, 2001.

Johnson, Todd M. and Kim, Sandra S., 'Describing the Worldwide Christian Phenomenon', *International Bulletin of Missionary Research* 29 (2) (2005), 80-84.

Johnson, Luke Timothy, *Brother of Jesus, Friend of God: Studies in the Letter of James*, Grand Rapids, MI: Eerdmans, 2004.

Johnson, Luke Timothy, *The Revelatory Body: Theology as Inductive Art*, Grand Rapids, MI: Eerdmans, 2015.

Kang, Namsoon, *From Colonial to Postcolonial Theological Education* in Werner, Dietrich et al (eds.), *Handbook of Theological Education in World Christianity: Theological Perspectives, Regional Surveys, Ecumenical Trends* (Oxford: Regnum Books International, 2010), 30-41.

Kanyoro, Musimbi, 'Reading the Bible from an African Perspective', ER 51 (1) (1999), 18-24.

Keller, Timothy, *Center Church: Doing Balanced, Gospel-Centered Ministry in Your City*, Grand Rapids, MI: Zondervan, 2012.

Keller, Timothy, *Galatians for You*, Epsom: The Good Book Company, 2013.

Keller, Timothy, *The Prodigal God: Rediscovering the Heart of the Christian Faith*, London: Hodder & Stoughton, 2000.

Kelly, J.N.D., *Golden Mouth: The Story of John Chrysostom – Ascetic, Preacher, Bishop*, New York: Cornell University Press, 1995.

Khiok-khng, Yeo, *What Has Jerusalem to Do with Beijing? Biblical Interpretation from a Chinese Perspective*, Harrisburg, PA: Trinity Press International, 1998.

Kierkegaard, S., *For Self-Examination; Judge for Yourself!* Kierkegaard's Writings 21 (Ed. and trans. Hong, H.V. and E.H.), Princeton, NJ: Princeton University Press, 1990.

Kling, Fritz, *The Meeting of the Waters: 7 Global Currents That Will Propel the Future Church*, Colorado Springs, CO: David C. Cook, 2010.

Kipling, Rudyard, *The Collected Poems of Rudyard Kipling*, (Wordsworth Poetry Library) Ware, Hertfordshire: Worsdworth Editions Ltd, 1994.

Kling, Fritz, *The Meeting of the Waters: 7 Global Currents That Will Propel the Future Church*, Colorado Springs, CO: David C. Cook, 2010.

Knight, W., *The Missionary Secretariat of the Rev. Henry Venn*, London: Longmans, Green & Co., 1880.

Koyama, Kosuke, 'Theological Education: Its Unities and Diversities', *Theological Education Supplement* 1:20 (1993).

Koyama, Kosuke, *Three Mile an Hour God*, London: SCM Press, 1979.

Kpipki, John, *God's New Tribe*, Accra: Hill City Publishing, 2003.

Kwast, L.E., 'Understanding Culture' in Winter, Ralph D. and Hawthorne, Stephen C. (eds.), *Perspectives on the World Christian Movement*, Pasadena, CA; William Carey Library, 1981, 397-399.

Kwiyani, Harvey C., 'Umunthu and the Spirituality of Leadership: Leadership Lessons from Malawi', *Journal of Religious Leadership*, 12, No. 2 (Fall 2013), 39-59.

Lampel, Joseph B., Mintzberg, H., Quinn, J., Ghoshal, S., *The Strategy Process: Concepts, Contexts, Cases, Fifth Edition*, Harlow, Essex: Pearson, 2013.

Law, Timothy Michael, *When God Spoke Greek: The Septuagint and the Making of the Christian Bible*, New York: Oxford University Press, 2013.

Levison, John R. and Pope-Levison, Priscilla (eds.), *Return to Babel: Global Perspectives on the Bible*, Louisville, KY: Westminster John Knox Press, 1999

Lewis, Bernard, *Notes on a Century: Reflections of a Middle East Historian*, Kindle Edition, London: Weidenfeld & Nicholson, 2013.

Lewis, Richard, *When Teams Collide: Managing the International Team Successfully*, London: Nicholas Brealey, 2012.

Bibliography

Lin, Y., *My Country and My People*, London: William Heinemann, 1936

Louth, Andrew (ed.), *Ancient Christian Commentary on Scripture: Genesis 1-11*, Downers Grove, IL: IVP, 2001.

Luther, Martin, *Luther's Works*, vol. 7, 'Lectures on Genesis', Pelikan, J. and Poellot, D.E. (eds.), St Louis, MO: Concordia, 1960.

Malina, Bruce, *The New Testament World: Insights from Cultural Anthropology*, Third Edition, Revised and Expanded, Louisville, KY: Westminster John Knox Press, 2001.

Mansell, Philip, *Levant: Splendour and Catastrophe on the Mediterranean*, London: John Murray, 2010.

Manson, T.W., *The Teaching of Jesus: Studies in its Form & Content* (Cambridge: University Press, 1935.

McGavran, Donald A., *Understanding Church Growth*, Grand Rapids, MI: Eerdmans, 1970.

McGrath, Alister E., *Christian Theology: An Introduction*, Hoboken, NJ: Blackwell Publishing, 2001.

Meeks, Wayne and Wilken, Robert, *Jews and Christians in Antioch in the First Four Centuries of the Common Era* (Society of Biblical Literature: Sources for Biblical Study, 1982.

Memory, Jim, 'How Can We Measure the Effectiveness of Church Planting?' in Van de Poll, Evert and Appleton, Joanne (eds.), *Church Planting in Europe: Connecting to Society, Learning from Experience*, Eugene, OR: Wipf & Stock, 2015.

Meral, Ziya, 'Türk Teologisine Doğru' (unpublished, Istanbul).

Mischke, Werner, *The Global Gospel: Achieving Missional Impact in our Multicultural World*, Scottsdale, AZ: Mission ONE, 2016.

Moberly, R.W.L., *Old Testament Theology: Reading the Hebrew Bible as Christian Scripture*, Grand Rapids, MI: Baker Academic, 2013.

Möller, Karl, 'Words of (In-)evitable Certitude?' in Bartholomew, Craig, Greene, Colin J D. and Möller, Karl (eds.), *After Pentecost: Language and Biblical Interpretation*, Carlisle: Paternoster Press, 2001.

Motyer, Stephen, 'Jesus and the Marginalized in the Fourth Gospel, in Billington, Anthony, Lane, Tony and Turner, Max (eds.), *Mission and Meaning: Essays Presented to Peter Cotterell*, Carlisle: Paternoster, 1995: 70-89.

Muller, Roland, *Honor & Shame: Unlocking the Door*, Bloomington, IN: Xlibris Corporation, 2000.

Muller, Roland, *The Messenger, The Message, The Community: Three Critical Issues for the Cross-Cultural Church Planter*, Third Edition, Surrey, BC: CanBooks, 2013.

Murray, John, *Collected Writings of John Murray*, Edinburgh: Banner of Truth, 1977.

Musk, Bill A., *Touching the Soul of Islam: Sharing the Gospel in Muslim Cultures*, Crowborough: Monarch Publications, 1995.

Mwombeki, Fidon R., 'The Book of Revelation in Africa', *Word and World* 15, No. 2 (1995), 145-50.

Newbigin, Lesslie, *Signs Amid the Rubble: The Purposes of God in Human History*, Grand Rapids, MI: Eerdmans, 2003.

Newbigin, Lesslie, *The Open Secret: An Introduction to the Theology of Mission*, Revised Edition, Grand Rapids: Eerdmans, 1995.

Neyrey, Jerome H., *Honor and Shame in the Gospel of Matthew*, Louisville, KY: Westminster John Knox Press, 1998.

Nida, Eugene, *Customs and Cultures*, New York: Harper, 1954.

Niles, D.T., *Upon the Earth: The Mission of God and the Missionary Enterprise of the Churches*, London: Lutterworth Press, 1962.

Nisbett, Richard E., *The Geography of Thought: How Asians and Westerners Think Differently – and Why*, Kindle Edition, New York: Simon & Schuster, 2003.

O'Carroll, Richard, *Generosity, Benefaction and Grace: A Contextual Theology of Grace Comprehendible to All Arabs from Poor Peasants to Powerful Politicians* (unpublished paper).

Padilla, C. René, *Mission Between the Times*, Grand Rapids, MI: Eerdmans, 1985.

Parratt, John, *A Guide to Doing Theology*, International Study Guide 35, reissued London: SPCK, 2012.

Pattison, Stephen, 'Management and Pastoral Theology' in *Pastoral and Practical Theology* (Wiley Blackwell Readings in Modern Theology), Woodward, James and Pattison, Stephen (eds.), Oxford: Blackwell Publishers, 2000, 283-297.

Payne, J.D., *Roland Allen: Pioneer of Spontaneous Expansion*, J.D. Payne, 2012.

Peristiany, J.G. (ed.) *Honour and Shame: The Values of Mediterranean Society*, London: Weidenfeld & Nicholson, 1965.

Peskett, H. and Ramachandra. V., *The Message of Mission*, Leicester: IVP, 2003.

Piper, John, *Adoniram Judson: How Few There Are Who Die So Hard!* (2012). http://www.desiringgod.org/articles/adoniram-judson-biography-free-ebook (accessed 6.10.17).

Piper, John, *Always Singing One Note – A Vernacular Bible: Why William Tyndale Lived and Died.* 31 January 31 2006. http://www.desiringgod.org/messages/always-singing-one-note-a-vernacular-bible (accessed 5.10.17).

Piper, John, *Brothers, We Are Not Professionals*, Nashville, TN: B&H Publishing Group, 2013.

Ramonet, Ignacio, 'The Control of Pleasure', *Le Monde Diplomatique*, May 2000.

Redford, Shawn B., *Missiological Hermeneutics: Biblical Interpretation for the Global Church* (American Society of Missiology Monograph Series), Eugene, OR: Pickwick, 2012.

Reimer, Johannes, 'Church Planting Connected to Society' in Van de Poll, Evert and Appleton, Joanne (eds.), *Church Planting in Europe: Connecting to Society, Learning from Experience* (Eugene, OR: Wipf & Stock, 2015: 80-89.

Bibliography

Richards, E. Randolph and O'Brien, Brandon J., *Misreading Scripture With Western Eyes: Removing Cultural Blinders to Better Understand the Bible*, Downers Grove, IL: IVP, 2012.

Said, Edward W., *Culture and Imperialism*, London: Vintage, 1994.

Sanneh, Lamin, *Disciples of All Nations: Pillars of World Christianity*, Oxford: Studies in World Christianity, 2007.

Sanneh, Lamin, *Translating the Message: Missionary Impact on Culture*, American Society of Missiology, Maryknoll, NY: Orbis, 1989.

Schreiner, Thomas R., *The King in His Beauty: A Biblical Theology of the Old and New Testaments*, Grand Rapids, MI: Baker Academic, 2013.

Shaw, R. Daniel and Van Engen, C.E., *Communicating God's Word in a Complex World: God's Truth or Hocus Pocus?*, Lanham, MD: Rowman and Littlefield, 2003.

Shenk, Wilbert, 'Henry Venn and Mission Thought', *Anvil*, vol. 2, No.1, 1985: 25-42.

Shorter, Aylward, *Toward a Theology of Inculturation*, Eugene, OR: Wipf & Stock, 1999.

Smith, George, *The Life of William Carey, Shoemaker and Missionary*, Kindle Edition, Harrington, DE: Delmarva Publications, 2014; first printed 1909.

Stone, Howard W. and Duke, James O., *How to Think Theologically*, Minneapolis, MN: Fortress Press, 1996.

Storti, Craig, *The Art of Crossing Cultures*, Second Edition, London: Nicholas Brealey, 2007.

Stott, John R.W., *Christian Mission in the Modern World*, London: Church Pastoral Aid Society, 1975.

Stott, John R.W., *The Contemporary Christian: Applying God's Word to Today's World*, Downers Grove, IL: IVP, 1992.

Stuart, Douglas Jonah in Carson et al (eds.) *New Bible Commentary*, Fourth Edition, Nottingham: IVP, 1994.

Sugirtharajah, R.S., *Asian Biblical Hermeneutics and Postcolonialism: Contesting the Interpretations*, Maryknoll, NY: Orbis, 1998.

Taylor, Dr and Mrs Howard, *The Spiritual Secret of Hudson Taylor* (New Kensington, PA: Whitaker House, 1997.

Tennant, Timothy C., *Theology in the Context of World Christianity: How the Global Church Is Influencing the Way We Think about and Discuss Theology*, Grand Rapids, MI: Zondervan, 2007.

Terry, John Mark and Payne, J.D., *Developing a Strategy for Missions: A Biblical, Historical and Cultural Introduction*, Grand Rapids, MI: Baker Academic, 2013.

Tompkins, Stephen, *David Livingstone: The Unexplored Story*, Oxford: Lion Books, 2013.

Van de Poll, Evert and Appleton, Joanne (eds.), *Church Planting in Europe: Connecting to Society, Learning from Experience*, Eugene, OR: Wipf & Stock, 2015.

Von Rad, Gerhard, *Genesis* (trans. John H. Marks; OTL; rev. ed.), Philadelphia, PA: Westminster, 1972.

Walker, Andrew G. and Parry, Robin A., *Deep Church Rising: Rediscovering the Roots of Christian Orthodoxy*, London: SPCK, 2014.

Walton, John H., *The Lost World of Adam and Eve: Genesis 2 – 3 and the Human Origins Debate*, Downers Grove, IL: IVP, 2015.

Werner, Dietrich et al (eds.), *Handbook of Theological Education in World Christianity: Theological Perspectives, Regional Surveys, Ecumenical Trends*, Oxford: Regnum Books International, 2010.

Wiedemann, T., *Greek and Roman Slavery*, London: Routledge, 1981.

Wilson, Andrew, 'Brothers, We Are Not Managers', *Christianity Today*, June 2015.

Wilson, Andrew and Rachel, *The Life You Never Expected*, Kindle Edition, Nottingham: IVP, 2015.

Winter, Ralph D. and Hawthorne, Stephen C. (eds.), *Perspectives on the World Christian Movement* (Pasadena, CA; William Carey Library, 1981.

Witherington III, Ben, *Paul's Narrative Thought World: The Tapestry of Tragedy and Triumph*, Louisville, KY: Westminster John Knox Press, 2004.

Witherington III, Ben, *The New Testament Story*, Grand Rapids, MI: Eerdmans, 2004.

Wright, Christopher J.H., *The Mission of God: Unlocking the Bible's Grand Narrative*, Nottingham: IVP, 2006.

Wright, N.T., *Church, Media and Public Life in a Post-Rational World*. Notes to a speech delivered at the Church and Media Conference 2016. http://themedianet.org/professor-nt-wright-church-media-public-life-post-rational-world/ (accessed 9.10.17).

Wright, N.T., *Paul and His Recent Interpreters: Some Contemporary Debates*, Kindle Edition, London: SPCK, 2016.

Wright, N.T., *Paul and the Faithfulness of God*, London: SPCK, 2013.

Wright, N.T., *The New Testament and the People of God*, London: SPCK, 1992.

Wright, N.T., *When God Became King: Getting to the Heart of the Gospels*, London: SPCK, 2012.

Wright, Robin, 'How the Curse of Sykes-Picot still haunts the Middle East', *The New Yorker*, 30 April 2016.